KU-159-944

Cardiff Libraries
www.cardiff.gov.uk/libraries

ACC. No: 05064469

ENGLAND'S CATHEDRALS

SIMON JENKINS

Little, Brown

LITTLE, BROWN

First published in Great Britain in 2016
by Little, Brown

Copyright © Simon Jenkins, 2016

The moral right of the author has been asserted.

All rights reserved.
No part of this publication may be reproduced, stored in a retrieval system, or transmitted, in any form or by any means, without the prior permission in writing of the publisher, nor be otherwise circulated in any form of binding or cover other than that in which it is published and without a similar condition including this condition being imposed on the subsequent purchaser.

A CIP catalogue record for this book
is available from the British Library.

ISBN 978-1-4087-0645-9

Designed by Osborne Ross
Printed and bound in China

Little, Brown
An imprint of
Little, Brown Book Group
Carmelite House
50 Victoria Embankment
London EC4Y 0DZ

An Hachette UK Company
www.hachette.co.uk
www.littlebrown.co.uk

For Hannah

CONTENTS

Left
Ely cathedral

PREFACE

This book is a companion to my *England's Thousand Best Churches*. It embraces all forty-two Anglican diocesan cathedrals in England plus Westminster Abbey and a selection of Roman Catholic cathedrals. Twenty-six of these date from the Middle Ages, that is before the English Reformation of 1536. They are conventionally known as 'the canon'.

I have included all cathedrals newly built or promoted from parish churches since the Reformation, as these were not included in the parish churches thousand. By the same token I have omitted, I must admit sadly, the so-called 'greater parish churches', notably Beverley, Selby, Sherborne and Tewkesbury, as they were covered extensively in that volume. I have also included Westminster Abbey. It was, briefly, a cathedral under Mary I and is known as a royal peculiar. It is in my view the 'cathedral of the nation'. The six Welsh cathedrals are covered in my *Wales: Churches, Houses, Castles* (2008). Scotland and perhaps Ireland are for another day.

There are today nineteen Roman Catholic cathedrals in England. All post-date Catholic Emancipation in the 19th century and many are barely distinguishable from parish churches. I have therefore chosen what I regard as the more outstanding ones. I include no Orthodox or other cathedrals as I found none that was regularly open, as are all Anglican and Catholic cathedrals.

I have awarded stars to cathedrals with mixed emotions. I regard each of the medieval cathedrals as outstanding in its own way, and ranking them panders to the unfortunate cult of the league table. But stars are undeniably popular, and they also help answer the question that has bombarded me since I embarked on this book. A ruling obsession of all cathedral enthusiasts is, 'Which is your *favourite* cathedral?' The obvious answer, that they are all favourites, will not suffice. So insistent did the question become that I feel it simplest to attempt a 'compare and contrast' answer here.

I came to regard Canterbury, in almost every respect, as the noblest church in England. It has a depth and variety of appeal that can absorb the visitor for a day, and some visitors for a life. I remain in awe of its status as a history book in stone. But it has an aloof beauty that I have found it hard to love. Beneath Canterbury stand the 'three elders' of cathedral England, mighty Durham, austere Winchester and eccentric Westminster. Again their majesty is undeniable, but again I admired them rather than submitted to their charms. Another group of popular cathedrals – York, Salisbury, Exeter and Norwich – have immense and diverse strengths, though none is at my top table.

Supreme in my affection are the 'three graces', Ely, Lincoln and Wells. They embody the qualities which, in my view, make the English cathedral unique in Europe. One is a sense of historical continuity, of the romanesque and gothic styles evolving over centuries before our eyes. Yet each has its own idiosyncratic flavour. Unlike many French cathedrals, these are individual creations, instantly recognisable as such. Another quality is richness of contents. These buildings are galleries of English art, displayed as carving in stone and wood, as statuary, leaf capitals, choir stalls, reredoses, stained glass, monuments and memorials.

If forced, as I have been so often, to choose between these three? It would depend on the season of the year and time of day, on the weather, the contrast of activity and calm in the interior and probably my own mood at the time. Like a Schubert trio, the individual instruments are but part of a more splendid whole. But I have to conclude that, most often, my favourite has been Wells. So Wells it is.

I am often challenged on how far I have respected the true purpose of a cathedral. Most practising Christians see it as a physical manifestation of their church's history and spiritual life, and find therein its principal reward. Cathedrals were, after all, built expressly for believers to use. I can only hope that this is enhanced by my appreciation of these majestic works of art and human enterprise. For the millions outside the church, including myself, cathedrals have an appeal that grows ever wider, despite falling church membership. Everyone who visits a cathedral should therefore remember that it can carry different meanings for different people. It is a place for all men and women.

I was accompanied on my visits by many silent companions who have gone before. It is no surprise that cathedrals are not short of admirers. The London Library has stack upon stack of volumes dating back through the 19th and 20th centuries. One recent cathedral bibliography contains three hundred and fifty entries over fourteen pages. Of writers who did not leave my side I most valued John Betjeman for his humanity, Alec Clifton-Taylor for his acerbity, John Harvey for his attention to craftsmanship, Nikolaus Pevsner for his exhaustive scholarship, Olive Cook for her opinionated eye, Paul Johnson for his splendid partiality and, most recently, Jon Cannon for filling these places with people and meaning. When referring to Pevsner's *Buildings of England*, I use the most recent editions, and try to name the actual contributor where it was known not to be the master himself.

Photographs are taken from a variety of sources, but notably from my *Churches* collaborator, Paul Barker of *Country Life*. Paul tragically died during the book's preparation. These are among his last published pictures, and the book is in part a tribute to him.

Friends who guided me on my travels are too numerous to list, but I would like to thank those who helped with the text, Jenny Dereham, Anne Locke and Tom Jenkins, and the editorial team at Little, Brown: Tim Whiting, Zoe Gullen and Zoe Hood, with, on the design side, Linda Silverman, Marie Hrynczak and Andrew Ross.

Any corrections suitable for a new edition will be gratefully received.

INTRODUCTION

The medieval cathedral is the most spectacular and lasting accomplishment of the English people. For over a thousand years cathedrals have towered over England's cities, towns and countryside. They are grander than palaces, castles or mansions. No building of such size was built until the Victorian age, seven centuries later. These cathedrals have been destinations of pilgrimage for those seeking consolation in faith or beauty in art. They have inspired preachers, painters and poets. Properly conserved, they should last for ever.

A cathedral is a church containing the seat, or *cathedra*, of a bishop. As such, it is distinct from other churches in being not parochial but an outpost of central authority, its bishop appointed by the head of the national church. Since the Reformation, this has been the monarch. Many cathedrals can date their foundation back to Augustine's papal mission to Kent in 597. The principal missionaries were the so-called black monks of the Benedictine order, whose monasteries (or 'minsters') were to form the basis of roughly half the medieval cathedrals.

The Synod of Whitby in 664 established the Roman rite and the supremacy of Canterbury over the Saxon church. This gave England an ecclesiastical unity that it did not achieve politically until the ousting, or assimilation, of the Danes almost four centuries later. The church was thus the earliest manifestation of a sort of united England, but since its loyalty remained, through Canterbury, to the pope in Rome, its relationship with the English crown was vexed, and remained so throughout the Middle Ages. It was not resolved until the Reformation.

Saxon cathedrals are the great ghosts of English history. All traces of them have vanished completely, other than some stone footings exposed in the close at Winchester. Cathedrals as we know them today originate entirely from after the Norman Conquest in 1066. William's invasion had initially been opposed by his feudal barons, who saw it as a personal dispute between William and England's king, Harold. To obtain their support, William had to go beyond merely winning the title to the English throne and consequent tribute. He had to evict the Saxon earls and promise their wealth to his supporters. He had also had to secure the blessing of the pope, with a pledge to reform a lethargic and corrupt English church. This blessing was secured by his close ally, Abbot Lanfranc of St-Étienne in Caen. It was these pledges that won the Battle of Hastings and led to the rebuilding of England's cathedrals and abbeys.

In 1070, William persuaded the pope to appoint Lanfranc as Archbishop of Canterbury in place of the Saxon Stigand. But as he imposed a ruthless order on his conquered land, he respected the diocesan geography and traditions of the Saxon church. He honoured Saxon saints judged worthy of reverence, such as Alban, Etheldreda and Cuthbert. While the fifteen Saxon dioceses remained mostly in place, a number of isolated

Previous spread
The parting of the ways: Wells' chapter house stair

cathedrals were moved into more easily defensible towns. Thus Lincoln moved its headquarters from Dorchester on the Thames north to Lincoln itself. The cathedral of Elmham in Norfolk moved to Norwich, and Selsey to Chichester.

What changed utterly was the arrival of a new cadre of ambitious Norman bishops, men such as Remigius of Lincoln, Gundulf of Rochester, Walkelin of Winchester and Losinga of Norwich. Of the Saxons, only the elderly Wulfstan of Worcester kept his job. At the same time, the monasteries were revitalised. Jon Cannon estimates that the fifty Saxon houses of 1066 had, by the middle of the next century, become seven hundred. A thousand monks and nuns became thirteen thousand. William's promise to the pope was honoured. So too was his promise to his supporters. Within two decades, ninety-five per cent of Saxon England south of the Tees passed into Norman ownership, with a quarter going to the church.

As symbol of his ascendancy, William chose to be crowned not in the Saxon capital of Winchester but in Westminster Abbey, on Christmas day 1066. This church had been built twenty years earlier in the Norman style by William's half-Norman cousin and claimed patron, Edward the Confessor. It was to form a symbolic as well as a stylistic bridge between Saxon England and its new rulers.

The Rage to Build

Shortly after the Conquest, in 1067, the cathedral at Canterbury suffered a severe fire. Lanfranc immediately began to rebuild it as a virtual copy of his home church in Caen. It signalled the start of what was the most sustained building programme in medieval history. Every Saxon cathedral was to be demolished. Wulfstan is said to have wept as his ancient church at Worcester crashed to the ground: 'We have destroyed the work of saints,' he said. 'We neglect our souls, so we can build up stones.' But build they did. The Norman cathedrals were so massive they were not to be outstripped in size until the erection of the Crystal Palace in the 19th century.

Within a decade of 1066, work had begun on cathedrals and major abbeys at Canterbury, Bury St Edmunds, Lincoln, Old Sarum, Rochester and St Albans. They were soon followed by Winchester, Worcester, Gloucester, Ely, Peterborough, Norwich and Durham. By the second decade of the 12th century, the rebuilding of virtually all the great Saxon churches had commenced.

Much debate has surrounded the purpose of this extraordinary aggrandisement. Clearly it went beyond the needs of the local population. A clue perhaps lay in the ambitions of the canons of Seville in Spain in rebuilding their cathedral in 1401. 'We shall build,' they declared, 'on such a scale that the world will think us mad.' For mad, the Normans would have substituted powerful. They built to show the English, and indeed all Europe, that this was an empire that would stay. The Normans, we should remember, were not French but 'northmen', descendants of Rollo the Viking, who had settled in Normandy as recently as the 10th century.

While Saxon architecture had been tentatively romanesque, Norman was emphatically so. The innovation the conquerors had shown in war was repeated on architects' drawing-floors and in builders' yards. Masons, carvers and carpenters – the 'free masons' of Europe – poured into England, their language a patois of Latin and French. They brought with them such design features as apsidal east ends, scalloped capitals, wall paintings and chevron decoration known as 'zigzag'.

England was thrust from being a northern backwater into the forefront of European architecture. While the new cathedrals and abbeys were not exceptionally high, they were prodigiously long. The builders of Winchester, St Albans and Norwich seem to have competed in rivalling Lanfranc's Canterbury. A buttressed stone vault rose over Durham's nave, the first on such a scale in Europe. New and lifelike carvings appeared in Canterbury's crypt and on the west front of Lincoln.

Only after 1135, with the 'anarchy' of Stephen and Matilda, did the frenzy abate, to be followed by the first great clash of authority between crown and church. In 1170, Henry II's quarrel with Thomas à Becket over ecclesiastical appointments led to the latter's murder. The deed outraged all Europe on account of the king's apparent complicity in the crime. This in turn led to gestures of piety on Henry's part, including monastic foundations by the Carthusians and a burst of cathedral rebuilding.

This piety coincided with a growing obsession with saints and the healing power of relics, much enhanced by Becket's death and instant canonisation. The flimsiest evidence of a miracle led to petitions to Rome for sainthood, the candidates being almost always recently deceased bishops of the relevant diocese. Shrines were established, cures promoted and (paying) pilgrims enticed from across the land. The English learned to travel. Cathedral chapters grew rich and were able to build lavishly to accommodate the new pilgrims.

Gothic Dawn (1170–1250)

This new activity coincided with the arrival from France of a new and revolutionary architectural device, the pointed arch. In 1174, shortly after Becket's murder, Canterbury was hit by a second great fire within a century, wholly gutting its east end. To some, this was a penalty for the murder, to others it was a golden opportunity properly to honour the new saint. The architect chosen to build a Becket chapel and shrine was a Frenchman, William of Sens, whose cathedral of that name was begun in the gothic style in 1140. He introduced pointed arches, leaf capitals and piers of black 'Purbeck marble', a stone able to take a dark, glistening stain that became a signature of the new gothic style in England.

English architecture now embarked on a restless, exhilarating development of the new French style, a development that was to continue through into the 20th century. Norman architects had relied on sheer mass to stabilise their walls and deliver sculptural punch. Their churches tended to look like castles. The new gothic brought space and light. The vertical stresses of the pointed arch permitted greater height, while lateral thrust could be resisted by buttresses, permitting greater width.

Gothic was most vigorously put to use in the new cathedral east ends. Here Norman apses, ambulatories and radiating chapels were gradually replaced by rectangular chambers known as retrochoirs, chiefly to accommodate pilgrims to the shrines of the proliferating saints. Today, these retrochoirs tend to be the most satisfying corners of gothic cathedrals, glades of Purbeck piers with shafts of sunlight fractured by stained glass. Some retrochoirs, as at Durham, Winchester and Lincoln, grew into grand halls, enhancing the drama of the approach to the shrine.

The presiding signature of the gothic was the lancet window, an aesthetically pleasing vehicle for the rhythmic play of light across stone. Such windows became universal, exemplified in the west front of Ripon and the Five Sisters of York's north transept. They were filled with stained glass, offering most pilgrims their first visual evocations of the Bible story.

With the pointed arch came the ornamental pier capital. Here the Corinthian acanthus leaf mutated into so-called 'stiff-leaf', then sprouted, waved and became 'windblown'. It saw its apotheosis in the astonishingly realistic capitals of Southwell chapter house. Such vegetation was often peopled with faces and scenes from domestic life. Capitals became a window on the Middle Ages, replicating in stone the wonders of illuminated manuscripts.

This burst of activity was halted in 1209 by the pope's 'interdiction', or excommunication, of King John, again over the matter of ecclesiastical appointments, and the flight of many bishops into exile. The subsequent rapprochement with Rome and the long reign of the pious Henry III (1216–72) was marked in 1219 by papal permission for a new cathedral at Salisbury, the first such project since the Conquest. With the later addition of a steeple, this soaring confection of buttresses and lancets was regarded as the ideal of the English cathedral, celebrated above all in the paintings of John Constable.

The word gothic for the new style did not enter use until the renaissance, and then as a term of derision. Goths were equated with vandals. In the more tolerant 19th century, the architect Thomas Rickman attempted to classify the style's three distinct periods, coining the terms Early English, Decorated and Perpendicular. These have stood the test of time, though as Early English was so manifestly French, the term Early Gothic is now more commonly used, as in this book.

Decorated Climax (1250–1350)

The reign of Henry III saw England at relative peace with France and prospering mightily on the export of wool. A new breed of courtier-bishop, arriving with Henry's assertive wife, Eleanor of Provence, embarked on a new bout of cathedral improvement. This was stimulated by Henry's extravagant rebuilding of Westminster Abbey after 1245, in honour of his revered forebear, Edward the Confessor. It was to be probably the costliest church in English history.

New building meant a new style, again imported from France. It was marked by the introduction and elaboration of window tracery, freeing wall openings to let in more light and carry more glass. Vertical mullions rose and fragmented into intersecting arches, or opened into daggers, tulips and tear-drops. The style was typified by the 'Heart of Yorkshire' window in York. Rickman dubbed it Decorated, and rightly so.

This period from the second half of the 13th century to the early 14th, the reigns of Henry III and the first two Edwards, was the apogee of English gothic design. Carvers in stone and wood, and artists in wall-painting and glass, saw the cathedral as their art gallery, to express both religious and secular imagination. Masons moved from one cathedral to another, inserting new windows and creating such glories as the Angel Choir at Lincoln, the chapter house at Wells and the longest vault in Europe at Exeter, festooned with carved bosses.

This outpouring of talent proved brief. Edward III's fascination with military chivalry ordained that cathedrals become settings for state ritual and displays of ostentation. The shrines of the Confessor at Westminster and Becket at Canterbury were crowded with tombs of royal and church celebrities. Decoration became lush. Shafts clustered round piers, ribs splintered into fronds, leaves were gathered into massive bunches. Purity of line degenerated into mannerism. At a time in the mid-14th century when gothic in France was evolving into the luxuries of Flamboyant, England seemed to reach a dead end.

Perpendicular Revival (1350–1530)

As if sensing this exhaustion, royal masons sent in the 1330s by the young Edward III to enhance his murdered father's tomb at Gloucester adopted a new form of walling. They enclosed the south transept and presbytery in a cage of vertical panelling. This all but eliminated the horizontal divisions of triforium and clerestory, creating a novel sense of height. Meanwhile, the new nave at York was built so wide that its vault had to be constructed of wood rather than stone. Suddenly architects turned their focus from decoration to space and volume, an eerie foretaste of the modernism of the 20th century. By 1330 Salisbury had finally received its steeple, the soaring embodiment of the new perpendicularity. For the remainder of the Middle Ages, size was to take precedence over adornment.

Left
Canterbury cathedral

Building everywhere came to a virtual halt with the Black Death of 1348. In some places, a quarter to a third of the population died, monks and masons, clergy and craftsmen included. New priests were ordained overnight. Laymen and even women heard confessions. Fields were not tilled and tithes went uncollected. A traumatised economy saw labour stirred into a brief Peasants' Revolt in 1381.

The institutional church was now challenged by a more questioning laity. Wycliffe and the Lollards preached the Bible in English and thousands flocked to hear itinerant mendicants of the new Dominican and Franciscan orders. Cathedrals since the Norman period had concentrated on growing their 'eastern arms', primarily as chancels and presbyteries for the clergy to say the Mass, and to accommodate paying pilgrim visitors. Naves, places of worship for the local laity, were left Norman, dark and draughty. Cathedral architecture was a reflection of class.

Now the laity and their preachers were clamouring for something better, and Perpendicular space was the answer. It saw arches flattened and simplified. Walls became stone frames for expanses of glass, often honouring the patrons who paid for it. Ceilings became a maze of ribs and liernes, culminating in the fantastic devices of the fan vault. We now trace the work of named architects such as Henry Yevele, creator of the nave at Canterbury, William Orchard of Oxford and John Wastell of Peterborough.

Though earlier gothic styles had evolved an Anglo-French flavour, Perpendicular was the first that owed nothing at all to France. It reflected a newly independent nation. Although the court still spoke French into the 15th century, English culture was detached from the Continent by the Hundred Years War (1337–1453). As that came to an end in defeat for England, the country was still rich enough to indulge in a senseless civil war between Yorkists and Lancastrians, the Wars of the Roses (1455–87). The pulpitums at Canterbury and York now displayed kings, not saints. Aristocrats and a new merchant class endowed chantries and chapels, coating them in boastful heraldry.

Civic and episcopal pride took the outward form of magnificent towers. Lincoln's three spires were reputedly the highest man-made structures in the world, higher than the Pyramids. Towers at Gloucester and Worcester were works of exquisite filigree carving. Finest of the towers was Canterbury's Bell Harry, designed by Wastell, a marvel of silvery limestone built from 1509. It was perhaps fitting that this great masterpiece of the gothic era should be completed on the eve of that era's demise. Within two decades, the English church faced its biggest upheaval since the Norman conquest.

The Reformation

As 1066 marked the start of the saga of the English medieval cathedral, so 1534 marked the end. Furious at the pope's refusal to annul his marriage to Catherine of Aragon, Henry VIII 'nationalised' the hierarchy of the English church, subservient to Rome since the Synod of Whitby. In 1534, he declared himself the church's earthly head. In 1536 and 1538, he dissolved first the small and then the large monasteries. A millennium of ecclesiastical history since Augustine was dissolved overnight. The English church was to be the Church of England.

Henry's nod towards the Protestantism then sweeping northern Europe was personally skin-deep. His Reformation was aimed at the abuses (and money) of church institutions rather than at their theology. The independence of monastic orders was crushed and their wealth seized, relieving the spendthrift king of frequent recourse to parliament for subsidies. Saints' shrines were removed, especially all traces of Becket, hated champion of papal power over kings. The Pilgrimage of Grace and other uprisings in support of the old religion were ruthlessly suppressed.

Nonetheless Henry, like the Conqueror before him, left England's episcopal geography more or less in place. Abbeys might go, but not cathedrals. In the case of a monastic cathedral, their monks often stayed on as canons. Only Coventry and Bath lost their status, but that was because they overlapped with Lichfield and Wells. The king also created new cathedrals from some former monasteries, as at Bristol, Chester, Gloucester, Oxford and Peterborough. To his death, he remained a devout man, troubled by his disloyalty to the Roman church.

The Reformation took hold in earnest on Henry's death, under his precocious teenage son, Edward VI (reigned 1547–53) and his archbishop Thomas Cranmer. Images, vestments and Latin were attacked and 'idolatry, superstition and hypocrisy' outlawed. Cathedral chantries were banned and their endowments confiscated. The assault on cathedral finances was mitigated only where endowments were transferred to local charities for schools and the poor. In 1549, Cranmer's revised prayer book was promulgated and the Latin mass ended.

There followed one of those hesitant reactions that often attend revolutions. Edward's death saw Henry's Reformation put into reverse. When Mary Tudor was crowned in 1553 by her favourite, Bishop Gardiner of Winchester, it was as if the old days had returned. Gardiner also officiated at her marriage to the Catholic Philip of Spain the following year, held in Winchester for fear of riots in London. The Te Deum was sung amid a display of Catholic ritual. Monks returned to Westminster Abbey. Unrepentant Protestant bishops were burned at the stake, including Cranmer.

Mary's counter-Reformation did not last. Like so many of her forebears, she quarrelled with Rome over her choice of archbishop and within five years she was dead. Her funeral heard Westminster's last Latin requiem. The next queen, Elizabeth I, was the embodiment of cautious moderation. Protestant bishops returned. Murals were painted over with the Ten Commandments. Communion 'cups' replaced popish chalices. The spymaster, Francis Walsingham, kept a keen eye on any sign of resurgent Catholicism.

The bishops, now owing allegiance to the monarch, were left with little but their palaces and the consolation of seats in parliament. The closure of the monasteries and the vesting of clerical authority in the state stripped the church of wealth and political influence. The cathedrals now entered a long period of decline. They lost their lucrative shrines, chapels and chantries. Protestant liturgy shifted the focus of worship from the east end of cathedrals towards the choir and nave.

The one purpose no Reformation could obliterate was memorial and monument. The English establishment continued to regard cathedrals as their mausoleums, with Westminster Abbey at the apex. While a cathedral's fabric might decay and its chapels crumble, aisles and chancels became ever more crowded galleries of the great and good of church and community. Religious craftsmanship switched from rood and reredos to tomb and monument, reflecting passing fashion without concern for gothic setting.

The Long Decline

The Civil War and the Commonwealth brought to cathedrals a reduced version of Henry VIII's Reformation. The war wreaked considerable damage. Cathedrals were desecrated by soldiers. Lichfield and Carlisle were in the thick of sieges and were partly demolished, Carlisle's nave remaining truncated to this day. To Cromwell, cathedrals were citadels of the enemy. When he stormed into Ely, he demanded the priests 'forebear altogether your choir service, so unedifying and offensive', and 'leave off your fooling' at the communion altar. The smashing of images, effigies and glass resumed.

The Rump Parliament of 1648 abolished all 'deans, chapters, canons, prebends and other offices and titles belonging to any cathedral or collegiate church'. It was even proposed to demolish Wells chapter house to raise £160 from the stone. Exemptions from confiscation were made only for cathedral revenues devoted to schools, almshouses and highways. Bishops were evicted from parliament.

The Restoration of 1660 was as good as its word. Diocesan officials quietly returned to their posts, altars and screens were restored and damage repaired. Buried images and glass hidden from iconoclasts were brought out of hiding. Charles II personally supervised the rebuilding of Lichfield. In Durham, Bishop Cosin conceived a stylistic reconciliation, with gothic used for sanctuary fittings and classical for the nave.

If cathedral buildings survived these turbulent years, the same was regrettably true of their governance. The bishops and their properties were protected by the House of Lords, where the bishops were to wield a virtual veto on reform into the 19th century. As cathedrals languished and bishops sank into the indolence and corruption later parodied by Anthony Trollope, parish churches assumed new duties in education and welfare. Worshippers sought sustenance elsewhere, flocking to the new non-conformist chapels.

One building fell outside these generalisations. In 1666, the Great Fire of London destroyed England's largest cathedral, St Paul's, which had towered over the city since the Conquest. So poor was its previous state that its demolition and rebuilding had been mooted for years. There was a brief debate as to whether its replacement should be a reinstated gothic building, but the commissioners, Sir Christopher Wren and crucially Charles II, agreed that classical was the style of the day. After many false starts, Wren produced one of Europe's most celebrated baroque monuments.

The 18th century brought little relief to the cathedrals' post-Reformation plight. The Georgian aversion to gothic was as much ideological as aesthetic. Gothic was archaic, respecting none of classicism's laws of proportion and balance. It seemed a throwback to a crude and undisciplined age. John Evelyn contrasted the 'faultless and accomplished' classicism, so evident in the new St Paul's, with the former 'congestions of heavy, dark, melancholy, monkish piles without just proportion, use or beauty'. Even Horace Walpole, champion of a new 'gothick' in matters of decoration, referred to the old gothic as 'venerable barbarism'. The medieval cathedrals seemed to evoke all that the renaissance and the Enlightenment were supposed to supplant.

This posed a peculiar challenge when gothic cathedrals required repair or when, like Hereford, they simply fell down. The most prolific restorer was James Wyatt, active at Durham, Salisbury, Lichfield, Hereford and elsewhere. A scraping operation in the 1770s devastatingly removed hundreds of images and a reputed two inches of surface stone from Durham. Wyatt even proposed the demolition of that cathedral's Galilee Chapel. He took down all of Salisbury's medieval glass and dumped it in a ditch. More damage was probably done to England's cathedral fabric through 18th-century restoration and neglect than through any Reformation iconoclasm.

Victorian Recovery and Revival

The hierarchy of the Church of England resisted reform well into the 19th century, even as Methodism and Dissent flourished and Roman Catholicism returned to strength. But the church could not resist the mood of change that followed the 1832 Reform Act. A new generation of leaders, such as William Howley, Archbishop of Canterbury, Charles Blomfield, Bishop of London, and Edward Pusey, leader of the Oxford Movement, led the charge. A new evangelical Anglo-Catholicism was to answer the challenge of Roman Catholicism and Nonconformity alike.

The Cathedrals Act of 1840 was drastic.

It ended sinecures, slashed patronage and centralised revenues under ecclesiastical commissioners. A huge sum of £300,000 a year was transferred from cathedral chapters to parish churches in the poorer parts of the country, notably industrial cities. Reform also entailed the most drastic reorganisation since the Reformation. New dioceses were created and bishops appointed. Ripon was made a cathedral in 1836, followed by Manchester, St Albans, Wakefield, Newcastle, Southwell and a completely new cathedral in Truro.

The most immediate effect of this revival was architectural. England's cathedrals were pulled back, many at the last minute, from decay and ruin. The Victorians left no building free from the restorer's brush and chisel, and often more severe tools. Mercifully, this coincided with a renewed interest in gothic design. In 1836, A. W. N. Pugin published a tract, *Contrasts*, initiating a cultural revolution that extended beyond the church into every aspect of art and design. As the Georgians had derided gothic as barbaric, Pugin tore into classicism as godless and pagan. To him, the Middle Ages had practised a true devotional style. The pointed arch was its glorious emblem, two hands praying to God.

Pugin was appalled at what the Georgians had done to his beloved cathedrals. When he saw Ely he burst into tears and declared, 'What has England done to deserve this?' Wyatt's work at Hereford led him to 'erupt in horror and dismay, the villain Wyatt had been there'. But Pugin's crusade also initiated a battle of styles among the goths themselves. From the 1830s, the Oxford Movement, the Camden Society, the Tractarians and the Ecclesiologists debated the significance of gothic for the new Anglo-Catholicism in terms that few could follow. Champions of Early Gothic battled with those of 'Middle Pointed', while Perpendicular was dismissed, at least initially, as degenerate.

A more sober response was that of a young architect, George Gilbert Scott (1811–78), pupil of the Regency classicist Robert Smirke. Scott was a larger-than-life Victorian who was to achieve a near-monopoly on cathedral restoration, among hundreds of other projects, both religious and secular. He did not waste time debating style, but rather approached each job with a scholarly respect for the original. His most successful contributions were in fittings, screens, choir stalls and reredoses.

Nonetheless, Scott was castigated by William Morris and the new Society for the Protection of Ancient Buildings for what they regarded as his excessive intervention. His restoration of Salisbury – much of it to correct Wyatt – may be perhaps blamed for the coldness of its interior. But Ely, Hereford, Lichfield, Gloucester and Ripon owe their survival largely to Scott's essential rescue. His total reconstruction of Westminster's chapter house was accepted as immaculate. Scott defended himself vigorously in lectures and articles and had no time for the cult of the picturesque ruin.

Scott's most spectacular collaborators were

Left
Lichfield cathedral

the glaziers. The loss of medieval glass through iconoclasm and neglect had been a tragedy, exacerbated by the Georgian preference for clear windows. The gothic revival in architecture was matched by its revival in glass. Stimulated by the Pre-Raphaelites in the 1850s, above all Burne-Jones, artists and craftsmen such as C. E. Kempe, William Wailes, Thomas Willement, John Hardman, and Clayton & Bell were kept busy for the remainder of the century. There is hardly a cathedral in England that does not contain work by some of their number.

Meanwhile, the Roman Catholics responded to a surge in demand. English cities were receiving thousands of Irish immigrants each year, driven by the famines of the 1840s. New churches were permitted after Catholic 'emancipation' – admission to public and university appointments – in 1829. Bishops and cathedrals were allowed in 1850. This led to a spate of the churches built in the 1830s being elevated to cathedrals, fifteen in all.

Most were designed by the Catholic Pugin, chiefly under the patronage of the Catholic Earl of Shrewsbury. Pugin was the antithesis of Scott, described by Christopher Martin as 'obstinate, bigoted and brilliant'. His ambition was curbed only by shortage of money, resulting in relatively modest churches in Birmingham, Newcastle and Nottingham. His altarpieces and Lady Chapels remain among the most exquisite works of Victorian design. Later in the century, Catholic cathedrals became more grandiloquent, as in Arundel and Norwich and, above all, Westminster.

The 20th Century

The 20th century could not match the 19th for productivity, yet new cathedrals continued to appear. Nor did they escape the style wars that had consumed the Victorians. In the case of Westminster in 1894, the Catholics commissioned J. F. Bentley to design a cathedral emphatically not in the gothic style, to avoid any confusion with the abbey down the road. In 1901, Liverpool's Anglican diocese commenced a heroic exercise in gothic revival, under Scott's grandson, Giles Gilbert Scott, which was to take half a century to complete. This choice of gothic in turn drove Liverpool's Catholics to repeat their Westminster paranoia. They went initially for classical revival with Sir Edwin Lutyens, switching after the Second World War to modernism with Frederick Gibberd. Anglican affection for gothic lingered on in Guildford's tepid new cathedral, begun between the wars. The last great shout of the style came in 2000, with the Perpendicular tower of Bury St Edmunds by the gothic revivalist Stephen Dykes Bower.

The consensus after the Second World War was that a modern church should profess a modern architecture. The boldest 20th-century works were Anglican Coventry and the two Catholic cathedrals in Liverpool and Bristol's Clifton. The most eccentric commission was of the neo-classicist Quinlan Terry for an elegant Catholic cathedral in Brentwood. Most of these new churches relied on modern stained glass, notably by John Piper, to enliven often bleak interiors. The glazier was to be the salvation of the modernist cathedral.

In the last quarter of the 20th century, the number of cathedral worshippers began to fall drastically, by some 5 per cent a year. This paralleled a similar fall in parish church attendances. The 1994 relaxation of Sunday trading laws dealt a further blow. With the turn of the millennium, this predicament suddenly changed. While parish church numbers continued to fall, cathedral attendances rose in fifteen years from 25,000 to 35,000 a week, almost 30 per cent. There was also a continued surge in tourist visitors, topping ten million a year.

This revival was variously attributed to more accessible services – notably mid-week evensong – and invigorated musical and social activities. Cathedrals were attracting a wider public, in search of a communal, cultural or meditative experience rather than a purely religious one. The sociologist Grace Davie ascribed to cathedrals the attraction of what she calls 'vicarious religion … a desire for anonymity, the option to come and go without explanation or commitment'.

This new appeal might seem puzzling. England's cathedrals were committed to a set of beliefs increasingly distant from the overwhelming majority of its population. Anglicanism was, by the turn of the 21st century, a minority sect. Muslims alone were on their way to outnumbering them as regular religious participants. The cathedrals evoked Philip Larkin's account of Anglicanism as 'A shape less recognisable each week / A purpose more obscure.' The relationship of English people to the Anglican liturgy and its architecture was mysterious. Yet a quarter of adults who professed no religious belief claimed to have visited a cathedral in the past year. For whatever reason, they wanted to come. I find it hard not to attribute this appeal to the sheer beauty of the buildings and their contents, a constancy handed down to today's church from the start of the Middle Ages.

Cathedrals in the 21st Century

As a result of this revived popularity, the modern cathedral has, unlike most other Christian churches, the prospect of expansion and development. At the time of writing, ten English cathedrals charge for entry, reducing dependency on fund-raisers and the Church Commissioners' investment advisers. The 'big six' cathedrals no longer need support from the church's central funds: Canterbury, York, Durham, St Paul's, Winchester and Salisbury. These cathedrals have staff and volunteers running into hundreds. As other civic institutions suffer from the drift to London, provincial cathedrals have taken on a portfolio of new functions, as concert halls, theatres, art galleries and places of local assembly. Most cathedrals lie in desirable enclaves and have become economic magnets, bringing prosperity to their host towns. Cathedral cities, rather than industrial ones, are the new growth centres of provincial England.

Left
Lumiere lighting of Westminster Abbey west front

This means that, for the first time since the 19th century, cathedrals can think of how to boost their cultural contribution to the community, assuming roles that many publicly funded institutions can no longer sustain. As Christian places of worship, they can reach out to replicate their earlier incarnation, as missions for the faith in an increasingly faithless society. In particular, they can support hard-pressed parish churches.

As someone who appreciates cathedrals as works of art and architecture, I would also like to see them be innovative in other ways. For over a century, they have been severely conservative about their fabric. The gothic cathedral was designed as a picture book, an illustration of the Christian narrative in sculpture, paint and glass. Stripped naked of most of this illustration at the Reformation, it has remained naked ever since. Stone is left bare. Colour is rarely restored to surfaces. Niches are left empty of statues. I am sure medieval masons would be surprised and disappointed by what we have allowed to happen to their masterpieces.

A few cathedrals have revived the spirit of the medieval tradition, attempting to integrate old with new. Modern architecture has made discreet but notable additions to Wells and Norwich. The vaults of Exeter and Bristol were re-coloured by E. W. Tristram in the mid-20th century. Painted sculptures in Ripon and St Albans give a glimpse at how a medieval screen might have looked to its creators. Such a vision was fleetingly recaptured when the west front of Westminster Abbey was spot-lit in the 2016 Lumiere Festival. Such was the precision of the projection that clothes, faces, hands were individually coloured, as if with a paintbrush.

If modern glaziers can replace stained-glass windows in almost all English cathedrals, surely modern artists in other media could do the same. Eroded screens and empty niches gape painfully from the west fronts of Exeter and Wells among others, and from Durham's Neville screen. The chantries and chapels of the Perpendicular age were designed to be brightly painted. There is no reason but a barren 20th-century modernism that prevents us from painting them now. The reinstated St Teilo's church in Cardiff's St Fagans Museum is still the only accurate reproduction of a medieval interior. Not one exists in England. These are all ideas that newly confident church authorities should be able to grasp.

English medieval cathedrals have passed through difficult times since the 16th century. In many ways, their post-Reformation colleagues have been lucky in being smaller and more adaptable to modern needs. But all buildings reflect the vicissitudes of history. Today's cathedrals are reviving as custodians of a vital strand of English culture, and as custodians too of civic as well religious ritual. Millions who have no commitment to Christianity are drawn to their embrace, to feel their spirits uplifted by beauty. They remain what they were a thousand years ago, the closest England comes to the sublime.

HOW TO VIEW A CATHEDRAL

Almost all medieval cathedrals descend from Norman ancestors. They belong to a stylistic family that extended across Europe, termed romanesque and then gothic. English cathedrals, while heavily influenced by movements on the continent, came to acquire a personality of their own. The historian of English gothic, John Harvey, wrote that 'German cathedrals crush by superhuman size, Spanish cathedrals are the dark and throbbing heart of a sombre mysticism, Italian cathedrals are the theatrical properties of children at play.' The great works of France were accepted by Harvey as having a surface supremacy, but he saw them as aloof places, 'remote and near to perfection ... but having all things, they lack charity'.

English cathedrals tend in comparison to be homely places. They are longer rather than higher than those of France, and most were built piecemeal, not in one coherent campaign. Most are in a patchwork of styles, and are more interesting because of it. In addition, having experienced Reformation and revolution before most continental countries, England did not see its cathedrals stripped as bare of contents as those, for instance, of Germany and France.

Each English cathedral is idiosyncratic. When we enter Wells or Ely or the chapter house at Southwell, we are witnessing the creation of free spirits and lively minds. The masons were reflecting not the edicts of an authoritarian church but, at least in their decorative ingenuity, the lives of the communities round them. There is no perfect English cathedral, but there is a perfection of cathedrals.

Cathedrals are almost all 'oriented', that is built with the altar at the east end. Their features are therefore most easily described by the points of the compass. Ancient cathedrals are in the form of a Latin cross, with four arms linked at a crossing over which there tends to be the main tower and arms pointing north, south, east and west.

The longer western arm is the nave, the space once used by the laity to hear the Mass being conducted at the opposite, eastern end of the church behind some sort of screen. Cathedral naves are composed of arcades, or rows of arches raised on pillars or piers. Behind the arcades are flanking aisles, supplying extra space for worship, and for chapels and altars. These arcades have above them a lesser tier of arches, called a triforium, with above it a row of windows or clerestory, allowing light down into the nave.

The wooden roofs of the Norman period were superseded by gothic stone vaults. These vaults, supported by internal or external buttresses, comprised cross ribs springing from the piers below. These were tiercerons. Later in the Middle Ages, they developed linking lierne ribs and eventually fans and pendants with carved bosses at their junctions.

The east end of the nave, usually starting at the crossing, was marked by a screen or pulpitum. This was single-storey, sometimes containing an inner chamber, with on top a musicians gallery and a rood sculpture depicting the Crucifixion. These roods were almost all destroyed at the Reformation, but many later returned. The Victorians tended to remove pulpitums as barriers to communal worship, sometimes installing metal or wooden screens permitting a view of the choir beyond. Such a view was then often obstructed by the placing of large organ cases in the space above.

The north and south arms of the crossing are known as transepts. The north transept tended to be the entrance for pilgrims making their way to the shrine, while the south was for monks and clergy accessing the cloister and monastic quarters, though this was by no means always the case.

The eastern arm is, or was, the business end of the cathedral, variously called the chancel or the presbytery and embracing the choir and the sanctuary with the high altar. This was for the use of monks and clergy, and for pilgrims visiting shrines.

During the Norman period, the sanctuary was completed to the east by a semi-circular apse, as in most French cathedrals. This was lined with chapels accessed from a curved ambulatory or promenade. Further to its east was often a Lady Chapel dedicated to the Virgin Mary. Towards the end of the 12th century, these apses were mostly replaced in England by square east ends forming retrochoirs. These were primarily to aid the circulation of pilgrims round shrines.

While the Reformation deprived cathedrals of most of their decorative flourish, notably statues and murals, much still remains. All cathedrals have carved choir stalls, with misericords of domestic scenes under their seats. The bishop's throne is usually of exaggerated height. Although most medieval altarpieces or reredoses have gone, their Victorian replacements are being recognised as important works of art in their own right.

Cathedral transepts and eastern arms are usually fringed with chapels, dedicated to saints and more recently to local regiments. To these are frequently added chantries founded and endowed by wealthy individuals, but banned at the Reformation. Alongside them are arrayed monuments and memorials to the great and good of the city and diocese.

Cathedral exteriors tend to be off-putting, in that they are heavily restored or, if not, badly eroded. Norman exteriors are more decorated that gothic ones, adorned with zigzag and blind arcading. Most still carry some gargoyles, statues and grotesques, original or Victorian copies. Almost all cathedrals have cloisters, that most satisfying genre of medieval architecture, and chapter houses.

Towers were usually the last part of a cathedral to be built or re-built, often in the perpendicular style of the 14th and 15th centuries. There is no greater pleasure on leaving a cathedral than to look back and see these majestic structures still dominating their surroundings as they have for centuries. They are a reminder of all we have seen without and within. They are the cathedral's final signature, its wave of farewell.

ENGLAND'S CATHEDRALS

Carlisle
Newcastle
Durham
Ripon
York
Blackburn
Bradford
Leeds
Wakefield
Manchester
Liverpool
Sheffield
Chester
Lincoln
Southwell
Derby
Nottingham
Leicester
Peterborough
Norwich
Lichfield
Birmingham
Coventry
Ely
Bury St Edmunds
Worcester
Hereford
Gloucester
Oxford
St Albans
Chelmsford
Brentwood
Bristol
London
Rochester
Canterbury
Wells
Guildford
Salisbury
Winchester
Arundel
Chichester
Portsmouth
Exeter
Truro

STAR RATING

★★★★★

Canterbury
Durham
Ely
Lincoln
Wells
Westminster Abbey
Winchester

★★★★

Chichester
Exeter
Gloucester
Lichfield
Norwich
Peterborough
St Paul's
Salisbury
Southwell
Worcester
York

★★★

Bristol
Carlisle
Chester
Coventry
Hereford
Liverpool
Oxford
Ripon
Rochester
St Albans
Westminster RC

★★

Bury St Edmunds
Liverpool RC
Manchester
Newcastle
Sheffield
Southwark
Truro

★

Arundel RC
Birmingham
Birmingham RC
Blackburn
Bradford
Brentwood RC
Bristol RC
Chelmsford
Derby
Guildford
Leeds RC
Leicester
Newcastle RC
Norwich RC
Nottingham RC
Portsmouth
Wakefield

Tu es Christus Filius Dei Vivi

ARUNDEL RC

Our Lady and St Philip Howard

Prominent setting on South Downs, Victorian stage-set sanctuary

★

Arundel cathedral towers on a ridge above the Arun valley, over-topping even neighbouring Arundel Castle, seat of the Howards, Dukes of Norfolk. The two buildings are Victorian rather than medieval – though the core of the castle is part Norman, part Georgian. In the early 19th century, picturesque romanticism dictated that buildings be subordinate to landscape. By the 1860s at Arundel, buildings are emphatically in charge.

Despite the Roman Catholic Howards losing some heads during the Reformation, Anglican tolerance allowed them to remain the premier peers of England, with their lands largely intact, as they are today. The chief constraint at Arundel was their inability to worship in the ancient parish church, uncomfortably sited within the castle enclosure, although they retained the use of the former chancel as a walled-off mausoleum. Thus, in 1868, the young 15th Duke decided to mark his coming-of-age by building a new church across the road from his castle. Nine years later, he was to celebrate his marriage with an even bigger one in Norwich (*see* page 185).

The church was dedicated to Our Lady and St Philip Neri when it was declared a cathedral in 1965. Eight years later, it was re-dedicated to a Tudor member of the family, St Philip Howard. He had been imprisoned in the Tower of London for treason, though never charged, and died there of dysentery in 1595, his faithful dog at his side. He was declared an English martyr, along with thirty-nine others, and the Forty Martyrs of England and Wales were made saints together in 1970. His shrine (with dog) is in the church.

The duke chose as architect a fellow Catholic, Joseph Hansom, best known for a small 'safety' carriage, patented as the standard urban taxi or Hansom cab. He also designed the magnificent Catholic church of the Holy Name of Jesus in Manchester. The duke was insistent his church was to be grand and prominent. Hansom's church was a massive assertion of post-emancipation Catholic pride, High Victorian imagination applied to religious triumphalism. It was completed in 1873.

The cathedral is exceptionally tall, more French than English, unless a better parallel is with Ludwig of Bavaria's Neuschwanstein. The nave, transepts and apse are positioned to maximum effect on a spur of the

Left
The apse: Sussex speaking French

hill, visible for miles across the Sussex plain. There is no spire, only a fleche. The rest of the exterior is encased in neo-gothic features, crockets and aggressive pinnacles. At close quarters, they seem heavy and ungainly, the niches mostly empty of statues. Some of the carving is left unfinished, as if intended merely as stage scenery.

The interior has presence by virtue of sheer height. The clustered shafts of the piers are theatrical, framing the sanctuary and apse, while the transepts are as high as the nave. The ambulatory lies behind eleven graceful arches. Hansom was a master of gothic space.

The walls carry much pious Catholic statuary. We look in vain for masters of late-Victorian art such as G. F. Bodley or Edward Burne-Jones. The darkly glowing windows are by Hardman & Co.

Left
Cathedral, church, castle

BIRMINGHAM

St Philip

Baroque church, Burne-Jones windows

★

Birmingham's older buildings litter the city centre like poor relations, told by the city fathers to stay out of sight of the great god Traffic. The result is not town planning but a car crash. Luckily, the Anglican cathedral retains some dignity in its churchyard off Colmore Row. As parish church, it was a rare provincial example of England's flirtation with baroque during the reign of Queen Anne. It was given cathedral status in 1905.

The church's architect in 1709 was Thomas Archer, Birmingham-born and best known for St John's, Smith Square in London. Whilst in Rome, Archer studied not classical ruins but the works of Borromini and Bernini. His design for a new church for his home town was to be worthy, if not of Rome, then at least of the emerging capital of the Midlands.

The tower rises from a simple pediment to a series of concave faces in true baroque style. The bell stage carries paired pilasters, again emphasising depth and movement, rising to scrolls, a dome and a lantern. Baroque motifs are repeated in the windows and doorways, elegant and sophisticated. The nave exterior has a parapet with urns.

The interior is small but architecturally rich, more banqueting hall than place of worship. Its character suffered from two 19th-century alterations. The first was a gallery inserted behind the arcade in the aisles, turning graceful columns into dumpy supports and slicing the windows in two. The second was an extended chancel inserted in the 1880s by J. A. Chatwin in preparation for promised episcopal status. Two arcades of giant columns jut into the choir, altering the balance of the interior.

Although Chatwin's intention was clearly to echo Archer's baroque, the impact is entirely late Victorian. It is intriguing to compare our response to gothic cathedral insertions, which so often seem pleasing to the eye, to these classical variants, which can seem crude. To pass from Birmingham's nave to its chancel is to pass from Handel to Gilbert and Sullivan.

As the Georgians loved clear glass, so the Victorians hated it. Chatwin's chancel is dominated by Edward Burne-Jones' east window. Burne-Jones, a local boy like Archer, was commissioned to design three

Left
Burne-Jones' Ascension

windows for the 1880s upgrade. They were made, as usual, by Morris & Co. They depict the Nativity, Crucifixion and Resurrection. The donor, a Miss Wilkes, was deeply involved in the design, for some reason forbidding the depiction of any oxen. The windows were designed by Burne-Jones when in his maturity, the figures big and the heads small. They loom over the chancel in a blaze of reds and blues. He was so pleased with their setting that he offered a fourth window, of the Last Judgment, which is under the tower. They are so powerful as to dictate the character of the interior. The altar screen is beautiful 18th-century ironwork. The choir stalls, pulpit and lectern are modest.

Left
Victorian chancel emboldens Queen Anne nave

BIRMINGHAM RC

St Chad
Pugin masterpiece, Hardman window, St Chad relics

Compared with the respect shown by the city of Birmingham to its Anglican cathedral, Catholic St Chad's is a discarded orphan. A. W. N. Pugin's elegant profile once rose over the factories and canals of the crowded gun quarter. It now rises over a wilderness of concrete and tarmac, sandwiched between two roaring thoroughfares.

The cathedral is pure Pugin, product of his burst of creative energy to meet Catholicism's voracious demand for new churches after emancipation in 1829. St Chad's was to be the first new cathedral built in England since the Reformation, and it cost a mere £20,000. It was erected in just two years, 1839–41, and it was granted cathedral status in 1852.

Why Pugin chose 'north German' gothic is obscure. It is unlike his other churches of the period. The twin spires framing the west front might come from Lutheran Saxony rather than Midlands England – though Pugin asserted that it was 'totally different from any *protestant* erection'. In 1940, the building had a lucky escape when a bomb pierced the roof, bounced down the nave and then exploded, in the process fracturing water pipes which extinguished the flames.

The redbrick exterior is plain and understated, sitting just yards from the inner ring road. This heightens the drama of the interior. To Pevsner, the contrast of exterior and interior is 'a surprise'. To Betjeman, it 'fairly takes the breath – it soars to the heavens'. The nave is a forest of tall piers, like slender redwoods which, at the crossing, burst into colour and decorative richness. The crossing arches are painted in spirals. The roof pitch is continuous over nave and aisles, again brightly painted.

Pugin's hand is noticeable everywhere, in the chapels, altarpieces, sculptures and stained glass. Though not a big church, St Chad's exudes the confidence of the gothic revival before later variants, and arguments, took hold. The one regrettable change was the 1960s removal of Pugin's screen, spoiling the ascending drama of the sanctuary beyond.

The furnishings by Pugin's studio continued the language of the master into the 20th century. His grandson, Sebastian Pugin Powell, designed St Edward's Chapel at the north-west corner. Its windows tell the story of the rescue of the relics of St Chad, patron saint of Mercia, from Lichfield cathedral at the Reformation. They were hidden by

Left
Gothic Saxony Midlands-style

Left
Immaculate restoration: Pugin's Lady Chapel

recusants until brought to Birmingham the day the church was consecrated in 1841.

A window in the north aisle was donated by glaziers working for the Birmingham firm of John Hardman, Pugin's close collaborator. Panels at the foot of the window show craftsmen engraving the glass for the panels directly above. The north transept window, by Pugin's son-in-law, John Hardman Powell, is a masterpiece of 1868, a swirl of ovals depicting the Virgin's Immaculate Conception, including the scene of Pope Pius IX promulgating this novel dogma in 1854. The ovals are united by a sinuous ribbon with inscriptions. Hardman Snr can be seen in the bottom left-hand corner, in prayer.

The Lady Chapel is almost entirely by Pugin, including the windows. At its entrance stands a statue of the Virgin, a Dutch work donated by him and claimed to be the first statue of Mary erected in an English church since the Reformation. Also by Pugin is the high altar, an evocation of gothic revival which Pevsner compares to his thrones in the Houses of Parliament. A gable forms a canopy over a tabernacle, with deep cusps front and back. The relics of St Chad lie in a casket in pride of place, surrounded by angels, statues, golds and reds.

Over the west entrance stands the organ whose magnificent case was designed in 1992 by David Graebe, clearly in tribute to Pugin. We can leave St Chad's to face the ring road with a lighter heart.

BLACKBURN

St Mary the Virgin

Regency nave, modern sculpture

★

The former cloth town of Blackburn may be a shadow of its old self, but it is justly proud of its new cathedral quarter in the blighted central area. As elsewhere, specifically in Sheffield, Derby and Leicester, these historic buildings are hoped-for stimulants to urban renewal, magnets for visitors where conventional slash-and-burn rebuilding has failed. Normally, this magnetism requires an enclave of other old buildings to attract new uses and incoming residents. In Blackburn's case, there was none and modern architecture has had to suffice. For once, the exercise appears to be working.

Blackburn claims documentary evidence of Christian activity since 596, implying possible continuity from a Romano-British settlement. The later medieval church of St Mary was rebuilt in 1826 by a Manchester architect, John Palmer, gutted by fire in 1831 and then restored. The style is Regency gothic, with a substantial tower and a nave interior with a ribbed vault. The decision to make Blackburn a new diocese in 1926 spurred a plan for a large central tower and east end, in the manner of Bury St Edmunds or Chelmsford. The architect was W. A. Forsyth. This was barely started when war and expense brought a halt.

A new design for a lantern rather than a tower was produced in 1962 by Laurence King and this was completed in 1967 with the cathedral itself being consecrated in 1977. The lantern, evocative of Ely only insofar as it is a lantern, comprises an octagon of sharp pinnacles from which emerges an exceptionally thin spike. Since it must balance a beefy west tower, the profile is weak, but is relieved by stained glass in the lantern. During the day, it casts a red light over the crossing; after dark, it is a colourful focus in the town centre.

Blackburn's interior is a light-hearted space, chiefly thanks to Palmer's Regency arcades and elegant vault. The latter has colourful ribs and cobwebby tracery in the aisles. Eastwards, the focus is on the Forsyth/King chancel, a perspective of descending arches over choir and sanctuary, beneath the modern lantern. The new work is warmed by white plaster walls with soft sandstone dressings. The marriage of Regency, interwar and post-war design works surprisingly well, showing the adaptability of gothic to all ages.

Left
Architecture as urban renewal

THE ROYAL BRITISH LEGION

This light-heartedness is tempered by the work of John Hayward, artist-in-residence during the 1970s rebuilding. Hayward collaborated with King, designing the statuary, glass, furniture and altar. As such, Blackburn represents a remarkable partnership of artist and architect. However, the outcome is an obsession with nails, spikes and agony, reminiscent of Coventry. The corona over the crossing depicts, says the guide, a crown of thorns 'emphasising the costly pain of the cross'. A statue on the west wall of Christ the Worker by Hayward shows him apparently transfixed on a loom, symbol of Blackburn's textile past. Paintings by Penny Warden lining the nave depict Christ's 'agony, trials, suffering and death'. These are brittle, uncomforting images, although they give the cathedral an undeniably aesthetic potency.

Relief comes tucked away in the north transept, some jolly medieval misericords imported from Whalley Abbey. They include the customary fox preaching to geese, a satire on a cunning clergy and a gullible people. At least the Middle Ages knew how to laugh.

Left
Ancient and modern at the high altar

BRADFORD

St Peter

Maufe conversion, Pre-Raphaelite glass

East of Bradford city centre is the hillside enclave of Little Germany, base of the German-Jewish merchants who traded in the town's worsted cloth in the mid-19th century. The area of italianate warehouses and fawn-coloured walls is a precious survivor of the sweeping demolitions that hit Bradford in the 1960s and later, under its city engineer, S. G. Wardley. Perched above Church Bank is the old parish church, whose elevation to cathedral status in 1919 presented an architectural challenge. Yorkshireman Edward Maufe, working on the severely restricted site, demolished and rebuilt the east end and clamped buildings round the tower, which are used as cathedral offices; these were opened in 1963. The result is not so much modern as modernised.

Bradford cathedral is compact. The stolid Tudor tower of 1508 is like a stout wedge driven into the ground to stop the building sliding downhill. The porch is big enough for a village wedding. A similar quaintness is dominant inside. The nave was completed in 1458. Unadorned Perpendicular arcades carry a simple clerestory with no triforium. The walls are roughcast stone, unplastered, and the roof has open wooden beams. A plain Perpendicular window lights the west end. We might be in a rural Pennine village.

The view east hints at something grander. A wide arch frames the crossing, flanked by Maufe's coolly elegant triple lancets to north, east and south. Maufe is more successful here than at his later Guildford cathedral in generating gothic grace and movement. The walls are white with sandstone dressings, a pleasant contrast to the crumpled old drawing-room of the nave.

Bradford is chiefly notable for its Victorian stained glass, much of it from a donor in the 1850s who was linked to the Pre-Raphaelite Morris partnership. The group was responsible for three striking portrait windows of 1863 in the new Lady Chapel. The south transept is a gallery by C. E. Kempe depicting the Life of Christ, suffused with his favourite green light. The north transept has William Morris glass of martyrs and saints, while specifically north-British saints are by the firm of Shrigley & Hunt. Though no friend to daylight, these Victorian windows form an ideal companion to a gothic interior. All of them, in chancel and nave, are compatible in style, a rarity in an English church.

Left
Two-tones of gothic: chancel from nave

BRENTWOOD RC

St Mary and St Helen

Classical atrium spliced onto Victorian church

Even fans of the Essex town of Brentwood would not call it handsome but, squeezed in behind the central crossroads, the cathedral is an architectural delight. In 1917, the town's modest Roman Catholic church was made the seat of the new diocese of Essex, and in 1989 money was found for a church commensurate with that status. The donors were anonymous, enabling the bishop, Thomas McMahon, to claim that the money arrived 'through the intervention of Divine Providence'.

McMahon shrewdly commissioned his cathedral from the neo-classical Essex-based architect Quinlan Terry. Terry proposed a renaissance hall at right angles to the existing church, whose nave he retained. The gable of the old church peers out from behind the new cathedral like an ancient aunt who refuses to vanish when visitors come to the front door.

The exterior is a typical Terry exercise, as if the entire enclave were an Italian provincial square. The former priest's house and diocesan buildings were embellished, showing what a sensitive hand can do with unpromising material. The cathedral façade has the architect's typical touches, a Doric portico, Portland stone pilasters, Venetian windows and a lantern on top. The only nod towards the former church is that the walls are of rough ragstone.

Brentwood's interior is almost surreal. We could be in a Venetian atrium, flanked by renaissance arcades and lit by clerestory windows and the lantern. This directs light down onto the altar which stands in the middle of the church, like Henry Moore's altar in St Stephen's Walbrook in the City of London. The bishop's seat presides over the ceremonies beneath swirling chandeliers. White is the dominant colour, including the furnishings, with features picked out in grey.

In the background lurks the old church, its shadowy gothic arches flitting behind Terry's classical arcade. Here the choir has been located sideways on, with the old chancel to the left redefined as a chapel. The furnishings were designed by Terry, altar table, organ case, choir stalls, lectern. It is an Essex triumph.

Left
Renaissance in Essex backstreet

BRISTOL

The Holy and Undivided Trinity

Unique flying vaults, star-burst tombs, recoloured Lady Chapel

Bristol is a cathedral in one act, but an act that is architecturally unique. The Augustinian abbey was under the patronage of the medieval Berkeleys and was virtually their private monastery. At the turn of the 14th century, the family began to rebuild the abbey's eastern arm but was then caught up in the civil war between Edward II and his queen Isabella. The Berkeleys were allies of the Marcher lord Roger Mortimer, Isabella's lover, and were thought complicit in Edward's murder in 1327 in their eponymous castle to the north of Bristol. A Berkeley spent time in prison but the family returned to favour under Edward's warrior son, Edward III.

The relationship between the abbey rebuilding and the politics of the day is much debated – not least in Jon Cannon's excellent history of the cathedral. Was it penance or ostentation, or both? What is certain is that the new presbytery at Bristol is unlike any other big English church of the period. Its aisles are as high as the choir and retrochoir, forming what amounts to a stately great hall, while the old Norman nave fell into ruin in the 15th century. Most Bristolians worshipped elsewhere, notably in the much larger church of St Mary Redcliffe across the harbour. Nonetheless, the Augustinian abbey was made the seat of the new bishop of Bristol by Henry VIII in 1542. The derelict nave was replaced by houses and a new one not built until the 19th century.

The approach to Bristol from the east is notoriously bleak: its city planner, Nelson Meredith, demolished most of what remained of the old town after the Second World War. The turn uphill at College Green brings some relief, mostly in glimpses of side streets and courtyards. But there is something lifeless about the cathedral, half medieval, half Victorian, as it sits across the old green, now stripped of its former trees. The building needs cleaning and the area cries out for architectural rescue.

The cathedral's nave was added by G. E. Street in 1868–88 and the west front by J. L. Pearson. Most of the exterior stonework is Victorian. The Elder Lady Chapel can be seen clinging to the north side of the chancel, a survival from the Early Gothic abbey. To the east, the hall plan is immediately evident in the unusually high windows with horizontal transoms.

Left
Chancel vault with hall-church aisles

Magnificat anima mea Dm̄n et

meus in Deo salutari meo

Previous spread
Lady Chapel in gothic colours

Right
Sacristy with communion niches

Far right
Tombs 'with the luxuriance of Seljuk portals'

The entrance into the 19th-century nave is confusing since Street designed it in deferential imitation of the east end, making it hard to distinguish the medieval from the Victorian parts of the building. It is best therefore to pass straight to the crossing, and see the nave afterwards.

We know that the east-end rebuilding was begun in 1298 but not completed until the 1350s. Why the monks decided on radical innovation is unclear. One suggestion is that the Berkeleys intended to evoke the interior of a noble castle, at a time when Arthurian ritual was a court obsession, though this seems odd in a monastery.

The height of the transepts, aisles and windows infuses the interior with light and space, a foretaste of the Perpendicular style that was soon to emerge with dramatic effect at neighbouring Gloucester. The central vault over the choir and presbytery is of four main bays, wide rather than high. The ribs swoop upwards, but rather than meet at the ridge are fractured into cusped liernes. The effect is to make the ridge look like a row of bomb craters.

The presbytery vault is divided from the aisles by arcades of piers, their mouldings devoid of capitals. Since the vault is the same height as the aisles, there is no triforium and no clerestory. The aisles thus act as flying buttresses to the presbytery, with horizontal bridges from the arcade to the outer wall. Above these bridges rise transverse vaults, their ribs sprouting like orchids from their centres.

These strange forms have evoked many metaphors, mostly nautical. Pevsner grants Bristol 'the saltiest history of any [cathedral] in England'. The monks had their own revenue-generating quayside in the harbour and the vaults, 'formed like flaring trusses and flying ribs, smack of sails and rigging – or of shipwrights' timberwork'.

In other words, the old abbey cannot be divorced from Bristol's maritime tradition and from styles brought back by sailors from the orient. The remarkable tomb niches set into the walls take the form of five-pointed stars in sweeping concave frames. A similar feature can be found in the north porch of St Mary Redcliffe. That church's guide gives it 'the luxuriance of Seljuk portals in Asia Minor or the stucco work of Islamic Spain'. It has even been traced to Isfahan in Persia.

South of the presbytery is the Berkeley Chapel, reached through an ogee arch. Its tiny vestibule appears to be a dry run for the aisle roofs, with the same skeletal un-ceiled ribs. Along the wall below are decorated niches with shelves, in one of which appears to be a sink with a flue, apparently for the baking of

communion wafers.

The chapel, which displays more 'oriental-gothic' motifs, contains a Berkeley tomb visible from both the chapel and the aisle. The frieze below was believed to come from Bristol's former Whitefriars monastery. Its design looks far from Bristol, beyond even the Christian world. This was English gothic at its most flamboyant, before its stifling by the Black Death. The chapel's treasure is a rare medieval brass chandelier which contains figures of the Virgin and St George.

The east end of the cathedral is completed by the Lady Chapel. This is the same height as the presbytery, with a Decorated reredos and full complement of star-burst tombs. These were much restored by J. L. Pearson in the 19th century and recoloured by E. W. Tristram in the 20th. At the junction with the north aisle is a monument of 1558 to the cathedral's first bishop, Bishop Bush, deposed by Mary I for being married. Though classical, it has a medieval cadaver as an effigy, as if the counter-Reformation Catholics were making a point. The cathedral does not let us see its misericords, which reputedly depict vulgarity and nudity.

In the south transept is a much-eroded Saxon sculpture, The Harrowing of Hell. This shows Christ trampling Satan underfoot, with the redeemed waiting patiently to one side. The work dates from before the Conquest, *c*1050. One arm of the monastic cloister survives, its traceried arcade filled with medieval and Victorian stained-glass portraits, enjoyable to see at close quarters.

The cloister leads to another Bristol treasure, its Norman chapter house. This appears to be as it was when built in the mid-12th century. Its vault is supported by ribs covered in zigzag. The stalls have friezes of intersecting arcades, fluted and beaded. The lunettes above are filled with a profusion of woven diapering, as if they were tapestries of stone. The east window glass is modern, engraved with the names of deans.

The west end of the cathedral can now be appreciated diminuendo. Street told the authorities in the 1860s that he wished his revivalism to respect 'similarity at a distance', so an expert could see his work was not the same as that of the medieval presbytery. It would surely have been better for this master of neo-gothic not to have mimicked but to have done his own thing. As it is, we have a worthy pastiche rather than variations on a gothic theme. Pearson was later summoned to finish the towers and replaced Street's closed pulpitum with the present elegant screen.

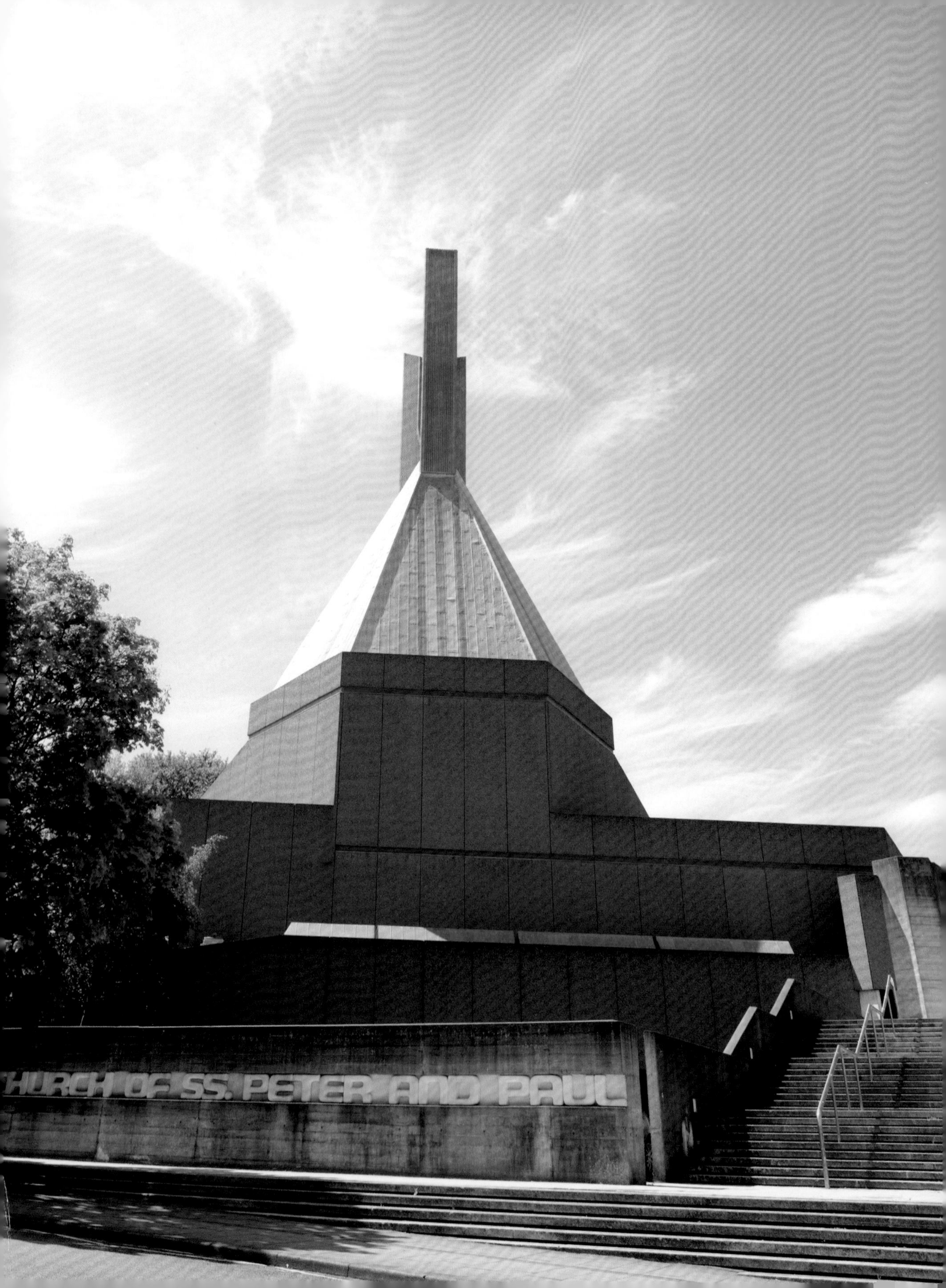
HURCH OF SS. PETER AND PAUL

BRISTOL RC

St Peter and St Paul

Modernist church, stained glass

Bristol's Catholic cathedral is emphatically called Clifton to distinguish it from its Anglican sister. A small site, a limited budget (£600,000 in 1968) and a Lateran decree for congregations to be as near as possible to the altar promised a degree of intimacy. The idea that brutalist architecture can be redeemed by coloured windows may be a cliché of post-war churches, but Clifton's ubiquitous concrete is not aggressive and, as at Liverpool's Catholic cathedral, a wigwam church almost in-the-round is spatially exciting.

The building was designed by Percy Thomas Partners to sit unobtrusively among the italianate villas and terraces of suburban Clifton. Its exterior shape is largely concealed by trees. Panels of soft brown aggregate build up from a raised deck into a double pyramid, crowned by a bell-tower of elongated fins. Except from the west, it is hard to appreciate the overall shape intended by the architects.

The interior carries more conviction, even though described as 'an irregular hexagon subdivided internally into varied polygons. The controlling module for all angles and dimensions is an 18-inch equilateral triangle.' The west door gives directly onto a shallow auditorium facing what amounts to a stage, on which stand the lectern, throne and large altar. The backdrop is an expanse of blank wall.

The effect is theatrical rather than participatory, with the congregation seated on metal chairs as if waiting for the show to begin. Above the 'audience' is a lattice of concrete beams enclosing wooden acoustic cones. The stage is lit from the tower, further enhancing the dramatic effect.

The most intimate part of the interior is the narthex containing the Blessed Sacrament Chapel and the baptistery. The font in the latter is by Simon Verity, with doves round its base. The area is lit by abstract stained-glass panels which allegedly depict Pentecost and Jubilation. They undoubtedly soften the harshness of their setting. But Clifton has little of the subtlety of Liverpool's Catholic cathedral, embodying as it does the spartan ethos of the 1970s. God is firmly locked in shuttered concrete.

Left
Clifton's wigwam modernism

BURY ST EDMUNDS

St James

Dykes Bower's Perpendicular tower, Clayton & Bell glass

★★

Bury St Edmunds was among the great Benedictine abbeys of Saxon England, claiming allegiance direct to Rome. It was founded by the Viking king Cnut (Canute) in 1020 as the shrine of St Edmund, killed in 869 by Cnut's predecessors by being used for target practice. The old abbey became a model of monastic degeneracy, rich and constantly at war with the local citizens. It was burned out *c*1150, damaged in a riot during the 1381 Peasants' Revolt, rebuilt and again burned and rebuilt shortly before the Dissolution. It was subsequently demolished. Stone fragments lie entombed in the lawns of the municipal park like eroded Henry Moores. Two gatehouses, one Norman and one gothic, survive, plus an arcade picturesquely built into the walls of a terrace.

On the street front of the old enclave stood a church for the use of the townspeople. This was rebuilt in the 1500s by the celebrated Perpendicular architect John Wastell, builder of Bell Harry Tower at Canterbury and the fan vault at King's College Chapel in Cambridge. As the 'people's' church, it survived the demolition of the abbey and was restored and reroofed by George Gilbert Scott in the 1860s.

The church was raised to cathedral status in 1914 for the new diocese of St Edmundsbury and Ipswich as St Edmundsbury cathedral, but only in the 1960s was money found to commence the requisite expansion. Plans were drawn up by Stephen Dykes Bower, the George Gilbert Scott of 20th-century English cathedrals and doyen of the gothic revival (or survival). Dykes Bower's death in 1994 and his legacy of £2m made it possible for his work to be completed, with the addition of a new tower supported by the National Lottery.

The west front gives directly onto the street opposite, Angel Hill, adjacent to the Norman gate of the old abbey. On the lawn to the south is a statue by Elisabeth Frink representing St Edmund (1974). From here, we get a view of Dykes Bower's exterior, notably his elegant East Anglian flushwork and the new tower over the crossing. We have to look twice to realise that this is completely new, a work of the 21st century. Dykes Bower justly wrote that it 'should look not different, but natural and harmonious … the exercise of skills and craftsmanship not extinct but only neglected and under-used'.

The interior offers variations on a Perpendicular theme. Wastell's

Left
Gothic revived for the 21st century

original nave is spare and pure, indeed modernist in feel. The arcades are tall, their piers bare of all but rudimentary mouldings and with no capitals. During restoration, Scott argued with the church council over whether the new roof should be steep or shallow, pleading that shallow was the Perpendicular way. He lost, and the result is that Wastell's arcades tend to disappear into the rafters.

The nave's true character is set by its aisle windows designed by the subdued medievalists Clayton & Bell. The west window, a Last Judgment by Hardman & Co, is garish in contrast, as is Scott's font with its enormous 20th-century cover, repainted by Dykes Bower. Flanking the west door are two monuments of mid-Georgian pomposity, to Chief Justice James Reynolds (d.1739) and his wife, attended by podgy cherubs; both are by Henry Cheere.

Dykes Bower's crisp, light-filled crossing is a perfect foil to Wastell's nave. The vault was not completed until after his death and is by way of being his memorial. He was convinced that gothic was all about space modulated by bright colours – red, greens, blues and gold on vaults, furnishings and woodwork. The vault is composed of demure piers that soar upwards to explode in four bursts under a blue sky filled with stars. The bursts – too jazzy to be called fans – are in red and green, like the tails of exotic birds of paradise.

North of the chancel are two calm chapels, of St Edmund and of the Transfiguration, the former housing a German medieval reredos. They are serene works of 20th-century gothic, in contrast to the vivid colours outside, demonstrating Dykes Bower's deft handling of gothic space.

Left
Dykes Bower's birds of paradise

CANTERBURY

Church of Christ

Perpendicular nave, site of Becket murder, Chichele chantry, Henry IV tomb, romanesque crypt carvings, medieval glass

★★★★★

Canterbury is England's premier cathedral. It is also the nation's most exhilarating gothic building. From Bell Harry Tower to Becket's martyrdom, from the ghosts of Chaucer's pilgrims to the Norman crypt capitals, it forms an incomparable collection of medieval art. I once sat in Yevele's Perpendicular nave on a spring afternoon and watched the sun's rays wander back and forth through the arcades as a choir rehearsed Mozart's C-minor Mass. It was an unforgettable marriage of sight and sound.

Canterbury's inspiration, like Westminster's, always lay in France. King Ethelbert of Kent's marriage to a Frankish princess in 580 led to his conversion to Christianity and to Augustine's mission to Britain in 597. He founded the first cathedral, possibly on the site of an old Roman church. Five hundred years later, the invading Normans demolished the old building and deposed its Saxon archbishop, Stigand. William I replaced him with his trusty lieutenant, Lanfranc, Abbot of St-Étienne in Caen.

Lanfranc's new cathedral was in the Norman style, built by Norman masons and using Norman stone. It was greatly enlarged after 1093 by his successor, Anselm, with transepts, a choir and apsidal east end. Beneath the choir, Anselm constructed an extensive crypt, a cathedral in miniature, with nave, aisles and side chapels arranged amid a forest of twenty-two columns. This crypt survives and is the most vivid relic of Anselm's church.

Barely a century later, Canterbury witnessed an event that ensured its pre-eminence throughout the Middle Ages. On the afternoon of 29 December 1170, the archbishop, Thomas à Becket, was murdered by followers of the Plantagenet king, Henry II. Such a deed, committed at a cathedral altar, horrified all Christianity. The cause was the archbishop's refusal to submit to the king's authority, chiefly in matters of church appointments. Within moments of Becket's death, townspeople flocked to dab their garments in his blood and miracles were instantly reported. A monk, Gervase, left a diary of the period following Becket's murder and recorded that, 'The blind see, the dumb speak, the lame walk, the sick are made whole from all manner of disease.'

Becket's murder, ostensibly by a king, struck at the power of the

Left
William of Sens brings the gothic to England

Left
Bell Harry and the cathedral at night

Following spread
Fan-vault interior of Bell Harry

Roman church across Europe. Yet such was the reaction that this power was enhanced. As Henry craved forgiveness – securing Becket's canonisation within just two years – Rome reasserted its sovereignty. Becket became the object of a fanatical (and highly profitable) cult, making Canterbury a premier destination of pilgrimage from all over Europe. Money poured into the cathedral's coffers and the shrine grew so splendid that, three centuries later, even the sceptical Erasmus was lost in admiration.

When, in 1536, the 'Becket question' was abruptly answered by the onset of Henry VIII's Reformation, Becket's shrine in the Trinity Chapel was dismantled and all traces of him were to be eradicated in churches across the land. The cathedral became no longer an outpost of the Vatican on British soil but emphatically the citadel of the new Church of England.

Any visit to Canterbury must start with the prospect of the cathedral from afar. In 1890, the American critic Mariana Van Rensselaer declared the view of its three towers from the adjacent Kent hills the finest in the land. It should be seen, she wrote, on 'one of those summer afternoons when the witchery of sloping light enhances the charms of colour, and shines through the perforations of far-off pinnacle and parapet'.

Of these towers, the central Bell Harry is supreme. It was completed in 1509 to the design of John Wastell and named after its donor, Prior Henry. It ranks among the final glories of the Perpendicular age, as perfect in profile, proportion and decoration as is Salisbury's spire.

The cathedral originally had two west towers. The first of these was replaced in 1458 but the second survived until its collapse in 1832, when it was replaced with a copy of the first. The buttressing of these towers is heavier than Bell Harry, a little ungainly as a result, but the overall effect of the three towers from a distance is that of a fantasy Tudor palace. There are even miniature pennants flying from the pinnacles.

The remainder of the exterior is largely a reflection of the interior. Canterbury is second only to Winchester in length, mostly by virtue of its extraordinary eastern arm, rebuilt after a devastating fire that destroyed Anselm's building in 1174, just four years after Becket's murder. The fire had left only the nave and eastern side chapels standing. Such was the trauma, wrote Gervase, that when a temporary altar was erected in the surviving nave, 'the grief and distress of the sons of the Church were so great … they howled rather

Left
Pilgrims at Becket's shrine

than sang matins and vespers'.

The monks of the priory – as custodians of the cathedral – now faced a remarkable opportunity. Becket's shrine, then in the crypt, was as lucrative as any in Europe. It needed a mausoleum worthy of such an attraction. The monks duly 'called together both French and English architects' for a grand consultation. The outcome was the arrival of the most famous architect of the age, William of Sens. He won the job, says Gervase, 'on account of his lively genius and good reputation … the work of a different fashion from the old'.

Above all, William had pioneered the pointed or 'broken' arch at Sens cathedral outside Paris. It is even conjectured that a pointed blind arch in the wall of the south choir aisle was William's sample demonstration. For the next century and a half, Canterbury was to realise his vision. Every element in the plan was to elevate a new Becket shrine as a pilgrim attraction. This took total precedence. The old nave was left to languish in Norman darkness while pilgrims crowded the transepts, crypt and presbytery.

A visit to the cathedral must start, somewhat uncomfortably, at the end of its story and progress to the beginning. The entrance is directly into the Perpendicular nave, which is that of a very different church from that of the eastern end. It was begun in 1378 and completed in 1405. The contrast with Anselm's Norman and William's tentative gothic is total. The nave's architect was the royal mason, Henry Yevele. He was required to construct his building on the old Norman piers and this meant that, to achieve spectacular effect, his only tool was height. The height is indeed astonishing. Nine bays of rolling shafts soar upwards before splaying out into a lierne vault. Nothing impedes their ascent, certainly not the recessed triforium and clerestory. The only visual punctuation on the piers are two shaft-rings, described aptly by John Newman (in Pevsner) as 'a mere whispered interruption'.

The light source into the nave from aisles and clerestory is hidden behind a corrugation of vast trunks. Yet when shafts of sunlight burst through them, they dance with refracted colour. The climax of the show is the west window, great sheets of reset Norman and later glass, a picture book of Bible scenes. These include the famous depiction of Adam delving in the Garden of Eden.

The font, now located in the north aisle, is a renaissance work of 1637 in black and white marble beneath a tabernacle rich in rococo scrolls. Nearby, a classical pediment by Nicholas Stone frames a bust of the composer

Left and opposite
Pier capitals

Orlando Gibbons (d.1625). The spectacular canopy of the archbishop's throne was probably designed by Nicholas Hawksmoor and carved by Grinling Gibbons. It is in the form of two trios of fluted columns linked by an arch, strangely at ease beneath Yevele's gothic vault.

The crossing at Canterbury is raised on a platform which acts as a performance space for the nave, with the transepts as wings and the nave as auditorium. Over it towers the fan vault of Wastell's Bell Harry Tower, best seen by lying on the ground beneath it and gazing upwards. It is so refined it looks more 18th century than medieval. Eight semi- and quarter-circles of ribs spin in mid-air like fan-dancers. The capitals and bosses are brightly coloured, as is the central roundel, all lit by side windows. The work was commissioned by Henry VII's archbishop (and tax-efficient chancellor) John Morton, reputedly to celebrate his elevation to cardinal. It was completed in 1509.

As backdrop to the crossing, the pulpitum divides the east and west arms of the cathedral. It dates from the 1450s and is formed of a portal flanked by six statues of English kings, allegedly Ethelbert of Kent and Edward the Confessor followed by Richard II, Henry IV, V and VI. Like the similar screen in York, this was a work of political propaganda, eulogising the house of Lancaster. The iconoclasts respected these secular masterpieces, confining destruction to saints.

The south transept introduces the first great display of Canterbury's stained glass, its collection being second only to York's. The main south window contains tiers of 15th-century figures and shields, while below are 12th-century depictions of Christ's ancestors, including an alert and expressive Methuselah. This 'ancestor' window has probably the most ancient glass extant in England, some of it believed to date from Anselm's pre-fire cathedral. Reset in a Perpendicular frame, it is a wonder of medieval art.

The north transept signals a change in key. We now enter the pilgrims' zone of the cathedral, shifting from grand ceremonial to mystical pilgrimage. It begins with the reputed site of Becket's murder, the so-called Martyrdom. The fatal altar is marked by a grim modern sculpture of jagged swords, by Giles Blomfield (1986). Overlooking it is the chantry of Archbishop Warham, determined to lie as close as possible to where Becket met his end. Warham died in 1532, narrowly escaping the denouement of Henry's Reformation.

Next door is the gloomy Lady Chapel,

overlooked by two Jacobean monuments. One is to Dean Fotherby (d.1619), its chest encrusted with ghoulish skulls. The other is to Dean Boys (d.1625), who sits at a desk, looking up towards the altar, apparently surprised at death calling him from his books. Overhead is a fan vault of 1468, hovering in the darkness as over some mysterious banqueting hall.

From the Martyrdom, steps lead down to the crypt, the most extensive and impressive in England. It dates from Anselm's first Norman cathedral and is high enough to have its own windows. Low piers and vaults stretch in all directions, so that any division into naves, aisles and side chapels can seem confusing.

The pier capitals are among the finest works of Norman carving in England. Apparently carved in situ – some are unfinished, others even un-started – they vary from the geometrical and floral to entire stories carved in stone. Almost all are either comical or violent, with jugglers, animal musicians, men fighting beasts, wyverns fighting dogs. The historian T. S. R. Boase wrote of them that 'The snapping jaws are never far behind men's heels ... frail, naked humanity is for ever caught in the coils'. To Newman, these capitals constitute 'the most ambitious, most finely conceived, and best preserved early romanesque sculpture in the country'.

In the centre of the crypt is an evident intrusion, the Chapel of Our Lady of the Undercroft, candle-lit and with delicate Perpendicular screens. Into its side is cut a rich monument to Lady Mohun in fashionable dress, and another to Archbishop Morton, both heads furiously mutilated by iconoclasts – perhaps victims of the latter's taxation. A side chapel of 1361 was created by the Black Prince in thanks for the Pope allowing him to marry his cousin, Joan, the 'fair maid of Kent'. It was long allocated to French Huguenots escaping from persecution across the Channel.

Of the other crypt chapels, St Gabriel's is the best preserved. Its capitals are satirical, with animals playing musical instruments. The walls carry an almost complete set of Norman murals (*c*1130), rediscovered after being walled up. We can only wonder how the rest of the crypt must have looked when covered in such pictures dancing in the light of flickering candles.

The pilgrim route now leads from the Martyrdom along the north choir aisle. For pilgrims who might have travelled hundreds of miles from home, this was the visual and emotional climax of the journey. As they progressed eastwards from the transept, they would have climbed ascending steps, lined with chantries, monuments, murals and

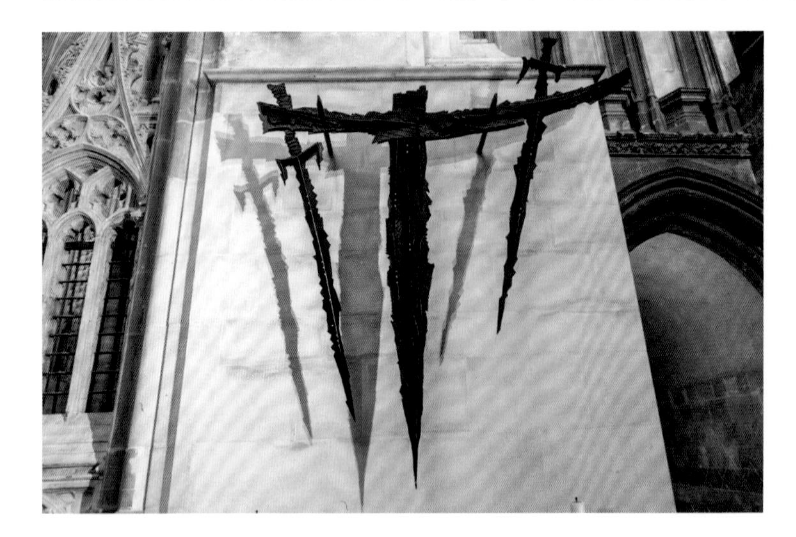

windows. Overhead were arcades with pointed arches, such as few pilgrims would have seen elsewhere. There was the smell of incense, the sight of candles flickering and the sound of monks chanting.

Erasmus in the 15th century recorded this progress as 'a pilgrimage within a pilgrimage'. It was faith as theatre, the purpose being to overawe the pilgrim, uplift the spirit and extract donations. It is near impossible even for modern Christians to think themselves into the responses of these people, witnessing something so utterly different from their everyday experiences, infused by a belief that they were encountering the aura of the Almighty, with Becket as intercessor. It was both a religious and a commercial phenomenon. Canterbury's pilgrim income was believed to be second only to Rome's.

The cathedral's eastern arm is essentially the church as created by William of Sens after 1174 and completed by 'William the Englishman', who took over after the first William was crippled by a fall from scaffolding in 1179. In planning his new structure, the first William faced a challenge. The fire had left two chapels standing at the east end of the choir and these had to be retained even as he pushed the new Becket shrine further east. This meant constricting the aisles past the chapels before opening them out again for the shrine. Beyond the shrine, there was a further constriction for the Corona Chapel, which was to house Becket's heart separate from the shrine. As a result the walls of Canterbury's eastern arm seem to bulge in and out, creating a sense of baroque excitement.

To purists, the Early Gothic of William's eastern arm is unsophisticated. The rounded piers of the arcades remain Norman in form. Their capitals are heavy, of a style found as far afield as Norman Sicily. Acanthus leaves grip the tops of the columns like Corinthian capitals in a Greek temple. The arches are still 'transitional' or barely pointed. The Purbeck shafts framing the triforium allow neither a horizontal nor a vertical rhythm to predominate. Unsophisticated it may be, but we are here witnessing a critical moment in what was to be the greatest stylistic innovation in European architecture.

The first portion of the arm, the choir, is unspectacular. The stalls are medieval but lack the customary canopies, whilst those backing the pulpitum are classical, of 1682. The Victorian archbishop's stall is enormous. The tempo only rises as the sanctuary is reached. This is flanked by chest tombs and chantries of a quality second only to Westminster Abbey. The finest, in the north choir aisle, is

Left
Blomfield's Becket sculpture

Right
Henry IV

the tomb of Archbishop Chichele (d.1443), a Perpendicular triumphal arch, peopled with saints and bishops and angels, brilliantly coloured and maintained by Chichele's foundation, All Souls College, Oxford. The only disconcerting feature is the gruesome cadaver lying beneath.

Across the aisle are two survivors of what would have been high points of the pilgrim route, windows telling the story of the New Testament as foretold in the Old. There were once twelve. In the north-east transept is a 12th-century rose window representing Moses, a Norman relic of Anselm's church.

We now ascend past the 'squeezed' entrance of the ancient St Andrew's Chapel to reach the Trinity Chapel and former site of Becket's shrine. When the commissioners arrived in 1538 to dismantle it, its coating of gold and precious stones was so rich that the Venetian ambassador declared it 'passing all belief'. It was said to fill twenty-one carts which were to be taken to London for sale. All that remains is a simple Protestant candle.

Overlooking the site of the shrine is one of Canterbury's great treasures, the tomb of Henry IV (d.1413) and his wife Joan of Navarre. The effigies are carved in alabaster and reputedly a close likeness of both. Henry was buried here because Westminster Abbey at the time was declared full, although his enemies said it was because he was a usurper. Across the ambulatory is a chantry dedicated to Edward the Confessor, with carved Perpendicular screen and fan-vault.

Canterbury's medieval glass is now in full flow, much of it re-arranged and infilled by the Victorian craftsmen Clayton & Bell. The windows in the Trinity Chapel portray the many miracles of St Thomas. Those in the Corona Chapel portray the events of the Crucifixion. The glass is complemented by medieval tiles, some brought back by crusaders from the Levant and surviving round the site of the shrine in rich browns and yellows. Canterbury here offers total immersion in the art of the Middle Ages.

On the south side of the chapel is the tomb of the Black Prince (d.1376), a warrior prince in gilded copper armour. Beyond we reach St Anselm's Chapel, with a wall painting of St Paul shaking off a viper. Guarding the chapel from the aisle is the tomb of Archbishop Meopham, a strange 14th-century design in black Tournai marble.

Continuing round the ambulatory to regain the south transept, we finally reach St Michael's Chapel by the main south transept, dominated by the tomb of its donor, Lady Margaret Holland (d.1439), lying flanked

by her two husbands. The rest of the chapel is post-Reformation, of the 17th century. Suddenly we have left behind kings and archbishops and entered a world of military bravura. The walls are crowded with banners and Jacobean monuments.

The cathedral close retains the ambience of a medieval enclave. Walls, gates and the outbuildings of the old priory quarter survive. Beyond the north transept lies the great cloister, dating from the Norman cathedral but much amended, its walks rebuilt in the Perpendicular period. The doors into the monastic chambers form a textbook of gothic decorative devices, scallops, dogtooth, zigzag, stiff-leaf, crockets, leaves and grapes.

The cloister vault is composed of liernes inserted by Yevele's pupil Stephen Lote and are adorned with some 850 bosses, mostly heraldic. A boss in the north-east corner depicts the murder of Becket, but with room for only two murderers. The screens to the central garth carry ogee arches, lending the place a gently oriental air.

Off the cloister is the chapter house, an oblong hall with a wagon roof of *c*1400, covered in decorated panels forming a patchwork. Beyond are the ghosts of the dissolved priory, fragments of a lost city within a city. The jutting staircase of the monastery's North Hall is the most notable survivor. Dating from Becket's day, it has an elephantine entrance stair more Roman than romanesque.

Canterbury is the most visited English cathedral and therefore can be the most crowded. Yet its vastness can embrace all-comers. Just as its history straddled the Middle Ages from Conquest to Reformation, so its architecture covers the spectrum from Norman to Perpendicular. Canterbury is the story of the English cathedral, complete unto itself.

Left
Tomb of the Black Prince

SIC DEVS DILEXIT MVNDVM

CARLISLE

The Holy and Undivided Trinity

East window, Brougham triptych, exposed misericords

★★★

Carlisle is England's second-smallest medieval cathedral (after Oxford). It sits tucked away on the edge of the old city in a close next to the castle. From the outside, its two-bay stump of a Norman nave looks as if it got the worst of a nasty fight, yet its east end is mannered and suave.

The city of Carlisle was the Roman empire's northernmost outpost. Throughout the Middle Ages, it was never quite sure if it was in England or Scotland. In 1122, Henry I built a castle here and founded an Augustinian priory under a Saxon prior, Athelwold. Few canons or monks cared to join him.

A decade later, Henry promoted the priory to cathedral, but to little effect. The new canons proved uncertain in their allegiance and Carlisle was so unpopular with its bishops that they built themselves a handsome church at Melbourne in Derbyshire, as if willing to go no further into here-be-dragons territory. Only in 1218 did Hugh of Beaulieu arrive to rebuild the east end and give the place some dignity. That church was gutted by fire in 1292 and had to be rebuilt again.

Carlisle was embroiled in Edward I's Scottish wars, as the king used it as his forward base. It was from here that he set out in 1307, desperately sick and propped on his horse, to lead his army north and to his death. Not until the mid-14th century were repairs to the old structure completed and a new east window installed. The cathedral survived the Reformation, but more trouble ensued in the Civil War when the nave was mostly demolished by a Scots army to shore up the castle. It was never rebuilt.

In contrast, the post-fire east end is a 14th-century building of sturdy buttresses, pinnacles and complex tracery, but its friable red sandstone has needed constant restoration, giving it a Victorian overlay.

The south door leads into the crossing and what remains of the nave. Two heavy circular piers stand like proud but bereaved parents, overlooking what they have lost. The vaulting shafts halt before reaching the clerestory, as if even the original builder has been called away to a more important job. The west wall is filled with lancets, the Victorian glass by Hardman & Co. A small altar by the 20th-century gothicist Stephen Dykes Bower has been created beneath it.

In the north transept is Carlisle's treasure, the Brougham triptych of

Left
Cumbrian sophistication: Decorated east window

Right
Misericords: harts and mischevious mermaid

the Crucifixion, made in Antwerp *c*1520. It is a joy to see such a masterpiece on display in a church and not spirited away by an avaricious museum. Above is a poignant window commemorating the five daughters of the Victorian Dean Tait, all of whom died of scarlet fever in just five weeks. When the news of the tragedy reached the wider world, a national surge of sympathy led even Queen Victoria to contribute to a memorial appeal. One of the girls had always misread the 23rd Psalm as, 'Though I walk through the lily of the valley of death.' Each window pane duly contains a lily in her honour.

Carlisle's choir and eastern arm are cut off completely from the crossing by the pulpitum and organ. The Norman south aisle arch is badly distorted, making the passage east all the more dramatic. The chancel is Early Gothic, much enhanced by Decorated windows after the 1292 fire.

Late-15th century choir stalls display elaborate canopies. Much to the cathedral's credit, the misericords are tipped up and fully visible. I recommend the mischievous mermaid under the chancellor's seat. The backs of the stalls facing the choir aisles carry painted panels of scenes from saints' lives, a well-preserved medieval strip cartoon.

Immediately east of the choir stands the renaissance Salkeld screen, named after the last dean at the time of the Dissolution. The screen dates from 1541 and is thus one of the earliest works of renaissance art in an English cathedral. Its classical tracery is crowded with arabesques and acanthus scrolls, the panels enclosing medallions with human heads in relief. Above the screen, the 14th-century pier carvings depict Labours of the Month in fine domestic detail. One depicting February has a man pouring water from his boot. Stalls, screen and capitals thus form a charming trinity of ancient English craftsmanship.

Carlisle's great east window is among the best in England. It is of nine lights rising to flowing tracery, suggesting two spoons either side of a tulip. The upper portion still has medieval glass, while that below is by Hardman & Co. The plethora of this firm's work lends a welcome harmony to Carlisle's windows.

Carlisle may be a modest cathedral but it retains the traces of an attractive, if battered, close. The medieval fratry survives, now housing the excellent library. Gatehouses, cloister arches, hall and deanery populate the cathedral in soft pink stone.

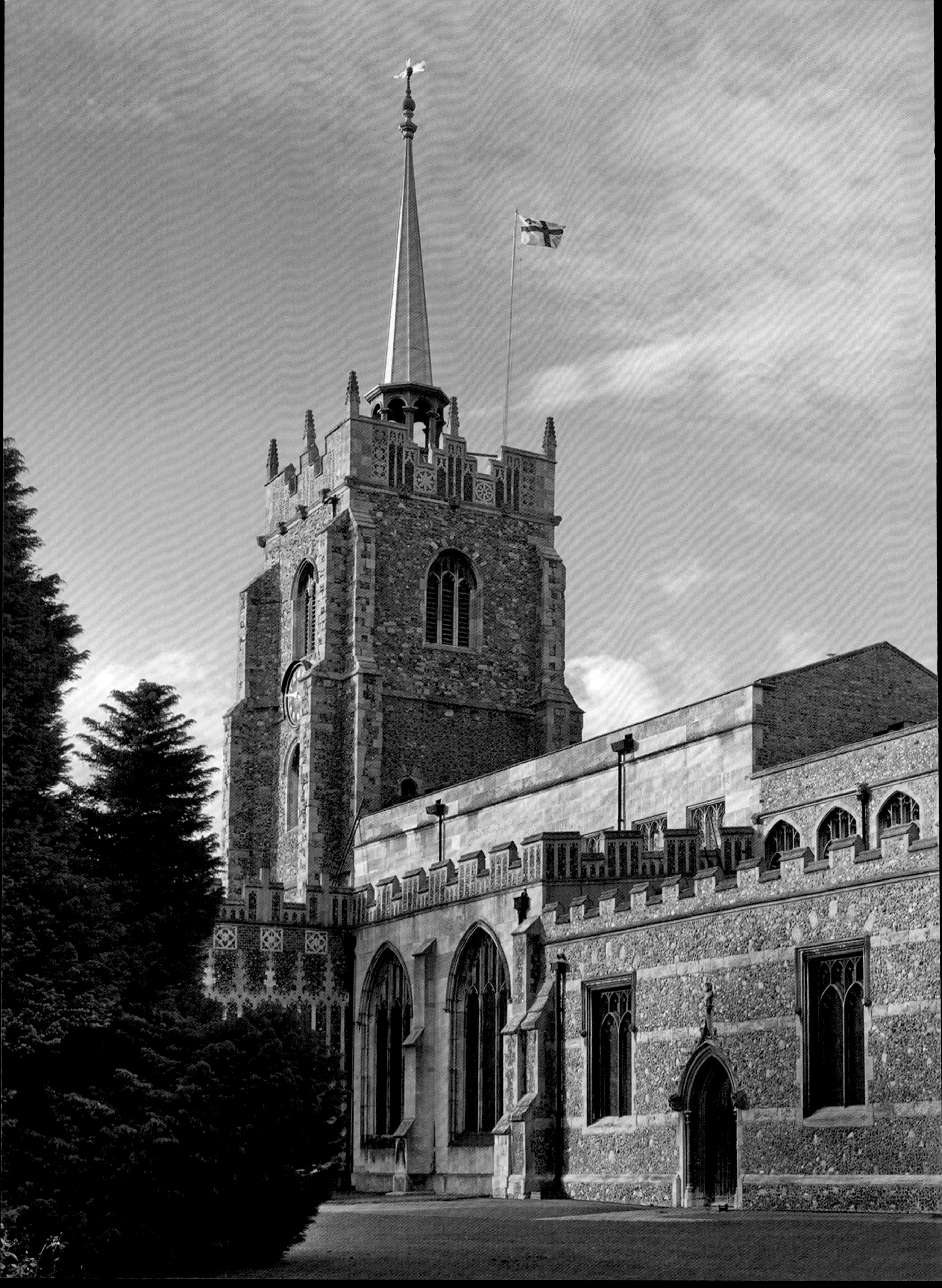

CHELMSFORD

St Mary, St Peter and St Cedd

Colourful conversion, Mildmay tombs, neo-Byzantine icons

★

The 20th-century Church of England created new bishoprics as fast as it lost congregations. But bishops came cheaper than cathedrals. When in 1913 Chelmsford won what the guidebook calls 'a bad-tempered contest' to be cathedral for East London, there were ambitious plans for a new building. As with many elevated parish churches at the time, all were aborted and the existing church had to make do until, in 1923, two extra eastern bays by Sir Charles Nicholson were added. The present cathedral is like a cheery old lady carrying rather too much baggage for her years.

The exterior is that of a typical East Anglian church, crowned with a narrow 'Hertfordshire spike' of a spire. Most prominent is the two-storey south porch, covered in original flint flushwork, which Nicholson tried to imitate less successfully in his chancel extension.

The interior was reordered over the course of the 20th century, most recently by Robert Potter in 1983. Its Perpendicular austerity is relieved by colour, notably the Georgian blue and gold ceiling panels and Stephen Dykes Bower's subtle colouring of the chancel roof. The slender arcade piers give the nave a feeling of spaciousness, while the tower arch is elegant, filled with tiers of organ pipes.

Chelmsford is enlivened by its furnishings and patronage of modern art, the most successful in a modern cathedral. A number of memorials to the lords of the local manor, the Mildmays, begin with a Tudor tomb of 1571, recording eight boys and seven girls. Two centuries later, the Mildmays go rococo, with flowing flames and fat putti. A frontal by Philip Sanderson (2004) in the Mildmay Chapel records the various foundations of the Ionan rite, from Lindisfarne to Saxon Bradwell on the Essex coast. Here is displayed Beryl Dean's lovely Byzantine-style cathedral banner (1960).

Outside the chapel in the north transept is a modern mural of the Tree of Life by Mark Cazalet, reminiscent of Samuel Palmer's magic apple tree. The cathedral has two works by the Austrian wartime artist Georg Ehrlich, of Christ the Healer and the Bombed Child, the latter a poignant pietà.

Left
Essex flushwork vernacular

CHESTER

Christ and the Blessed Virgin Mary

Choir stalls, chapter house vestibule, Gladstone/Disraeli corbels

Chester is a boisterous urchin of a cathedral. It is squeezed into the centre of the old city, and is draped with placards promising tea and platitudes. Legend gives it a past as a druidical temple followed by a Roman one, before becoming the shrine of St Werburgh under the patronage of Alfred the Great's daughter, Ethelfleda. On the border with Wales, the town of Chester resisted the Norman invasion and was, like Durham, subjected to palatinate (that is, quasi-imperial) powers. Its ruler was the Conqueror's wanton and profligate nephew Hugh Lupus, Earl of Chester. In 1092, he founded a Benedictine monastery, filling it with Norman monks who became rich on confiscated land in the northern Marches.

The monks, based in what was a garrison town, were as disreputable as their founder. They were later reprimanded for hunting, womanising, profiteering and wild hospitality. One abbot was ordered to have two monks sleep in his chamber 'to safeguard his reputation'. The building of the Norman church proceeded in fits and starts. The monastic choir and cloister were sumptuous, while the nave allotted to the townspeople was a more modest affair. Much the same procedure applied to the gothic rebuilding, which progressed slowly westwards from *c*1250 for over a century. The monastery became a cathedral in 1541 after the Dissolution.

Chester's exterior suffers from heavy-handed restoration. When George Gilbert Scott arrived, he found it 'decayed as to reduce it to a mere wreck, like a mouldering sandstone cliff'. The exterior is almost all his work, much of it a redesign, including the tower with its odd corner turrets. Yet the informal jumble of façades sits comfortably into the medieval street pattern. Indeed, at one point it is hard to tell what is cathedral and what Barclays Bank. The Victorians retained one old tradition, carving satirical corbels. The east corner of the south transept has Gladstone and Disraeli, the one attacking Rome and the other defending the Empire.

Sandstone, when weathered, becomes a dirty red-black. Inside, however, it is a pleasant grey-pink. As restored by Scott, Chester's nave and chancel keep their 14th-century coherence, with Decorated arcades forming an orderly rhythm the length of the church. The nave has a

Left
Early Gothic elegance: chapter house vestibule

Perpendicular clerestory, the chancel an earlier triforium of blind arcading. There are lierne vaults and gilded bosses throughout.

The west window is a colourful 1960s work by Carter Shapland. It depicts various northern saints in a cubist/medieval style against a blue background. In the north-west corner, the baptistery is framed by tall Norman arches; in the south-west is an old consistory court, its 17th-century fittings still intact. Here wills and church tenancies would have been disputed with papers spread over the large table in the centre. It could convert today into a serviceable magistrates' court.

The north transept contains further Norman remains, with battered triforium columns reputedly salvaged from the ruins of Roman Chester. In the crossing, near a beautiful mosaic by Scott, stands the Greene memorial. This is a 16th-century depiction of a local mayor and his wives, their hands cut off by iconoclasts for being shown praying, and thus 'popish'.

The south transept is more ambitious, with four chapels on its east flank. They have the generous proportions of the Decorated style, with flowing 'tulip' tracery in their windows. A large late-Victorian window of the Triumph of Faith is by the firm of Heaton & Butler. The transept contains the monument to the Cheshire magnate the 1st Duke of Westminster, his names Hugh and Lupus indicating his descent from the first Earl of Chester. His life straddled the Victorian era, from 1825 to 1899, and he paid for much of Chester's restoration.

We now reach the cathedral's glory, its choir stalls. They date from the 1380s and are attributed to William and Hugh Herland, the royal carpenters. The carving is intricate.

Left
Monastic comfort: the Herland stalls

Opposite
Refectory pulpit: eating the word

Left
Disraeli corbel

Below, nodding ogees form miniature oriels, while above are tabernacles with tiny windows behind. Each is a work of intense imagination, rising to a crescendo of invention on the east side of Scott's screen. Under the seats are misericords, many a mischievous satire on the leisure activities of the monks. Some were said to be so indecent that the Victorians regrettably removed them. While much of the surrounding woodwork is Victorian, an elephant-and-castle bench-end is original, clearly carved by someone who had never seen an elephant.

The rest of the interior is so restored as to look new. Behind the high altar, St Werburgh's shrine guards the Lady Chapel. Here we are back in Early Gothic, with graceful lancet windows, their glass by the north-country medievalist William Wailes, in the style of an early missal. The arches and vault ribs were repainted in their original colours in the 1960s. A boss depicts Becket having his head cut open.

Chester retains many of its conventual buildings. The cloisters, heavily restored and now glazed, retain the monks' wash basins and study carrels. The celebrated Chester mystery plays would have been transcribed here. The monks reputedly had to work through winter, breaking the ice in their inkwells each morning, so perhaps they were entitled to less ascetic pastimes. Gardens, a magnolia and a fountain fill the charming garth.

The cloister is home to two remarkable chambers. The chapter house vestibule is Early Gothic of *c*1230, its rounded ribs rising uninterrupted from base to vault with no trace of a capital. John Harvey sees traces of German gothic in this entrancing design. The chapter house itself is rectangular and an immaculate essay in what I call lancetry, its windows rising from floor to ceiling. The east window depicts scenes from Chester's history by Heaton & Butler.

Also off the cloister is the grand refectory with a modern hammerbeam roof, appropriately now the cafeteria. Into one wall is set the original refectory pulpit reached up via an internal stair. From here, sacred texts (we assume) were read to the monks at mealtimes. I am sure visitors would appreciate a revival of this tradition.

CHICHESTER

The Holy Trinity

Transitional nave and retrochoir, Arundel screen, Piper tapestry, modern art

★★★★

The last bastion of English paganism was not in some upland fastness but, according to Bede, in the rolling hills of Wessex. It was here in 680 that the cantankerous Wilfrid of Ripon, exiled from Northumbria after the Synod of Whitby, sought to redeem his reputation by converting the heathen. He founded a new abbey on the coast at Selsey and built new churches in the interior, one of which survives at Corhampton near Winchester. After the Conquest, the Norman desire to concentrate churches in towns led them to move the abbey to the old Roman city of Chichester and make it a cathedral.

Chichester is a friendly, popular cathedral. In the 1960s, Ian Nairn (in Pevsner) called it a 'well-worn, well-loved, comfortable fireside chair'. It sits cosily on the edge of the old city, prominent but not dominant. Its exterior is an amiable kaleidoscope of styles, patched together as the old structure aged and crumbled. None of the Decorated windows of the Lady Chapel quite matches another. The north tower of the west front is Victorian, by J. L. Pearson, almost a replica of the south one but not quite.

Chichester's free-standing bell-tower dates from when churches built on soft ground hung their bells in separate chambers, to minimise collateral damage should the bells fall and demolish the crossing tower. Despite this, Chichester's crossing tower collapsed in 1861, falling in a matter of seconds, said a local report, 'as one telescope tube slides into another'. George Gilbert Scott rebuilt it facsimile, reinstating every bit of carving he could find in the rubble. The bell-tower remains splendidly intact.

Chichester's interior has strong visual coherence. This it owes partly to its rebuilding after a fire in 1187 and partly to its poverty thereafter. The upper storeys were rebuilt in the Early Gothic style, while the lower ones remained from the earlier Norman church. We therefore see Purbeck shafts added to Norman piers, and stiff-leaf capitals jostling heavy Norman ones. Overhead is a gothic ribbed vault. This so-called transitional moment in medieval architecture has always confused critics, wondering if the masons somehow knew what was coming with the gothic revolution. I prefer to see it as a period when builders used romanesque and gothic motifs to answer differing decorative needs, like

Left
Tower from bishop's garden

Left
Norman nave, Arundel screen

a musician using major and minor keys.

Chichester is not a long cathedral and the view east is interrupted by the controversial Arundel screen. The screen is Perpendicular and was dismantled and put into store by purists of the Early Gothic revival in 1861. A Victorian guidebook says the zealotry of the time was 'not always with discretion, not always with knowledge, wisdom and taste … rash ardour, often without the hesitation of true reverence'. A century later, the screen was put back, no less controversially. While it leaves a clear view of the roof to the east, it obscures the choir, and so today reduces the impact of John Piper's vivid tapestry.

Norman or gothic, the nave itself is supremely elegant. Creamy limestone is articulated by dark Purbeck shafts. There are excellent views down narrow side aisles that form an unbroken ambulatory round the interior. Cathedral aisles are my special pleasure, corridors of light and shade, galleries of art and places of repose. Chichester's best view is from the north-west corner, east down the nave aisle and south across the narthex to the baptistery. On the wall is a Tudor brass to William Bradbridge, 'thrice maior of this cittie'. Another memorial (1830) is to a local MP, William Huskisson, for 'relinquishing this station when yielding to a sense of publick duty', an allusion to his being killed by the *Rocket.* The Fitzalan effigies in the north aisle show a knight and his lady, her leg unusually crossed towards him. They hold hands, a rare moment of medieval devotion captured in stone.

The crossing has the retooled look of Scott's post-collapse restoration. The transepts to either side are the original Norman ones but much restored. In each is hung a Tudor wooden panel painted by Lambert Barnard in the early 16th century, recording the bishops of Chichester and the kings of England. They are said to be the largest paintings of Tudor scenes in England. We see Wilfrid's arrival at Selsey and Henry VIII's visit to Chichester in full pre-Reformation splendour. The panels were commissioned by the bishop, Robert Sherburne, who greets Henry to his seat. Sherburne also commissioned Barnard to paint murals over much of the cathedral interior. These were painted over at the Reformation, repainted under Mary I and again over-painted on her death. Tudor artists were never idle.

Whatever the opinion of the siting of the Arundel screen, it is a superb work, one bay deep and with a narrow central arch separating two wider ones on either side. Beyond we glimpse the choir, overseen by

Piper's tapestry reredos, almost as prominent as Sutherland's at Coventry. It is a blaze of reds and blues depicting the Trinity and the elements. It asserts what, in my view, is the 20th century's most lasting gift to English cathedrals, which is needlework in banners, tapestries, frontals and kneelers. The choir stalls have original misericords, one with a fiddler trying to kiss a girl dancer whilst still playing. Above is the organ case incorporating 17th-century decorated pipes by Thomas Harris, thankfully moved from on top of the screen, where it really did block the view. Other cathedrals, please note.

The south choir aisle contains two treasures, romanesque reliefs of Christ visiting Mary of Bethany and of Christ raising Lazarus. They have been dated to *c*1125, carved possibly for a former rood screen and resembling similar carvings in Hildesheim and Cologne in Germany. Their agonised humanity compares with the worldliness of the paintings in the Roman villa at nearby Fishbourne, which are twice their age. Between the panels is the wall tomb of Bishop Sherburne, patron of the transept pictures, who died in 1536 after 'steering a prudent course at the Reformation'. The design remains medieval, the bishop presented as a smart young man in alabaster. The paint is modern, right down to the fingernails.

Chichester's retrochoir was dedicated to Sussex's patron saint, Richard of Chichester, a conservative, vegetarian ascetic who held out for church sovereignty under Henry III. He was forced to leave his cathedral and wander his diocese. There were many miracles following his death in 1253, and he was canonised just nine years later, with a shrine established to his cult. Richard was author of the popular prayer ending with the words,

Left
Piper's tapestry reredos

Left
Hand in hand: knightly affection

to 'know Thee more clearly, love Thee more dearly, follow Thee more nearly', albeit an Edwardian translation of the Latin original. An austere statue of him by Philip Jackson stands near the bell-tower.

Like the nave, the retrochoir is in the transitional style, Norman in proportion yet gothic in detail. Purbeck shafts and stiff-leaf capitals sit beneath rounded arches. Here, wrote Ian Nairn, was 'the exact point of balance, perhaps in the whole of England, between romanesque and gothic … a medieval debate made visible'.

Chichester has long been a determined patron of modern art, some of it controversial. On the back of the reredos hangs a German tapestry by Ursula Benker-Schirmir, commemorating Bishop Bell, an opponent of the carpet bombing of German cities and advocate of post-war reconciliation. He is also commemorated in Oxford cathedral. The work is loud, almost fierce, vaguely suggesting Lady Thatcher emerging from a fiery furnace.

An adjacent window is by Marc Chagall, inserted in 1978, while the altarpiece in the Mary Magdalene Chapel is by Graham Sutherland (Noli me tangere, 1960) and that in the St John Chapel by Patrick Procktor (Baptism of Christ, 1984). The 14th-century Lady Chapel is brightly painted in the medieval style, even its capitals and vault ribs. It looks 'fairground gothic' but there is no reason to think it unauthentic.

Chichester's cloister is amiably asymmetrical, just three sides with wooden barn roofs rather than vaults. The central garth is called Paradise and is used for sculpture exhibitions. Its access to the cathedral is through St Richard's Porch, an elegant work of Early Gothic design composed of two arches on slender piers, with the saint's statue set in an oddly 'stretched' quatrefoil.

Beyond, there is no formal close but rather a medieval enclave that merges comfortably into the town, a cluster of bishop's palace, diocesan offices, almshouses and vicars' terrace. Everything in this corner of Chichester seems to fit. The short walk from the cloister through a maze of back streets to the Pallants neighbourhood is small town England at its most entrancing.

COVENTRY

St Michael

Spence addition to medieval ruin, Piper windows, Sutherland tapestry

An air of tragedy continues to hang over the city of Coventry. The Germans bombed it in November 1940, leaving its gothic cathedral of St Michael a charred ruin. That was hardly Coventry's fault. What happened next was a different matter. While Germany rebuilt many of its ancient city centres bombed by the British, Coventry's city fathers demolished most of what the bombs left standing, compounding destruction by war with destruction by planning. Today, the rebuilt German town of Lübeck is a World Heritage Site and rebuilt Dresden is visited by thousands. Few visit Coventry. It is a desolation of car parks, underpasses, shopping centres and warehouses, overlooked by the bleak campus of Coventry University.

While the town was self-harming, the Church of England had to decide the fate of its cathedral. St Michael's sandstone walls remained standing, together with the third-highest steeple in England, whose magnificence matches Salisbury's. The Victorians would have summoned Scott, Pearson or Street to rebuild the church facsimile but British architecture in the 1950s had no such self-assurance. Since a modernist Coventry was to rise from the ashes, so perhaps should a modernist cathedral.

The design competition for a new building adjacent to the ruin of the old was won by Basil Spence in 1951, the year of the Festival of Britain and a hoped-for new dawn in English architecture. Spence's plan was for a new cathedral at right angles to the ruins of the old, and to a similar medieval ground plan, with nave, choir, sanctuary and chapels; his was the only design to link the old to the new. He was allowed 'a total cost not exceeding £985,000' to spend. The cathedral was opened in 1962.

Despite this boldness, or perhaps because of it, a deluge of criticism ensued. Pevsner's lengthy entry for Coventry records such phrases as 'ugly factory … cockroach … gasholder … glorified dustbin'. To some it was too gothic and to others not gothic enough. The pro-modernist Pevsner broadly liked it though he admitted to finding some of its features 'corny'.

My own hesitation is with the air of morbidity that hovers over the place. Its themes of human pain and reconciliation had it dubbed as

Left
Sutherland's Christ in Majesty

Previous spread
New cathedral and old from the east

Left
Piper's baptistery window

'a cathedral for today', but barely a corner is without some reference, often macabre, to agony, violence and war. This may have seemed appropriate in the 1950s but today it seems obsessive. There is no sense of joy. I feel the Germans were right in their post-war reconstructions, to make peace with peace.

The former cathedral, an old parish church elevated to cathedral status in 1918, is now a walled 'enclosure of remembrance', the skeletal remains of its tracery gaunt against the sky. It forms a fine setting for the steeple, the tower being a slender 15th-century masterpiece of four stages, crowned by an octagon and spire. The bell openings have ogival gables covered in pinnacles, all in vivid red sandstone. Some old guild chapels survive and a World Monuments Fund project has conserved and repaired some of the medieval glass that was removed and stored during the war.

The apsidal east end is linked by a heavy modern porch to the new building next door. Seen from the ruin, the porch roof yawns over the old walls like a shark's mouth. The self-conscious newness jars with the more delicate medievalism of the ruin. But when seen from the steps below, Spence's structure clearly echoes the old. The bulge of the baptistery answers the bulge of the ruined apse. The clash of styles is eased by the new building being clad in the same pink-brown stone as the old. The more we look at it, the more the old building and the new can be seen as one composition. This is well done.

Attached to the exterior wall is one of Epstein's last works, a sculpture of St Michael defeating a cowering Lucifer. On the roof is a strange fleche, an archaic feature looking like a radio mast. Spence said it was 'to receive messages from Heaven', but it sits ill with the spire next door.

To early critics, Coventry's interior was like that of an aircraft hangar, despite being relatively small for a cathedral. The west wall is entirely composed of glass, and the wide expanses of undecorated concrete are hard on both the eye and the emotions. In fairness to Spence, he wanted the inside walls to have been of sandstone, but money was short.

The main nave has an arcade of slender piers and a lozenge pattern of roof members that might pass for liernes, suggesting a gothic vault. All this was a mere nod towards tradition, as the columns are structurally unnecessary.

Like many post-war architects, Spence relied on art to add visual interest to his modernism, and in this he was undeniably successful. The great west screen (liturgical west as the alignment is in fact north–south) is entirely of glass. It displays rows of angels, saints and

Left
Frink's altar cross

Opposite
Gethsemane chapel

apostles, most of them apparently in flight, engraved by John Hutton. It uplifts an otherwise cold space and, from inside, acts as a frame to the ruined walls beyond.

The adjacent baptistery is the star of Coventry. Its wall alcove rises the full height of the building and displays Spence's talent in manipulating space. It is overlooked by 195 small windows in an echo of the Perpendicular style. Their glass is the most satisfying of all John Piper's many cathedral works, constructed by his long-time associate Patrick Reyntiens. When Piper was at a loss for inspiration, Reyntiens suggested tossing a metaphorical bomb into the cathedral, creating an explosion of light. The vividness of yellows and reds suggest Donne's lines, that 'God comes to thee not as in the dawning of the day, not in the bud of the spring, but as the sun at noon.' When sunlight is refracted on the floor, this is a window to compare with York and Gloucester. The boulder-shaped font came from Bethlehem.

We now confront the view east from the entrance. Coventry's most problematic feature is the saw-tooth openings in the side walls. They are set at an angle, making them invisible from the back. This means that, initially, the view from the nave is of blank concrete walls. They carry biblical homilies in large letters – suggested to Spence by Pevsner – like some Puritan chapel.

The vista ahead is dominated by Graham Sutherland's east wall tapestry of Christ in Majesty, framed by organ pipes. It towers over the nave like a great Buddha, attended by four evangelists and with a bleak crucifixion at its foot. The prominent colours are yellow and green, lit by concealed openings in the adjacent wall. When first unveiled, the work was fiercely attacked. To some it was crude, to others intrusive. In Spence's original perspective, the figure of Christ was smaller and softer, more like a reredos.

The tension generated by the tapestry is maintained in the choir. Here the stalls have suspended open-work canopies above them, with organ pipes stacked behind. They look at first like flocks of birds, but they apparently evoke thorns, 'as symbol of humanity's difficult passage through life'. This theme is emphasised by an altar cross depicting a charred relic by Geoffrey Clarke. The lectern, pulpit cross and Tongue of Fire over the dean's stall are by Elisabeth Frink. Another tangle of thorns screens the Lady Chapel. We almost expect to see Coventry's mendicant friars traipsing the steps, sporting blood-stained backs.

On reaching the choir and turning back

towards the nave, we at last gain the force of Spence's coup de théâtre, the ten vertical stained-glass windows, 70ft high, let into the side walls. Designed by Lawrence Lee of the Royal College of Art, they emerge as the power behind the whole design, galvanising otherwise leaden concrete walls. Coventry's plainness is redeemed by colour.

Behind the chancel are subsidiary chapels dedicated to various abstract nouns, service, unity, suffering, guilt and forgiveness. They offer a gallery of nails, thorns, charred crosses, weeping women and tragic Madonnas. The Gethsemane Chapel is a relief: behind its screen, predictably of thorns, is a splendid kneeling angel in gold mosaic by Steven Sykes.

On my last visit, Coventry's windy piazzas were deserted, a depressing sign of failed architecture. The 20th century destroyed one of England's most charming small cities. The best thing the 21st century could do is simply rebuild it as it was before, as its legacy to the 22nd. That is what the Victorians would have done, and they would have been right.

DERBY

All Saints

Baroque church, ironwork screen, Cavendish tombs

I visit Derby with a heavy heart. In the 1960s, the city fathers devastated one of the leading centres of the Industrial Revolution in Georgian England. They demolished rows of 18th-century houses and a square, and St Alkmund's church. They then drove a through-road along the bank of the river below the cathedral, despite there already being a by-pass. The partially preserved enclave now marketed as 'Derby Cathedral Quarter' is as much a memorial to what Derby lost as to what remains.

The parish church of All Saints became Derbyshire's cathedral in 1927, but by then only the tower remained of the medieval building. Beautifully proportioned, it still punctuates the Derby skyline. The rest of the church was demolished in 1723 by the then vicar, Michael Hutchinson, to so much local protest that the workmen had to labour overnight. A new building was commissioned from James Gibbs, architect of St Martin-in-the-Fields in London, who partnered the distinguished Midlands architect Francis Smith of Warwick. The strain of raising the necessary money drove Hutchinson mad and he died before the new church was complete.

Gibbs was clearly sensitive to local controversy. He kept the exterior simple, since 'the plainness of the building makes it less expensive and renders it more suitable to the old steeple'. But he showed no such restraint inside. It is a handsome space, with all the gaiety of the period. Bold arcades enliven but do not obstruct the width of the nave. A gallery with an organ loft runs across the west wall. The only substantial change came with cathedral status, when the east end was extended by Ninian Comper and his son, Sebastian. This was completed in 1972 and includes a prominent baldacchino, whose severe white-and-gold classicism contrasts with Gibbs' uninhibited baroque.

The cathedral's pride and joy is its ironwork screen running across the church between nave and sanctuary. The style is English rococo, designed in 1730 by a local ironsmith, Robert Bakewell. The guide rather archly calls it 'delicate as lace and intricate as a fugue'. It is thought Bakewell may have studied in London under Jean Tijou, the French Huguenot master of the Hampton Court gates. The screen is surmounted by the coat of arms of George II. More gates by Bakewell stand outside the main entrance.

Left
Nave with rococo screen

P. M
ELIZABETHÆ
IOHANNIS HARDWICK de HARDWICK in agro DERB: Armigeri filiæ fratriq: IOHANNI tandem cohæredi
primo ROBERTO BARLEY de BARLEY in dicto com: DERB. Armig. nuptæ
poſtea WILL.° CAVENDISH de CHATSWORTH Equ: aur: (thefaurario cameræ Regibus HENRICO VIII EDOARDO VI° ac MARIÆ Reginæ
quibus etiam fuit a ſecretioribus conſilijs)
Deinde WILL.° S.T LOW militi Regij ſatellitij capitaneo;
AC ultimo prænobili GEORGIO comiti SALOPIÆ. deſponſatæ.
Per quem WIL.M CAVENDISH prolem ſolum̃odo habuit; filios tres, ſcil: HENRICVM CAVENDISH de TVTBVRY in agro STAFF. Armig:
(qui GRACIAM dicti GEORGII comitis SALOPIÆ filiam in uxorem duxit) ſine prole legitimâ defunctum,
WILL.M in Baronem CAVENDISH de HARDWICK, nec non in comitẽ DEVONIÆ. per ſereniſsimũ nuper Rege IACOBVM euectum,
Et CAROLVM CAVENDISH de WELBECK Equ: aur: patrem honoratiſsimi WILL. CAVENDISH de Balneo militis Bar: OGLE jure materno
Et in uicecom: MANSFEILD, comitem Marchione ac Ducem de NOVO CASTRO ſuper TINAM et comitẽ de OGLE merito creati
Totidemq: filias; ſcil: FRANCESCAM HENRICO PIEREPONT Equ: aurato, ELIZABETHAM CAROLO STVARTO LENOXIÆ comiti
Et MARIAM GILBERTO comiti SALOPIÆ enuptas.
Hæc inclitiſsima ELIZABETHA SALOPIÆ comitiſsa
Ædium de CHATSWORTH, HARDWICK et OLDCOTES, magnificentiâ clariſsimarum fabricatrix.
Vitam hanc tranſitoriam XIII.° die menſis Februarij
Anno ab incarnatione D.NI MDCVII.° ac circa annum Ætatis ſuæ LXXXVII. finiuit.
Et glorioſam expectans reſurrectionem ſubtus jacet tumulata.

Derby is rich in furnishings. Within the sanctuary is a bishop's throne, a Greek Orthodox piece acquired by a local vicar in an Istanbul market in 1927 and upholstered with Derby needlework. The nave pulpit is ostensibly Georgian but actually Victorian, of 1873. The classical font is modern but of Gibbs' design. Memorials of Derby's great and good fill the walls, some of them transplanted from the medieval church.

Of these, the principal ones are of Derbyshire's prominent Cavendish family, gathered together to the south of the sanctuary. Over them presides the matriarch, Bess of Hardwick, her tomb designed by the architect of Hardwick Hall, Robert Smythson, seven years before her death in 1608. It was presumably with her approval. On its completion, it was said that 'it wanteth nothing but setting up'.

Round Bess were buried over forty members of the Cavendish/Devonshire family. These include Caroline, Countess of Bessborough (d.1760) in a classical pose by J. M. Rysbrack, and Georgiana, Duchess of Devonshire (d.1806). Since the mid-19th century, the family has been buried at Edensor, near Chatsworth, which seems appropriate. Monuments elsewhere in the church are recorded as by Roubiliac, Nollekens, Chantrey and Westmacott, forming, with Rysbrack, a royal flush of church memorial sculptors.

On either side of the altar are two vivid yellow windows by the Welsh artist Ceri Richards. Designed in 1965, they are said to depict All Souls and All Saints. The guidebook explains that the first 'represents the human soul emerging from its physical limitations, while the All Saints window depicts its consummation'. As they are abstract we must take this as read.

Left
Cavendish splendour: Bess of Hardwick

DURHAM

Christ, the Blessed Virgin Mary and St Cuthbert

Prominent setting, Norman nave, Galilee Chapel, Neville screen, Cuthbert shrine, Chapel of Nine Altars

★★★★★

Durham is a colossus among England's cathedrals. In the famous view from the railway, it stands proud on its promontory above the River Wear – a view that caused John Betjeman to plead for the job of Durham station-master. From Framwellgate Bridge below, it merges with its castle in a mighty tableau of Norman power, painted by J. M. W. Turner and Thomas Girtin. It is massive, muscular and slightly frightening. I once saw it after a visit to St Peter's in Rome, and realised there was no contest. Rome was a simpering upstart in comparison.

In 995, the monks of Saxon Lindisfarne were wandering through Northumbria with the coffin of their patron, St Cuthbert, seeking refuge from invading Danes. One day, so it is said, the bier suddenly proved too heavy to be moved. At this point, a cow that had bolted stood fast on a rocky outcrop overlooking the Wear. Taking this as a sign from the saint, the monks lifted the immediately obliging bier, followed 'the dun cow' and built a church on the spot.

After the Conquest, the Normans appreciated the site's military value and supplied it with a castle, a Benedictine monastery and, from 1093, a cathedral. They would be lords of the north and none would question it. Durham's 'prince bishops' would enjoy palatinate (that is, quasi-imperial) power as absolute rulers of the borders, defending them against Scots and Danes alike. The cathedral was completed in just forty years, with St Cuthbert's shrine as its centrepiece. It was soon among the most popular pilgrim destinations in England.

Even today, the route from the old town to the summit of the rock has a sense of expectation, winding through a tangle of old streets until opening on to a spacious enclave of medieval buildings unique in England. The north side is filled with the castle and Norman keep, now used by Durham University. To the west, a terrace overlooks the gorge below, with the hills of County Durham beyond. To the south is the cathedral, a great brown cliff of stone, sometimes shimmering gold in the sun, sometimes dark with rain-swept menace. Nowhere better evokes Auden's description of England's cathedrals as 'Luxury liners laden with souls, / Holding to the east their hulls of stone.'

Durham today remains essentially the cathedral built by the Normans,

Left
Norman potency: the nave piers

Previous spread
Castle and cathedral over the Wear ravine

Opposite
Zigzag elegance in the Galilee Chapel

although later additions predominate on the exterior. Nave and chancel stretch in equal proportion either side of the central crossing. The main tower is 15th-century, a curious design that seems to conclude with battlements above the bell stage, but finds a second wind and surges up a further stage. It is not so much handsome as powerful, as if its late-medieval builders could not forget the history below.

The two west towers are original, each a Norman keep in miniature, covered in arcading. They are spoiled only by 19th-century battlements in place of what were once spires. Beneath this west end, perilously overlooking the gorge, juts the Galilee Chapel. Legend holds that it was a Lady Chapel originally intended for the cathedral's east end, but the ghost of the misogynistic St Cuthbert undermined each attempt at a foundation, averse to women coming near his shrine. A more probable misogynist was its creator, the 12th-century Bishop de Puiset. A line in the nave floor still marks the point beyond which he would not allow women to pass into his church.

Durham's exterior was scraped in the 18th century losing, it is said, two inches and a thousand tons of ancient stonework and carving. Although the original stone must have been heavily eroded, we can never know what wonders were lost. At least the fearsome romanesque sanctuary knocker survives. A fugitive who grasped it was, in theory, allowed 37 days of safety in the cathedral to make peace with his enemies, or to escape, before being passed over to the authorities. The present knocker is a replica, the original being on display in the cathedral museum.

Durham's interior, begun in 1093, ranks among the great works of Europe's 11th-century architecture and is now a World Heritage Site. The nave arcades form an avenue of towering redwoods, each trunk rising from square plinth to cushion capital, alternately circular and composite. The piers are incised with fluting, diapering, spiral and chevron, the incisions once filled with metal, and presumably coloured. They convey intense confidence and power. Might a future generation restore them to their former decorative glory?

All other English cathedrals of this period have wooden roofs, since it was assumed a Norman arch could not support the weight of stone. Durham's vault is of stone – a daring and costly innovation for its completion date of 1135. The vault is not barrel-shaped but has ribs rising to what is, in effect, a forerunner of a pointed arch. The vault is supported by flying buttresses, hidden in the aisle roofs.

CHRISTUS
EST STELLA
MATUTINA QUI NOCTE
SAECULI TRANSACTA
LUCEM VITAE
SANCTIS PROMITTIT
ET PANDIT AETERNAM
CHRIST IS THE MORNING STAR
WHO WHEN THE NIGHT
OF THIS WORLD IS PAST
BRINGS TO HIS SAINTS
THE PROMISE OF
THE LIGHT OF LIFE
& OPENS EVERLASTING DAY

Left
'Frivolous' Tudor clock

It is strange that this device, so visually effective, was not to be imitated in any other cathedral for half a century. The most radical engineering breakthrough of the Middle Ages, the ribbed vault, was here initiated far from the cultural mainstream of Britain, and indeed Europe.

Every moulded feature of the nave is decorated with zigzag. It covers the arcades, triforium, clerestory and main vault, almost obsessively. There is no other decoration apart from a few monsters peering down from corbels. The side walls are lined with blind arcading. Otherwise, the nave is sculptural and spare.

An extraordinary contrast is provided by de Puiset's Galilee Chapel, reached through a door in the west wall. Its name derives from its role in the Easter ritual, Galilee being the supposed point of Christ's departure for Jerusalem. Although the arcades are Norman, they are a far cry from the potency of the nave. When it was built in *c*1175, pointed arches had already arrived in England, notably in William of Sens' rebuilding of Canterbury. Yet here we see old-fashioned round arches on spindly piers in a basilica-like chamber, reminiscent of the mosque-cathedral of Cordoba. Once so forward looking, Durham is suddenly archaic.

On the north side of the chapel lies the tomb of the historian of the early Middle Ages, the Venerable Bede. He was brought from Jarrow to Durham by monks in the 11th century, whether for safe keeping or in hope of pilgrim revenue, who knows? The chapel walls carry medieval paintings, the windows medieval glass. Late in the day, when suffused with western sunlight, this last cry of Norman design offers the most serene of spaces.

The west end of the nave is dominated by a Decorated window. It is of seven lights rising towards an arch, where the tracery constricts then bursts into a lovely lily pattern. By the north door is a contrast, the 'daily bread' window by Mark Angus and donated by Marks and Spencer in 1984. Its abstract colour supposedly illustrates the Last Supper, which looks to have been a terrible mess.

Opposite stands a font of 1663, with reputedly the tallest canopy in England. It was designed at the bidding of John Cosin, bishop of Durham, after the Restoration. Cosin, a high-churchman and friend of Archbishop William Laud, served the Stuart royal family in exile during the Commonwealth. On the Restoration, as a Protestant eager for Catholic reconciliation, he sought to fuse gothic and renaissance traditions in church design. He tended to gothic in (clerical) chancels and classicism in (lay) naves. Cosin also added the magnificent organ case near the south door.

The south transept is festooned with regimental and miners' banners. It is overlooked by a splendid Tudor clock with a pinnacled canopy and crown. It has 48 rather than 60 minute marks and was narrowly saved from being turned into firewood during the Civil War by being manifestly not liturgical. This cut no ice with the Victorians who removed it as 'too frivolous', but it is now restored. Next to it is the entrance to the central tower, 325 exhausting steps to a spectacular view over County Durham.

The choir stalls were installed by Cosin in 1665, reasserting the 'old religion' in their gothic form. He even gave them new misericords. Beyond them stands the grandiloquent bishop's throne, erected by (and for) Thomas Hatfield, prince-bishop for thirty-six years until his death in 1381. The throne, with Hatfield's prospective tomb beneath, is said to be taller even than the pope's in Rome, an extraordinary piece of episcopal egotism.

East of the throne stands the Neville screen and flanking sedilia. This exuberant work of Perpendicular art was donated by the northern grandees, the Nevilles, in thanks for St Cuthbert's intervention in the battle of Neville's Cross against the Scots in 1346. Though outnumbered, the northern armies defeated David II's invaders and captured the Scots king. The screen was designed by Edward III's master mason, Henry Yevele, and shipped from London in kit form. It soars upwards like a row of stalagmites in a limestone cave. They would once have been brightly painted and held 107 alabaster statues in their niches, but all were lost at the Reformation. The screen's nakedness is painful to witness, like a sculpture gallery with only the plinths remaining.

In the adjacent choir aisle are good modern windows. The Millennium Window by Joseph Nuttgens (1995) depicts scenes from Durham history in pastel shades. Next door, Tom Denny's Transfiguration window (2010) is a blaze of yellows and reds, crowded with figures gazing upwards in wonder. If modern art can fill windows, why can it not fill the Neville screen?

To the east, the cathedral changes gear. Norman arcades are replaced by the slender lancets of the magnificent gothic retrochoir, called the Chapel of Nine Altars. This eastwards extension of the old cathedral was begun by Bishop Richard Poore in the 13th century, presumably on the site of de Puiset's 'undermined' Lady Chapel. A veteran of the 1214 Fourth Lateran Council, Poore was founder of the new Salisbury cathedral

Opposite
Cuthbert's shrine and Neville screen

and one of the regents of England during the minority of Henry III. He was clearly a busy and an able man. In 1228, he was sent north as bishop of Durham to resolve disputes within the fractious Benedictine community. Medieval monasteries were rarely at peace with their neighbours or themselves.

Poore was attuned to the booming pilgrimage business and sought a new showcase for St Cuthbert's shrine. He placed the shrine itself on a platform directly behind the high altar reached up flights of steps in the most dramatic way imaginable. The original shrine was destroyed at the Reformation, but when Henry VIII's commissioners opened the actual coffin, they were shocked to see the saint's body was, as legend had declared, 'lying whole with his face bare and his beard as if it had a fortnight's growth'. This alleged sign of sanctity – or efficient embalming – so disturbed them that they retreated and wisely referred the matter to the king. Cuthbert's various relics are now in the cathedral museum. Over the shrine hangs a canopy by Ninian Comper, showing a vividly 20th-century image of Christ as a youth.

From the tomb, we descend to the Chapel of Nine Altars. This was in effect a great hall where crowds would have awaited their moment at the shrine. Its Early Gothic style echoes Poore's interior at Salisbury, evidenced by copious Purbeck marble. Its soaring height maintains the majesty of the Norman cathedral while the lancet windows suffuse the space with a sombre light.

The north window, however, is not lancet but a later Decorated insertion and in a most extraordinary form. The Joseph window has tracery on two planes, the inside one of intersecting bars, the outside of geometrical ones, with a wall passage in between. The intention is obscure but, to Pevsner, the effect of the window is 'one of breath-taking vigour and splendour'.

The nine altars that used to line the east wall are now reduced to three. The chapel is used for exhibitions and has rather succumbed to hoardings and clutter, but there is a moving Pietà (1981) by a local sculptor, Fenwick Lawson, in raw rough-cut wood.

Durham cathedral embraces England's most extensive monastic enclave. A quiet cloister with wide pavements and Perpendicular arcades gives on to a large Norman chapter house, a monks' dormitory, now a reading room, a kitchen and an undercroft. All are in the process of restoration, mostly being converted as museums or for diocesan use.

ANDREW · JAMES · JOHN · PHILIP · BARTHOLOMEW · THOMAS

ELY

The Holy and Undivided Trinity

Norman west front, crossing octagon and lantern, Lady Chapel carvings, Scott restoration

★★★★★

Ely is the great eccentric among English cathedrals. Once on a bright winter's day, I watched it from a distance, rising above a fenland fog like a castle in some childhood fantasy. Ely stands with Lincoln and Wells as one of my 'three graces'. After each visit, I am left in a state of wonder that England could have created such a place eight centuries ago.

The original abbey was founded in the 7th century by England's first female saint, Etheldreda. She was a local princess who fled from not one but two arranged marriages, then founded both a monastery and a nunnery. She died, it is said, a virgin and was duly the object of veneration and pilgrimage.

The abbey was reached by three causeways over the water. It was briefly the base of the Saxon rebel Hereward the Wake, and its isolation and independence was naturally of concern to the Conqueror. He entrusted the abbey to his cousin, Abbot Simeon of Winchester, with absolute power to deal with local trouble. In 1081, Simeon demolished and began to rebuild the abbey, and it became a cathedral in 1109.

As housing estates sprawl over the surrounding land, traditional views of this 'ship of the Fens' are disappearing, but the view from the south is still relatively pristine, showing the western and eastern arms divided by the famous lantern. When floating on a bed of trees in summer, they can appear like two cathedrals moored head to toe.

The original Norman building had no fewer than six towers, one over the crossing and another, which survives, over the west end, with two subsidiary towers over each of the western transepts. Ely ranked with Durham and Norwich as works of Norman ostentation, asserting the potency of conquest down the eastern flank of 12th-century England. Even so, by the end of the century the press of pilgrims to Etheldreda's shrine required expansion, leading to the customary rebuilding of the east end in the 13th century in a sumptuous Early Gothic style.

Disaster struck a century later when, in 1322, the crossing tower collapsed into the choir. The consequent reconstruction brought Ely its most prized feature, its central octagon and lantern. When a further catastrophe occurred at the end of the 14th century with the collapse of the north-west transept and towers, there was no pressure or no money to rebuild. To this day, Ely looks like the wounded veteran of some

Left
The ship of the Fens

forgotten war, the only un-rebuilt cathedral other than Carlisle. Paul Johnson makes a passionate case for the transept's reinstatement. To others, its mutilation is part of Ely's charm.

Though lopsided, the west front is still magnificent. The three remaining towers are romanesque architecture at its most sophisticated, displaying Anglo-Norman blind arcading from top to bottom. A blank wall seems to have been anathema to these masons. Pevsner points out that the south-west tower is adorned with freestanding shafts rising in front of the arch openings, as if it were temporary scaffolding. I have seen this nowhere else. The Early Gothic extension over the galilee porch, its arcading now gently pointed, adds effortless elegance. Three lancet windows rise above the galilee's double-portal, with floral tracery in its tympanum.

The remainder of Ely's exterior reflects its chequered history. The lantern's piercings, crockets and flying buttresses sit like a Decorated crown over the Norman transepts below, uniting and balancing the surrounding arms. The lantern is as much part of Ely's character as is the steeple at Salisbury, also built during Edward II's building boom of the early 14th century.

The south wall of the nave contains two works of Norman virtuosity, the prior's door and the monks' door (1135). Composed of spiralling tendrils, they are crowded with figures and motifs. The tympanum above the prior's door has a Christ in Majesty, attended by distorted angels with huge hands and feet. The monks' door is arched with a cusped trefoil, its mouldings an encyclopaedia of romanesque carving. Later gothic masters respected these extraordinary – and most un-gothic – portals and thankfully did not replace them.

Ely's interior is the only one I know that can be seen from the seat of a car, the result of the local council judging the west door needed a road a few feet in front of it. From whatever standpoint, the view of the nave is awesome. Framed by the tall western arch, the vista is of a colonnade of piers and arches, formal, relentless, dignified, the knights of Normandy towering in line abreast over the fenland rebels. There is no decoration or ornament, just a rhythmic alternation of rounded and shafted piers. Overhead is a wooden ceiling, painted by the Victorian muralist Henry Styleman Le Strange and, when he died, completed by his friend Thomas Gambier Parry, in warm reds and greens.

As we walk down the nave towards the crossing, Ely conveys a strange transformation. Instead of the enclosure of a crossing and

Previous spread
Octagon and lantern with Victorian decoration

Opposite
Romanesque portal: Christ in Majesty

presbytery, we become aware of a dramatic sense of space ahead. Suddenly the roof opens and a great opening soars upwards. It is one of the most exhilarating moments in English architecture.

When the Norman tower fell in 1322, it took with it the crossing and three bays of the choir. A monk/architect, Alan of Walsingham, was in charge at the time and is said to have fled Ely in despair. He recovered and devised as replacement not a tower but an octagon on eight piers, its vault acting as base for the lantern. This lantern rose to a second vault, each stage in turn suffused with light.

The story of the Ely lantern is enhanced by the mystery of its creation. If Alan of Walsingham was the original designer, the woodwork was by William Hurley who, as the royal carpenter, was paid twice the wage of the next craftsman in line. While the vault below is of stone, the lantern had to be lighter and of wood. This required eight colossal oak beams resting on sixteen beams, all hewn from trunks brought by water from Bedfordshire. Modern engineers continue to marvel at the skill of these masons and carpenters, working with none of the tools of modern construction.

At the apex of the lantern is a painting of Christ in Majesty, surrounded by panels of angels playing instruments, again by Gambier Parry. The panels fold back and give visitors to the lantern a view down into the cathedral; this is after a climb I recommend for those with a head for heights and an interest in medieval woodwork.

When seen from below, the octagon and lantern vaults seem both to radiate outwards and yet draw the eye towards their centre. In any light, they offer a kaleidoscope of lines and angles, the shafts playing diagonally over the crossing like spotlights chasing ghosts. They illuminate the pier capitals in the crossing below which form a tableau of the life of Etheldreda. Niches set into the side walls show apostles.

Eastwards, we reach an altogether different Ely. The collapse of the tower was used as an opportunity to rebuild the three western choir bays. The style conformed to the earlier gothic of the presbytery but is heavy with Decorated motifs. The main and triforium arcades have almost obsessive shafting and moulding, garlanded with stiff-leaf and studded with ballflower. Crocketed brackets drip down the spandrels. Overhead, the decorous tierceron vault of the sanctuary breaks into liernes above the newer choir. Victorian purists found a certain coarseness in this late-Decorated architecture of the 1320s and 1330s, sensing the impending advent of what they regarded as

Left
Scott restores Ely's majesty

the vulgar Perpendicular.

By the start of the Victorian era, Ely was in poor condition. On one of his rides, William Cobbett denounced it as 'in a state of disgraceful disrepair and disfigurement'. A. W. N. Pugin arrived and reportedly burst into tears: 'O God, what has England done to deserve this.' Only the arrival in 1850 of the ubiquitous George Gilbert Scott put matters to rights. The choir screen is one of Scott's earliest, replacing a stone pulpitum destroyed in the 18th century. It both opens and frames the view from the nave to the choir and altar, and became the model for similar screens in churches and cathedrals elsewhere. With organ cases repositioned, surviving stalls restored and a lavish reredos, Scott's mastery of gothic revival is nowhere on better display than at Ely.

The cathedral has memorials of quality if not of quantity. In the north aisle is a monument to Bishop Northwold (d.1254), original rebuilder of the east end of the cathedral, an essay in Decorated mannerism. In the south choir aisle is the tomb of John Tiptoft, Earl of Worcester (d.1470), lying in prayer between his two wives, both of whom look more than his equal. Both aisles terminate in chantry chapels, entered through elaborate Tudor screens. That on the north side is to Bishop Alcock (d.1500) and is Perpendicular in a final frenzied climax before the renaissance. Every canopy, every niche, every corner is crowded with monsters, flowers and musical instruments. Above is a pretty fan vault and pendant.

Opposite, at the end of the south aisle, is Bishop West's chantry (d.1533). Its screen is covered in statue niches emptied by iconoclasts, a gallery of frames without their pictures. Inside is a similar gallery, also much bashed about. The vault is panelled, with traces of renaissance detail, the foretaste of things to come.

Ely has no surviving cloister or chapter house. Instead, there is a Lady Chapel, built at the same time as the lantern but not finished until 1349. The chapel is a precious example of the Decorated style at its most accomplished. It was probably fashioned by John of Wisbech, whose reward was to die of the Black Death. The plan is a simple rectangle. A large window fills the east end with reticulated tracery, and the vault is the widest of the period in England (46ft). But the chapel's glory is the stone seats along the walls, like stalls in a chapter house. Their canopies of ogival and triangular gables undulate round the room in a continuous flowing line, voluptuously coated in leaves, crockets and figures. Each could be the page of an illuminated missal in stone, but stone

Left
Lady Chapel stalls: filigree in stone

Opposite
Lady chapel with ruined stalls

fashioned so meticulously it might be the work of silversmiths.

These stalls were defaced in the Reformation, when iconoclasts paid particular attention to the cult of St Mary and thus to Lady Chapels. As a result, it is a sad chamber, as if a bunch of drunken vandals had gone berserk with hammers, which is probably what happened. The niches and plinths would have contained statues of saints, brightly coloured, while the gable panels depicted biblical scenes in relief. It is hard to see how these walls might be restored to their former state. We are left with a fragmentary evocation of a vision lost. In the circumstances, David Wynne's Madonna (2000) above the altar seems a sentimental modern intrusion, in contrast to Peter Eugene Ball's evocative Christ in Glory (2000) above the nave pulpit.

Ely's original glass was lost to the ravages of time but it was replaced by the Victorians in the most complete programme of neo-medieval glass in any cathedral, over a hundred new windows in all. The east window tells the story of Christ's life by William Wailes. The finest sequence is of the gospels by Clayton & Bell in the south choir aisle. In the nave triforium is the Stained Glass Museum, including 13th-century roundels of the martyrdom of St Vincent. We can here compare originals with facsimiles by such Victorians as John Hardman, C. E. Kempe and William Morris, and also the master of modern stained glass, John Piper. Ely is a monument as much to the talents of these artists as to their medieval forebears.

EXETER

St Peter

West front statues, longest vault in England, coloured roofs, bishop's throne, medieval east window

Exeter is an immaculate cathedral, luxurious, confident and mature. Its single continuous vault is the longest in Europe, the climax of Decorated gothic as this complex style approached its zenith in the early years of the 14th century. The reign of Henry III (1216–72) had seen English architecture absorb its last great transfusion of French influence. This now flowered in the building boom of Edward II (1307–27).

After the departure of the Roman legions in the 5th century, Devon and Cornwall remained a land apart, with what is believed to have been an uninterrupted allegiance to Celtic Christianity. But as Wessex gradually asserted its dominance over southern Britain, Canterbury took charge of episcopal appointments. In 1050, the twin Cornish dioceses of Crediton and St Germans were combined under a new cathedral for Devon and Cornwall at Exeter. The Normans rebuilt the cathedral from 1112.

All that survives of this cathedral are the two towers flanking the nave, which remain Exeter's signature to this day. In 1258, Bishop Bronescombe attended the consecration of the new cathedral at Salisbury and returned intent on replicating its Early Gothic majesty at Exeter. But it was not until 1275 that demolition and rebuilding was started in earnest, and by now the prevailing style was Decorated. The progress of the work was recorded in what are called fabric rolls, accounts of money, labour and material coming onto the site, year after year, with a degree of detail unique in any European cathedral. Although a mason named Master Roger began Bronescombe's project, it was taken over in 1315 by the outstanding English architect of the day, Thomas of Witney, then master mason at Winchester. Thomas's cathedral is essentially the one we see today, the nearest to Salisbury in stylistic cohesion.

Exeter sits in a close of quiet contentment. There is no traffic. The north side is flanked by lawns and a backdrop of shops and town houses, with alleys connecting to the high street. To the east runs the old Roman wall. The tragedy of Exeter's 20th-century self-laceration, when the city fathers demolished such of the old town as Hitler's bombers left standing, is thus out of sight. This is one of the few cathedrals whose west front visitors can enjoy from outdoor cafés and restaurants.

Left
West front: kings in argument

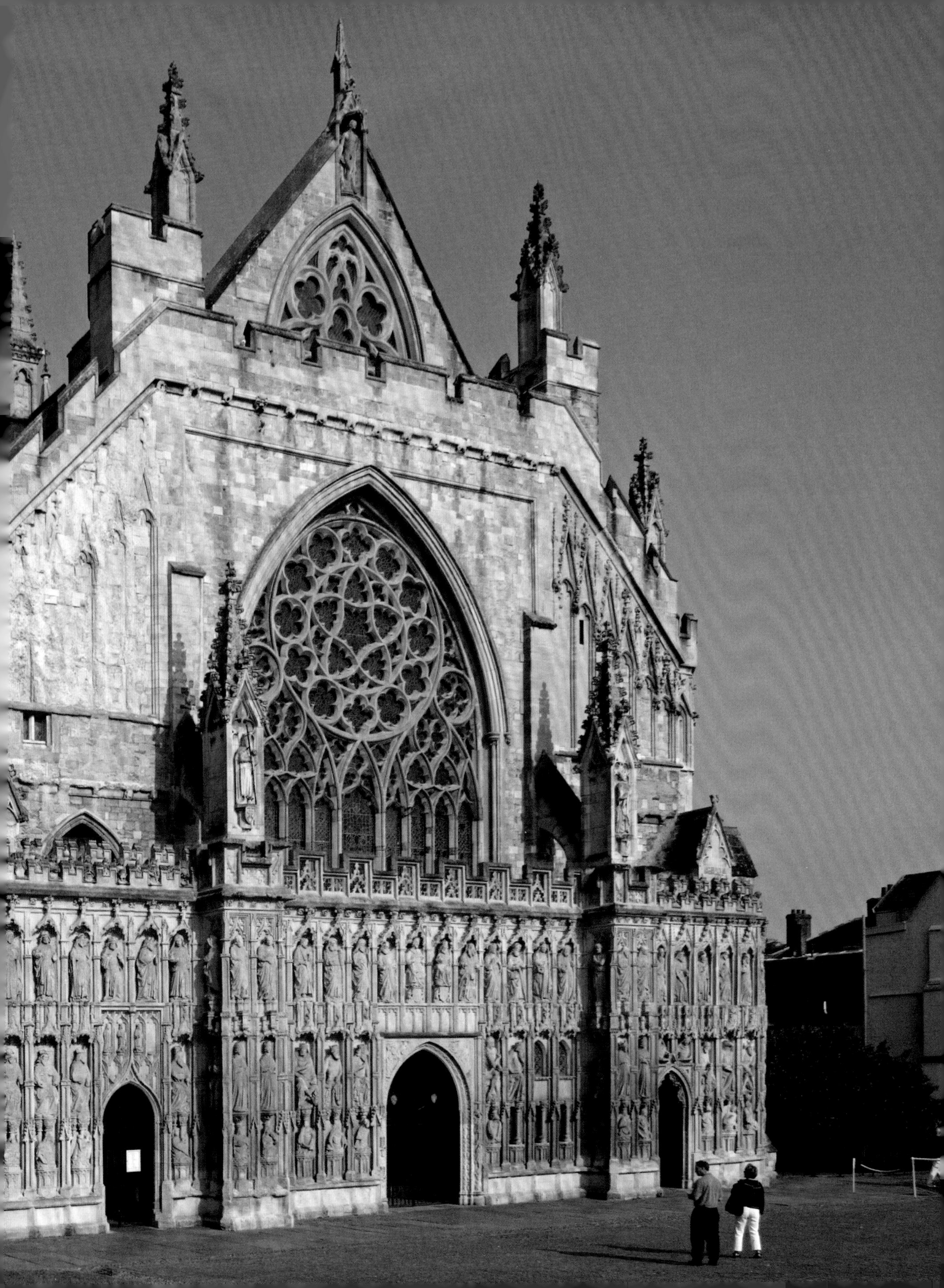

From every angle, the ancient Norman towers look endearingly antique, covered in blind arcading and crowned with turrets and triangular caps. They stand almost free of the intervening structure, relieving the monotony that afflicts England's longer cathedrals, such as St Albans and Winchester. The exterior of the nave and chancel are clad in deep flying buttresses, their pinnacles dominating the building's profile. Between the buttresses, we glimpse the cathedral's Decorated windows. Whether in the nave, chancel or clerestory, each is different, the tracery being mostly geometric, with added triangles, trefoils and quatrefoils.

Exeter's west front is a first intimation of the delights within. It is basically a giant Decorated gable of overlapping planes. A magnificent rose window is composed of cinquefoil discs encircling a wayward Star of David in a swirl of ecstatic tracery. Above it, a secondary window in the gable top peers like a face over a castle wall. In 1338, a new bishop, Grandisson, decided to make his mark on the then almost complete cathedral by fixing a low screen of sculpture to the west end. As Bronescombe had imitated Salisbury, so Grandisson would imitate Wells and Lincoln.

This screen was not completed until 1375, with Grandisson dead and the Black Death having carried away its probable designer, William Joy. It takes the form of a gallery with three tiers of statues, surrounding three diminutive but beautifully carved doorways. It is as if a row of pictures had been left leaning against an available wall. The lowest tier is

Previous spread
Norman tower, west front gallery

Left
The glory of Decorated: choir and sanctuary with bishop's throne on right

Left
The martyrdom of Becket

Opposite
Music on high: celestial orchestra

of angels, mostly so eroded as to be shapeless stones. The higher tiers are of kings and knights, then of saints and apostles. In spite of also being eroded, these figures retain personality and animation. They stand, sit, turn and pray. Two have their legs crossed and appear to be arguing with each other.

Exeter's interior is a burst of Decorated glory. Its 100yd undulation of shaft clusters, arch mouldings and vaulting ribs seems to disappear into the far distance. The architect of this work, presumably Master Thomas, was clearly accomplished in the latest gothic forms. Each pier has sixteen shafts, with eight mouldings to each arch. Visual interest is maintained by the use of different shades of stone – creamy limestone above, blue Purbeck marble for the main piers below. The triforium is a recessed arcade of trefoils, deftly recoloured. The clerestory windows are filled with the variegated tracery noticed from outside.

Exeter's roof is of incomparable exuberance. All eleven ribs in each bay spring from a single capital below the clerestory line, splaying out into the window openings and up to the central ridge. There are no liernes or subsidiary ribs, just a rhythmic movement. The rib joins are sealed with coloured bosses, which are bigger than the cathedral norm, making them easier to enjoy from below – whether with the naked eye, binoculars or a wheeled mirror. The cast is the familiar one of monsters, monarchs, biblical scenes and a vivid Becket martyrdom, interspersed with baskets of gilded foliage.

Attached to the north wall is Exeter's most popular internal feature, a minstrels' gallery, fronted by a frieze of colourful angels playing musical instruments. Since most cathedral ritual was confined to the choir, this implies a more active engagement of the nave congregation than is often supposed. The angels are, like the bosses, brightly coloured and astonishingly lively for medieval statues, each playing a different instrument, including a fiddle, a recorder, a Jew's harp, a portable organ and bagpipes. Research indicates that the statues may have come from elsewhere and were cut to fit into the bays.

Exeter's crossing does not really exist since there is no central tower. The two Norman side towers form notional transepts, broken into by tall arches that do not interrupt the onward march of the nave roof. In the south transept is the vigorously restored 14th-century tomb of the 2nd Earl and Countess of Devon; she was a de Bohun and her family's heraldic swans are at her feet. In the north transept is a 15th-century clock and, below it, an ancient

door with a medieval cat-flap. The cat was employed for a penny a week to keep down the vermin. Next to it is the Sylke chantry, with Tudor carving and wall painting.

The eastern arm of the cathedral is announced by the pulpitum, first of the furnishings by Thomas of Witney. Dating from 1324, it is of three arches topped by an openwork balustrade. The crockets and trefoils are stretched, almost tortured, to fulfil the designer's mannerist vision. From every nook peers an animal or a human face. The arch spandrels sprout foliage so undercut they might be about to fall into a basket below. Each panel of the balustrade contains a Jacobean painting of a biblical scene, replacing panels destroyed at the Reformation. They are an anachronism that sits happily in these rich surroundings.

The elaboration of Exeter's eastern arm partly compensates for the cathedral's medieval deficiency, its lack of a saint's shrine as a focus for pilgrimage. Though the choir stalls are a George Gilbert Scott reconstruction, the canopies, misericords, bishop's throne, sedilia and screens are all believed to be original, some recoloured. Some of the misericords date from the mid-13th century, that is from the earlier church, making them the oldest complete set in England. The seats are sadly kept down and are therefore invisible.

The most extraordinary furnishing is the bishop's throne and its early 14th-century canopy, again recorded as being by Thomas. He was paid the then enormous sum of twelve shillings to build it in a month in 1313. The canopy is telescopic in form, rising to the first nodding ogee arch in England, and set beneath an enormous pinnacle. The whole work would have been gilded and painted and, as a result, today looks uncomfortably bare. From this throne, William of Orange read out a 'declaration of peaceful intent' after landing at Brixham for his invasion of England in 1688.

The sanctuary contains Thomas's three stepped and effusive sedilia. Each has a gilded canopy with, above it, a niche with another canopy containing a statue. A pinnacle completes this wedding cake confection. To Pevsner, the Exeter sedilia rank among the finest works of 14th-century gothic, with 'all the intricacy and unrestrained spatial play … more easily seen than described'.

The view east now becomes complex. There is no reredos since that supplied by Thomas was lost. Instead, the sanctuary's east end is closed by two almost round arches, through which we glimpse the retrochoir beyond. By now, we are aware of Exeter's most distinctive characteristic, the enhancement of its gothic

Left
Tudor over-crowding: the Carew tomb

architecture by restored colouring. We have here the most extensive work of the 20th-century medievalist E. W. Tristram, who used tiny specks of original paint to research and recreate the original appearance of walls, vaults and statues. Most colourful are the roof bosses and corbels. Over the sanctuary hovers a mermaid, with a mirror and evident vagina. Such a portrayal of temptation may be theological, but the masons were surely having fun at the expense of the clerics below.

The choir aisles are lined with effigies of medieval knights lying in niches, as well as brasses and wall plaques of those killed in more recent combats. They form a narrative of what seems a nation continuously at war. In the north aisle is the tomb of Sir Robert Stapledon (d.1320), bashed but exquisitely carved; he lies attended by his (beheaded) squire, his groom and his horse.

The sanctuary arches act as bases for Exeter's great east window. Its original glass, though much reordered, is early 14th century and quite different in style from that of York and Canterbury. The architectural settings and frames are simple, the faces of saints and biblical characters vividly alive and, to that extent, quite un-medieval, notably the portraits of Isaiah, Abraham and Moses. This window must have formed an astonishing partner to Thomas's lost reredos below.

Exeter's east end would have been crowded with chapels and chantries, of which some dozen survive. The Lady Chapel, starting point of the Decorated rebuild, has vaults that fan outwards in a foretaste of those of the main roof. To Pevsner this vaulting was among the most advanced in England at the time.

The Lady Chapel walls are flanked with large gothic tombs, including a coloured effigy of Lady Dodderidge (d.1614), in high Tudor fashion, holding a skull. The chapel's west end is guarded by effigies of Bishops Bronescombe (d.1280) and Stafford (d.1419), the latter's alabaster covered in ancient graffiti. Both are beneath filigree Perpendicular canopies. In the centre is a fine bronze of Unfolding Love (2006) by Janis Ridley.

The lesser chapels each have personalities of their own. St Gabriel's Chapel vault has been completely repainted. St John's Chapel has a Carew tomb of 1589, with a knight and his lady spaciously accommodated, while their nephew is crammed on to a shelf beneath. In the Oldham Chapel is an original carved reredos, much bashed, and the tomb of Bishop Hugh Oldham (d.1519), replete with his rebus of an owl. Thanks to Tristram, Exeter conveys better than anywhere the experience of a great cathedral in its gothic prime.

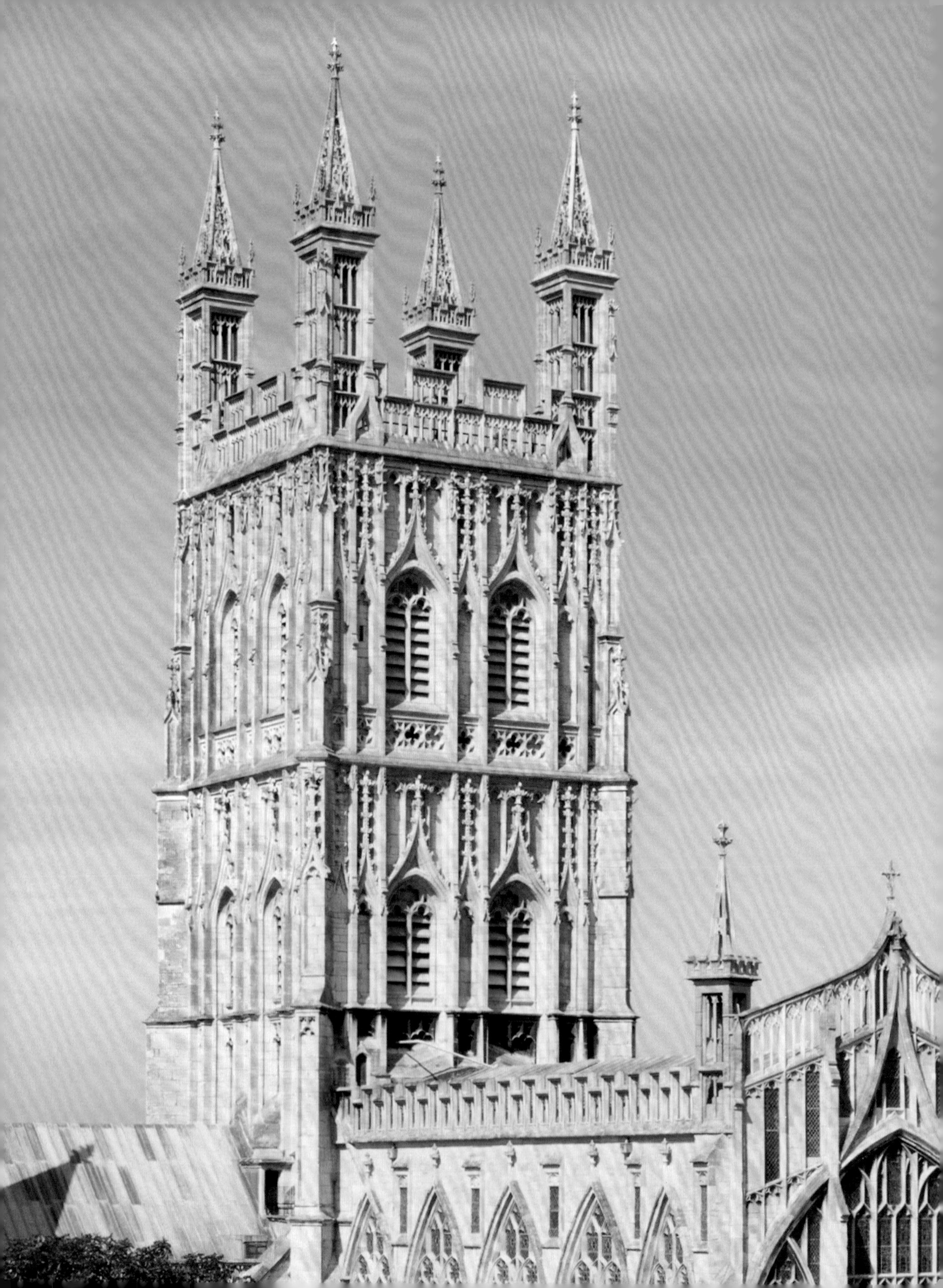

GLOUCESTER

St Peter and the Holy and Indivisible Trinity

Norman nave, earliest Perpendicular interior, largest medieval window, Edward II's tomb, fan-vault cloister

★★★★

A silver tower shimmering with ornament rises over the Severn valley. It was long a beacon for pilgrims descending from the Cotswolds or travelling upstream from Bristol, many to visit the tomb of the murdered Edward II. In the cathedral, they would find not just a king's tomb but an ancient Norman abbey which, partly thanks to that tomb, was to surge briefly into the forefront of gothic innovation, leading the way to the glories of English Perpendicular. Gloucester is the most exciting of England's smaller cathedrals.

The former Benedictine abbey was the creation of a giant of the Norman Conquest, Abbot Serlo, formerly a monk at Mont Saint-Michel. When he arrived in 1072, he found a monastery reduced to just two monks and a handful of novices. By the time he died in 1104, it was one of a chain of active monasteries the length of the Welsh Marches, embracing Hereford, Worcester, Shrewsbury and Chester. The story of the abbey was nonetheless uneventful until its fortuitous proximity to Berkeley Castle, scene of Edward II's murder in 1327.

Gloucester's Abbot Thokey, who had been a friend of the monarch, brought the king's body from the castle with elaborate ceremony. It was conveyed in a hearse adorned with golden leopards and attended by a procession of monks. The new king, the young Edward III, deliberately made the burial an event of political significance, glorifying his father's legitimacy against the uprising led by his mother and her lover, Mortimer.

No sooner had Edward II's body been laid to rest than miracles were reported in its vicinity, and pilgrims began to appear. The arrival of royal masons under the king's patronage led to the drastic conversion of the south transept and choir in the new style then appearing in London, to be known later as Perpendicular. The contrast between Gloucester's Norman nave and its 14th-century transept, choir and presbytery is a set text of English architecture. The rebuilding of the tower followed a century later. Impressed by the abbey's royal antecedents, Henry VIII made Gloucester a cathedral at the Reformation.

The new tower, the most prominent feature of the exterior, was begun in 1450 and clearly takes its cue from neighbouring Worcester. Its architect seemed to sense Worcester's (albeit modest) shortcomings and

Left
Stone imitates silver: the Perpendicular tower

sought something more refined. The gothic tension between horizontal and vertical lines is perfectly balanced. Two tall stages rise from the roof gables, while the bell-openings crowned with ogees are almost flush to the walls. Four lantern turrets linked by a pierced parapet complete the composition. The stonework is so finely carved that, in sunlight, it can seem crafted from gold.

Gloucester can only be understood, outside and inside, through its split Norman/late-gothic personality. This is immediately evident on the outside of the south transept, visible from the close. The wall is Norman, but random struts and supports seem to imprison the Norman work in later strengthening. Most cathedrals replaced their Norman features when converting to gothic. Gloucester encased them, at times almost imprisoned them, in gothic features. It is as if the locals refused to allow the royal masons from London to eradicate all trace of their old abbey.

The nave is uncompromising Norman. Cylindrical drum piers march east to the crossing. They rise to plain capitals, which act as bases for arches that leap from one pier to the next, carved with zigzag. The corbels are angry grotesques. The vault above is Early Gothic, springing from clerestory shafts that seem feeble compared with the columns beneath. To Pevsner, this vault was 'an elegant and graceful hat that hardly fits the rugged face below'.

In the south aisle, the hat becomes a muffler. Subsidence in the 1320s meant the entire south wall had to be rebuilt, but now in the Decorated style. The windows with butterfly-patterned tracery carry an abundance of ballflower, reputedly with 1500 separate balls. This really was the oddest of medieval decorative fads.

We now move east to the transept, and the shock is clear even to the most untutored eye. To Paul Johnson, 'There is no more exhilarating sensation in the whole of English architecture than the sudden emergence from the Gloucester nave-tunnel into late-medieval space and light … this blinding world of glass and wafery stone'. We are in the presence of the earliest surviving manifestation of England's one truly home-grown version of gothic, Perpendicular.

The style's origins are believed to lie in St Stephen's Chapel in Westminster and in old St Paul's, London, both long gone, hence the attribution of this part of the cathedral to Edward III's patronage. The London masons were clearly reluctant to demolish the east end of the abbey entirely – possibly because the parishioners wanted the old chapels to remain.

Opposite
Exquisite alabaster: Edward II effigy

Thus the concealing of the Norman walls in what amounted to a Perpendicular stone skin.

This was not easy. In the south transept, existing walls were shaved of stone, and new windows inserted beneath old Norman gables. Everything was covered in a lattice of soaring shafts and struts. The occasional Norman arch or window can be seen lurking behind the new panels.

The south transept contains a curiosity, a medieval wall bracket apparently carved by a master mason in memory of an assistant who fell to his death from the roof. St Andrew's Chapel, east of the transept, is decorated by the Victorian muralist Thomas Gambier Parry, wealthy creator of Highnam church not far outside the city, and decorator of the lantern of Ely cathedral.

Set into the north transept wall is an elegant screen (*c*1240) of three arches thought to be a former pulpitum. Such structures were moved aside by (conservation-minded) restorers eager to open up through-views from nave to choir. The astronomical clock is late Victorian art nouveau by Henry Wilson.

The choir and presbytery, not completed until the 1360s, presented the king's mason with a bigger challenge than did the south transept. They set out to turn the entire east end into what amounts to a single, aisleless chamber, a new chapel royal in glass and stone. Shafts rise from ground to roof, as if triforium and clerestory were mere stops on an elevator. The shafts then burst into tiercerons and liernes in the vault.

Gloucester's new vault ran continuously from the east through the crossing tower, but at this point it comes to an abrupt halt as the dimensions clearly did not fit. The architect, therefore, had to construct strainer arches to carry the vault over the transept arches, precursor of those in Wells. They are delicate structures, wonderfully serpentine in shape, creating beauty out of necessity. The vault bosses depict Christ surrounded by angels playing musical instruments.

The choir stalls below have tall ogival canopies. There are forty-six medieval misericords – including much-studied early ball games – plus those added by George Gilbert Scott. The Harris organ of 1665 may impede the view from the nave, but it does so with panache.

Gloucester's presbytery east wall is less a wall than the largest uninterrupted expanse of medieval glass in existence. It is composed of nine tiers of rectilinear panel tracery. The sides are splayed, turning it into a bow window, thus enabling even more glass to be carried. This window is known as the Crécy window,

Opposite
South transept:
enter the Perpendicular

thought to have been erected to celebrate the Battle of Crécy (1346), Edward III's first great victory in the war with France.

Jon Cannon sees the window as the summation of the presbytery and royal chapel. Its emphasis is on the sacredness of kingship 'laying out the entire feudal order like a management chart, from the heraldry of local barons at the base, running through the bishops … through the saints and the apostles, to Christ in Majesty at the top'. The figures, in red, white and blue, stand in elaborate architectural settings. The effect is lighter than most medieval glass, signalling the more subdued mood of the new Perpendicular. Other windows comprise a treasury of Victorian glass by Clayton & Bell, John Hardman and William Wailes. One by C. E. Kempe illustrates Gloucester's history.

Below in the presbytery lies the fount of Gloucester's late-medieval wealth, the tomb of Edward II. The tomb was allegedly supervised by Edward III in person and sits on a Purbeck base. The effigy is in the then novel material of alabaster, semi-translucent and easy to carve. There is no trace of Edward's reputed effeteness. He is depicted open-eyed and every inch a macho Plantagenet, with curling beard, orb and sceptre. Above rises a canopy of cinquefoil arches, gables and pinnacles, a transition from Decorated exoticism to the orderly verticals of Perpendicular.

Across the presbytery lies Edward's forebear, Robert Curthose (d.1134), William the Conqueror's eldest son. As such, he was bequeathed the senior inheritance of Normandy, while his brothers, William and Henry, went on to inherit the far richer lands of England. Never happy with this deal, Robert indulged in lifelong conflict with his brothers, to be eventually defeated and imprisoned in Cardiff. He expressed a desire to be buried in Gloucester and is represented by a later much-repainted oak effigy, about to draw his sword.

North and south ambulatory chapels are guarded by Perpendicular screens. The south was recently refashioned with a 'gothick' vault and swirling blue windows by Tom Denny (1993), said to represent Christ's appearance to Thomas.

Beneath Gloucester's east window is the entrance to the Lady Chapel, virtually a separate church and late Perpendicular (*c*1500). It is overlooked by a gallery with views both into the chapel and west into the cathedral. There are no real walls, just expanses of glass supporting lierne vaults encrusted with bosses. The glass is partly an assemblage of medieval fragments. It would be exhilarating one day

to try to reassemble these fragments and give these windows some meaning.

Side windows are mostly by the Arts and Crafts artist Christopher Whall, depicting saints and biblical stories free of the usual Victorian fussiness. Off the Lady Chapel are tiny chantries with fan vaults and singing lofts. One on the south side celebrates Gloucester organists, including music by Herbert Howells printed on the glass. On the north side is a memorial to the war poet and composer Ivor Gurney, with Denny glass depicting Gloucestershire's landscape. The whole chapel is a masterpiece of Tudor craftsmanship.

No cloister in England stands comparison with Gloucester, standard-bearer for the new Perpendicular. On a warm summer evening, the sun, filtered by coloured glass, floods its arcades. The roof is the first example in England of the half-cone vault, dating from the 1350s. The effect is of a row of seated ladies fluttering their fans in unison, the fans being so low that we can almost touch them. This design was to develop, in Oxford, Bath and finally Henry VII's Chapel at Westminster, into the most elaborate and exotic English contribution to the gothic style, reigning for almost two centuries.

A rare lavatorium survives in one range, with even a stone cupboard for towels. Another range has small carrels with individual windows onto the garden; in these, the monks would sit and study. The central garden, or garth, contains small hedges and a gentle fountain. From here, there is a good view of the tower, a blissful spot to enjoy the epitome of late gothic harmony.

Left
Cloistered fans in sunlight

GUILDFORD

The Holy Spirit

Simple neo-gothic interior, Arts and Crafts statues

As a child, I 'bought a brick' for Guildford. When later taken to see it in place, I was mortified. It was lost among millions of bricks, among cliffs of interminable, relentless brickwork. Disappointment still hangs about this place, lonely on its hill outside the town. Cars stream along the A3 below, scarcely noticing. Even the approach road has been likened to the entrance to a crematorium.

Guildford was created a diocese in 1927 and Holy Trinity Church in Guildford high street was used as its cathedral. A competition was then held for a new building and, in 1932, a proposal by Edward Maufe was declared best of 183 competitors. It is a poor comment on inter-war British design. If only art deco had not been vulgarised by super-cinemas and Hoover factories, how much more exciting might now be the new Guildford?

Maufe's chosen style was gothic, but not the academic gothic of Truro or the grandiloquent gothic of Liverpool's Anglican cathedral. Guildford is naked gothic, stripped of clothing and visual diversion as if desperate to be thought modern. Building began in 1936 but was halted by war. By the time it restarted in 1954, Basil Spence's Coventry was under construction and Guildford seemed not so much gothic revival as gothic exhaustion, with few ghosts even of Maufe's Arts and Crafts past. It was consecrated in 1961 and finished in 1966.

The site on Stag Hill rates in prominence with Lincoln and St Albans, and surely demanded stylistic drama. Instead, Maufe's exterior is clinical and downbeat, with traditional nave, tower, transepts and chancel in uniform brick with sparse stone dressings. The walls are pierced with tall lancets, barely more than slits. The entrance front has three lancets above three whalebone arches crowned by carvings. The door to the large St Ursula porch is Arts and Crafts, with the interior glass engraved by John Hutton.

That said, Guildford's exterior carries excellent contemporary statuary. Above the central door is the Hand of God by Alan Collins. Doors to the south transept carry Vernon Hill's bronze reliefs of men's and women's domestic and pastoral occupations – doubtless now politically incorrect. Above the door is a St John the Baptist by Eric Gill. Statues of the Virtues and the Gifts of the Spirit line the north and south walls, most of

Left
Gothic enfilade: the side aisle

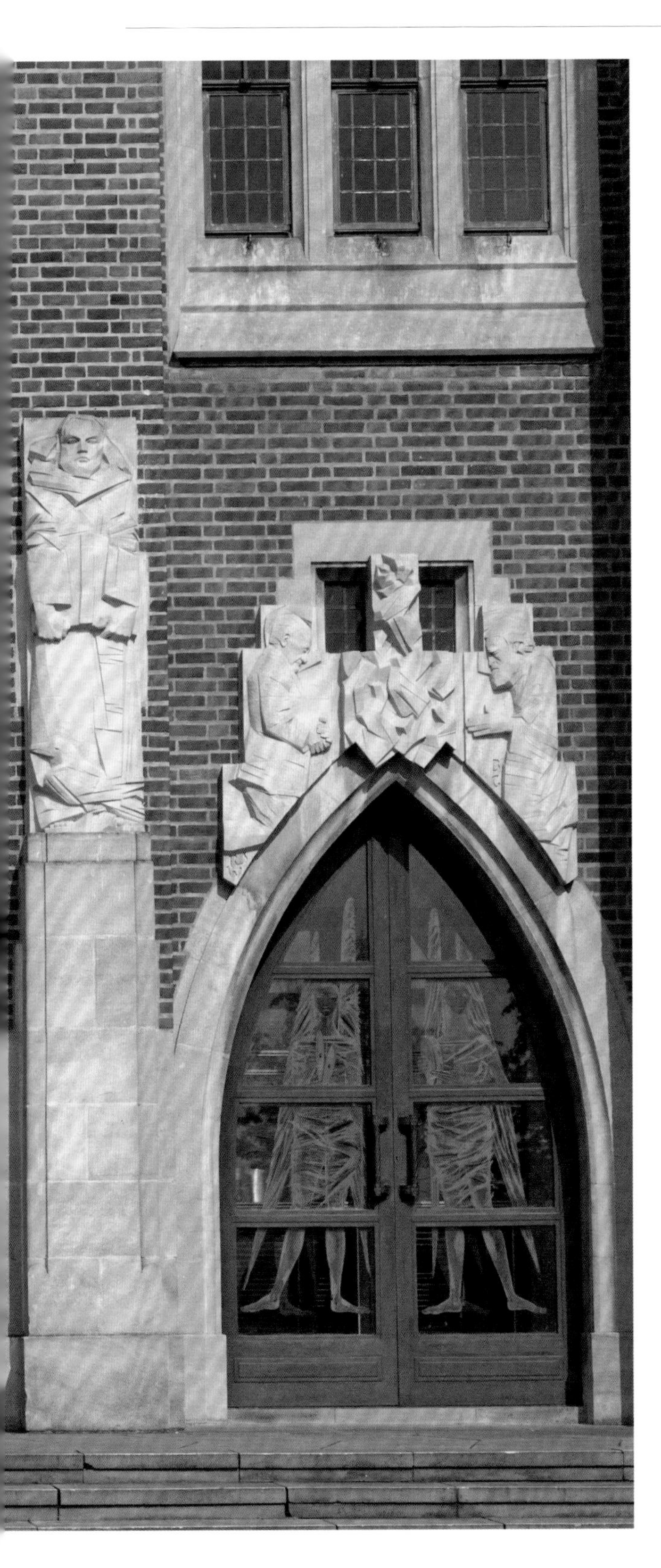

them by Alan Collins. His statue of Prudence is said to be of Maufe's wife of that name, including her favourite shoes. I particularly like Richard Browne's poignant Justice.

The interior is more accomplished than the exterior, and has grown on me since my first visit. Ian Nairn (in Pevsner) found it a 'well mannered, even mealy-mouthed, postscript to the gothic revival', but added that the interior displayed a 'sweet-tempered, undramatic curvilinear gothic … with a queer power of compelling not reverence but contemplation'. It certainly shows Maufe as a master at handling space, aided by the inherent elegance of the pure gothic arch (if there is such a thing), unadorned with capitals and rising sheer from floor to apex. Guildford is a series of variations on this theme.

The nave marches east from the entrance under plain arcades. The clerestory is confined to pinholes. The windows are opaque, deep-set and without colour, so from the nave we cannot see sun or sky, just a white tunnel of plaster with stone dressings. Only the Lady Chapel at the far end allows some colour and variety, notably in the panelled ceiling.

The most uplifting views are down the side aisles to the crossing, an enfilade of pencil-thin arcades in receding sequence. There is a serene play of light where the lofty arches meet the transepts, though the exhilaration of Liverpool and Giles Gilbert Scott's cross-cutting perspectives is missing.

Of the furnishing, the octagonal font has fish and water carvings on its bowl, and a surprisingly garish gilt font cover of interlocking doves. The choir shows few traces of Arts and Crafts or of its pre-war genesis. The nave lampshades and choir fittings are in the folksy style of the Festival of Britain.

Left
West front: Arts and Crafts relief

HEREFORD

St Mary the Virgin and St Ethelbert

Cantilupe cult, Audley Chapel, Mappa Mundi

★★★

Hereford is a cathedral of all-sorts, with medieval, Georgian, Victorian and even Edwardian blood in its veins. Its scholarly past – Hereford was even dubbed 'the city of philosophers' – bequeathed it England's finest cathedral library, including the treasured Mappa Mundi. It boasts a handsome tower situated, like neighbouring Worcester's, looking over the River Wye to the hills of Wales, but much of the interior is marred by unhappy restoration. This is despite being, for a period, one of the leading pilgrimage churches in England.

Hereford was declared a cathedral as early as the 7th century, the town being the recognised capital of the Mercian sub-kingdom of Magonset (now Herefordshire). It acquired the relics of St Ethelbert, an East Anglian king murdered by Offa in 794. The Welsh burned the cathedral to the ground in 1055 and it was one of the last cathedrals to be rebuilt by the Normans, consecrated in 1142.

The east end of this structure appears to have been adapted for pilgrimage over the following century, with a crypt below its Lady Chapel, but it was not until the reign of Henry III that dramatic change began. Hereford was an intellectual retreat in the Welsh Marches.

For whatever reason, its new bishop in 1240 was Peter Aigueblanche, Savoyard chaplain to Henry's teenage queen, Eleanor of Provence. He angered local people by appointing twenty fellow Savoyards to the chapter, though few took up residence. During de Montfort's rebellion in 1263, the Gascon dean of Hereford was murdered and Aigueblanche's own lands were plundered. The bishop, who spoke no English, had at one point to seek the safety of Hereford castle.

None the less, Aigueblanche survived until 1268 and began yet another rebuilding of the cathedral, blatantly in the cosmopolitan style of his royal master at Westminster, though he got no further than the east side of the north transept. It was the next bishop but one, Thomas Cantilupe (1275–82), who was posthumously to transform Hereford's fortunes. Excommunicated after an argument with the archbishop of Canterbury, he died in Italy on his way to seek a pardon from the pope. His successor, Richard Swinfield, was to prove the most skilful impresario of sanctification in the age of pilgrimage. He repatriated Cantilupe's remains (allegedly still bleeding), erected a shrine for them in

Left
Guarding the Marches: the tower over the Wye

the cathedral and publicised miracles. For two decades from 1287, the resulting cult ballooned into a mass hysteria.

Thomas Cantilupe's miracle count – over four hundred were 'certified' – was outstripped only by Becket's at Canterbury. They became 'the two Thomases'. This was even before his official canonisation in 1320. Madnesses were cured, children raised from the dead and wounded horses returned to service. Investigating Swinfield's bid for Cantilupe's canonisation, papal commissioners listed donations of 170 silver images of ships, 129 images of people, 108 crutches and 97 nightgowns. One year, 9000 pilgrims were noted to have passed through Worcester on their way to Hereford. Cantilupe was even said to have later cured victims of the Black Death.

Pilgrimage revenue resulted in the rebuilding of the cathedral, which proceeded well into the 14th century, although it was spasmodic rather than systematic. The chancel received Decorated windows. New stalls appeared in the choir. Perpendicular windows crowded Norman walls in the south transept. A north porch to receive pilgrims was given a Decorated extension and then a spectacular Perpendicular one, the Booth Porch, on the threshold of the Reformation in 1519, by when the Cantilupe cult had come to an end.

Later centuries hit Hereford hard. The west tower collapsed in 1786, taking with it the west front and part of the nave: these were replaced by the Victorians and then by a member of the Scott dynasty, John Oldrid Scott, in the early 20th century. The nave was restored by James Wyatt in the 18th century and the transepts and chancel by L. N. Cottingham in the 1840s. It is a stylistic jumble. The soft red sandstone has had to be heavily restored.

The west front is an odd composition, with immense jutting buttresses and a circular west window above a projecting screen. It looks best when floodlit at night. The strength of Hereford's exterior lies in its tower, exemplifying Decorated richness. Two stages of openings are framed by buttresses rising to pinnacles. These substitute for a spire, making elegant what might otherwise seem squat. Most extraordinary is the surface covering of ballflower, a craze for Decorated masons around the turn of the 14th century.

The initial view of the interior is disappointing. The Norman nave lacks the punch of Gloucester due to the alterations of Wyatt and Cottingham. Pier drums rise to effete capitals. Shafts are cut short before they reach the vault. Cottingham's changes, devoid of any unity, drove Alec Clifton-Taylor to despair: 'incompatible … formal dissonance …

Previous spread
Audley Chapel screen

Left
England meets Savoy: Cantilupe and Aigueblanche tombs

insuperable problem … change for the worse'.

The furnishings are better. The font is by the celebrated Herefordshire school of Norman carvers, lined with apostles and arcading. A knightly monument to Sir Richard Pembridge (d.1375) has him recumbent, but with a 'spare' right leg on the adjacent wall. This was a wooden replacement for a damaged original, showing the Order of the Garter on the wrong leg and kept for some reason when a correct replacement was inserted.

The crossing is a puzzle. The transepts are mostly Norman, with later windows, but how much is true Norman and how much Cottingham is unclear. What cannot be missed are Aigueblanche's changes to the east wall of the north transept, in obvious imitation of Westminster. The arcade is wholly 'un-British', with straight-sided arches like triangles. There are quatrefoils in the triforium and triangles in the clerestory. The Savoyard was emphatically imposing French taste on Hereford, presumably hoping to continue with it round the rest of the cathedral. For better or worse, he failed, but he left the cathedral with some stylistic dash.

In the transept below lie spectacular monuments to Hereford's two celebrities, Aigueblanche himself (d.1268) and the miracle-maker, Thomas Cantilupe (d.1282). The canopy over the first is in the latest Westminster style and worthy of that abbey, with three giant gables rising boldly on thin Purbeck shafts. Next door lies Cantilupe, but where Aigueblanche soars, Cantilupe squats. The tomb chest is surrounded by cinquefoil arches containing armed knights in a variety of poses. The actual effigy vanished in the Reformation. The monument has been transformed by a brightly coloured wooden canopy, with angels holding a copy of the Mappa Mundi. The canopy (2008) is by the iconographer Peter Murphy, in the style of a medieval original and a superb addition to the cathedral's furnishings.

The view from here to the south transept is dominated by a Te Deum window by C. E. Kempe, said to be his largest. On a side wall hangs a Swabian triptych (*c*1520) of the Adoration. Opposite are three abstract tapestries by John Piper which, on my last visit, looked alarmingly vulnerable to the sunlight.

Hereford choir was once closed by a jewelled metal screen designed by George Gilbert Scott and made by the Coventry metalworking firm of Francis Skidmore, one of his early group of designs that included Lichfield and Worcester. This was not a solid pulpitum, blocking the view, but a transparent screen, regarded by many as a great work of Victorian art. It was

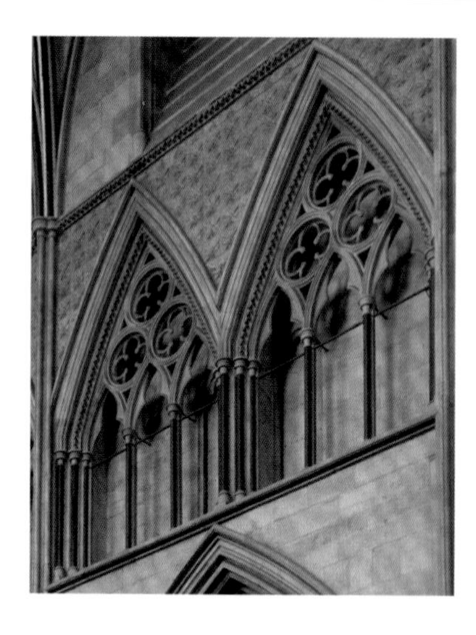

Left
North transept: Westminster on Wye

Opposite
The Grandisson tomb

astonishingly removed by the chapter in 1966 'as a hindrance to worship' and now resides, superbly restored, in the V&A in London. The choir is left strangely naked.

The east end of the sanctuary is closed by Cottingham's neo-Norman wall, with an arch topped by a gallery. The view through the arch to the retrochoir beyond is obstructed by what seems the dislocated spandrel of another arch that has lost its way. Next to the choir is the 1375 chantry of Bishop Stanbury, confessor to Henry VI. It is a fine Perpendicular casket, ornamented with panels and heraldry and roofed with fan vaulting. Outside, effigies of 14th-century bishops line the aisle walls, including Hereford's collection of brasses, rare in a cathedral as brasses were cheaper than carved stone and tended to indicate poverty.

Hereford's Early Gothic retrochoir is something of a relief; it is an elegant chamber of slender columns and stiff-leaf capitals and is the original site of Ethelbert's shrine. It gives onto the Lady Chapel beyond. Here lancet windows, with detached shafts and clustered mouldings, rise to a simple roof vault. Retrochoir and chapel are rich in reinstated colour. At the entrance to the chapel stands a new shrine to St Ethelbert, vividly painted in 2007 again by Peter Murphy.

In the Lady Chapel is the tomb of Peter de Grandisson (d.1352), armoured knight attended by the Virgin and saints. He lies in prayer with his feet resting on his dog. Opposite is the Audley Chapel, with a Perpendicular roof, upper watching gallery and gloriously restored painted screen with ghostly saints in the panels. Its windows celebrate the 17th-century Herefordshire writer Thomas Traherne and are by Tom Denny (2007) in vividly expressionistic tones. This is the sort of chamber in which English cathedrals excel. The Lady Chapel glass diffuses soft colours over the interior.

Hereford's cloister was largely destroyed by the collapse of the west tower but the east range survives, with flowing tracery in its openings. The cloister garth and chapter house ruin have been made into an intimate garden, while the old vicars' college has been converted into diocesan offices.

Facing the road is a new library and museum by William Whitfield, opened in 1996. Hereford's chained library of some 1500 books remains the largest such library in England. The *c*1300 Mappa Mundi is a national treasure, nearly five feet in diameter and the largest surviving medieval map in the world. The single sheet of vellum shows an extraordinary array of the geographical features of the then known world, albeit hard to identify today.

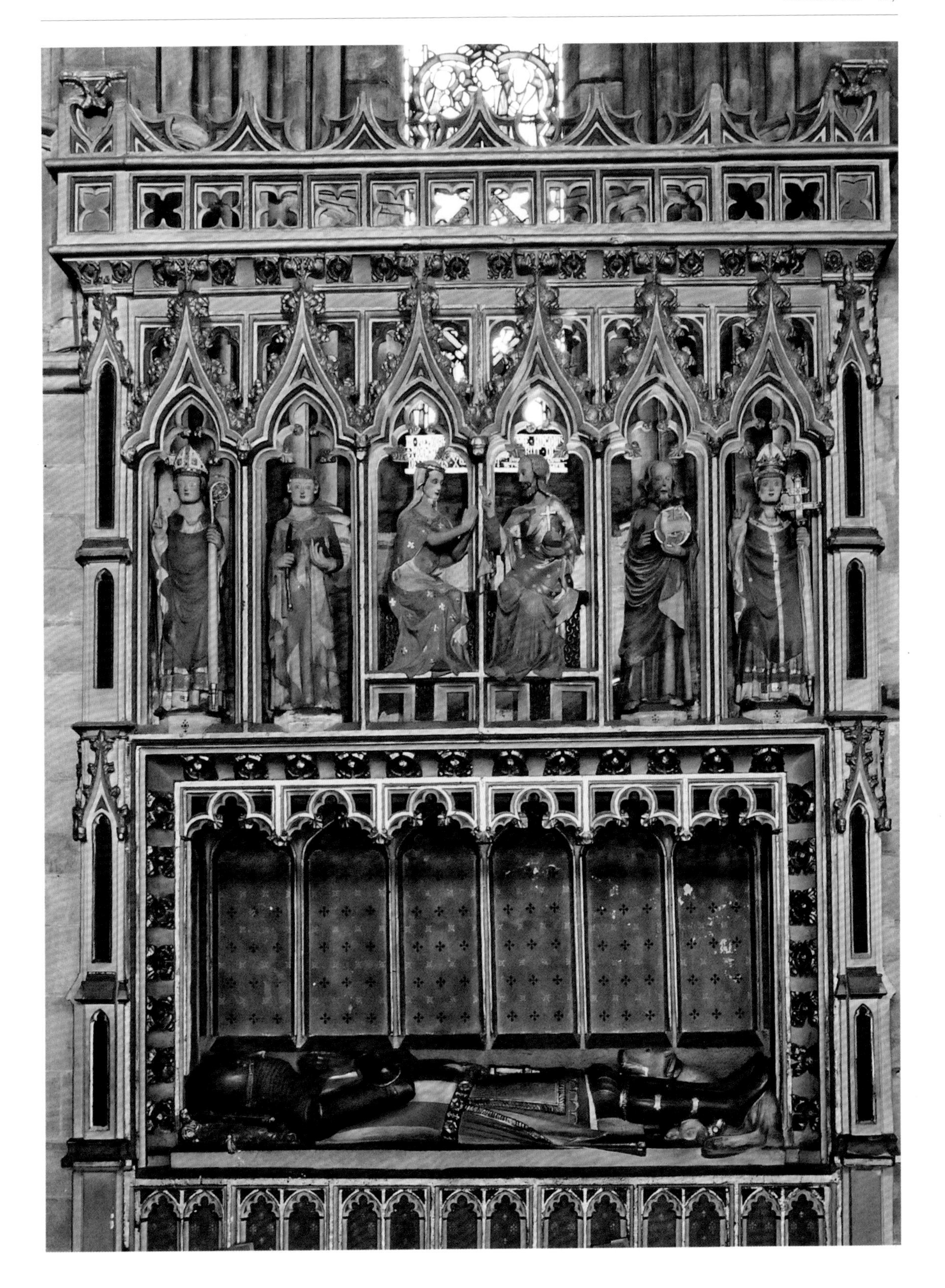

HOSANNA ✠ BENEDICTUS · QUI · VENIT ✠
OMINE · DOMINI ✠
HOSANNA ✠

LEEDS RC

St Anne

Arts and Crafts interior, Pugin altarpiece

Leeds lacks an Anglican cathedral, having ceded most of Yorkshire to York, Ripon, Sheffield and Wakefield. This is despite having a magnificent parish church in St Peter's. The city's Roman Catholic cathedral is modest, but occupies a central site provided for it after Leeds' previous Catholic cathedral was demolished for road widening. It is an accomplished work by a little-known Edwardian architect, J. H. Eastwood, in collaboration with S. K. Greenslade. It was consecrated in 1904.

The site restricted the plan to a square, with just four nave bays, short transepts and a chancel. The style is late gothic revival but with a distinctive Arts and Crafts overlay, much bolder than the contemporary Westminster cathedral. The west façade on Cookridge Street is rugged, as if hewn from a giant slab of silver limestone. The three central windows are deep-set, reminiscent of Peterborough. The rood over the entrance looks as if it is carved from the same rock as the door. The side walls are almost entirely composed of buttresses, giving the church a bombproof appearance.

The interior is stylistically eccentric. The nave piers carry gothic shafts but some rise not to the vault but to saints' niches. Likewise, the window tracery breaks into semi-fans, faintly art nouveau. The aisles are lined with chapels.

Most extraordinary is the chancel arch. This is in the manner of a proscenium framing the chancel and rendering the sanctuary reredos a dramatic climax. The eye is drawn to the tall gothic altarpiece of gilded wood, surrounded by swaying art nouveau mosaics of saints. All the work is by either Eastwood or Greenslade. The sanctuary was stripped of most of its decoration in the 1960s following the liturgical edicts of the Second Vatican Council.

The Lady Chapel off the south aisle is some compensation. It contains A. W. N. Pugin's altarpiece of 1842 from the previous cathedral. Recently restored, it is typical Pugin, with nine gabled niches and much decorative colour. The small statue of the Virgin with Child in the central niche is exquisite.

Left
Pugin's Lady Chapel altarpiece

LEICESTER

St Martin

Richard III's tomb, rococo gravestone

★

Every medieval cathedral craved a pilgrimage shrine to bring it lustre and lucre. None had to wait as long as Leicester. In 2012, this modest town church, elevated to cathedral in 1927, was transformed by the unearthing of the proclaimed bones of Richard III beneath an adjacent car park. His sole link with the city was to have been killed nearby, at the Battle of Bosworth in 1485.

Leicester's city fathers responded like medieval monks eager for a shrine on which to build pilgrimage revenue. They won a court case against Richard's DNA ancestors to keep the bones in the city, rather than see them transferred to Richard's home base of York. A handsome tomb and new visitor centre, the latter including the site where the remains were found, testify to their success.

What had been a parish church sits in an enclave protected to the north by a warren of 18th-century streets, but facing an ominously derelict space to the south. The exterior is Perpendicular, heavily Victorianised by Raphael Brandon in 1867. Its steeple is referred to by Olive Cook as 'heavy, insensitive and pedantically correct, Victorian historicism at its most forbidding'.

The north porch, by J. L. Pearson, is better and carries statues of Leicester worthies, a category generously interpreted to include Hugh of Lincoln with his swan. Inside, the nave has three aisles built to accommodate the city's guild chapels, some of which survive. Wooden roofs have been brightly repainted in original colours. Gilded angels and bosses are from the dissolved Greyfriars monastery (Richard's resting place since Bosworth). In St Dunstan's Chapel in the south aisle is a 16th-century Russian icon, The Hospitality of Abraham.

The crossing arch has Brandon's strangely stumpy piers, crowded with rings and capitals, and losing verticality in the process. The arrival of Richard and the need for a fitting chamber meant the sanctuary was brought forward into the nave and given a new bishop's throne. This seat is a bizarre furnishing, a geometrical design in primary colours and surmounted by a massive sheet of dark wood rising and tilting to form a drooping cross (by the Draisci Studio). It looks uncomfortable in every sense.

The new throne and crossing arch overwhelm the handsome neo-

Left
Sanctuary with bishop's chair

gothic screen to the retrochoir beyond, where Richard's bones were reinterred in 2015. His tomb is a simple block of stone with a deeply incised and suitably austere cross. The guide states that Richard was 'flawed like the rest of us', which seems a bit hard on the rest of us. Of the side chapels, that of Christ the King has an east window by Christopher Whall, in pastel blues and pinks and a relief from the heavy Victorian glass round about. St Katharine's Chapel houses memorials of the local Herrick family, including the poet Robert Herrick (1591–1674), shown in a window with his extraordinary Roman nose. In the north aisle is (or was) the pall used to cover Richard's coffin before it was interred. I find even Leicester's modest celebration of this appalling monarch hard to take.

The churchyard has been substantially remodelled to accommodate Ricardian paraphernalia. There is a statue of Richard horseless but sword in hand in one corner. Another less successful one takes the form of a row of steel slabs supposedly depicting his death at Bosworth. Elsewhere in the garden is a gravestone to Richard Barns (d.1762). In the most exquisite rococo frame, its loops and swirls are what is known to calligraphers as 'striking'. It is the loveliest thing anywhere near the cathedral.

Left
My kingdom for a horse

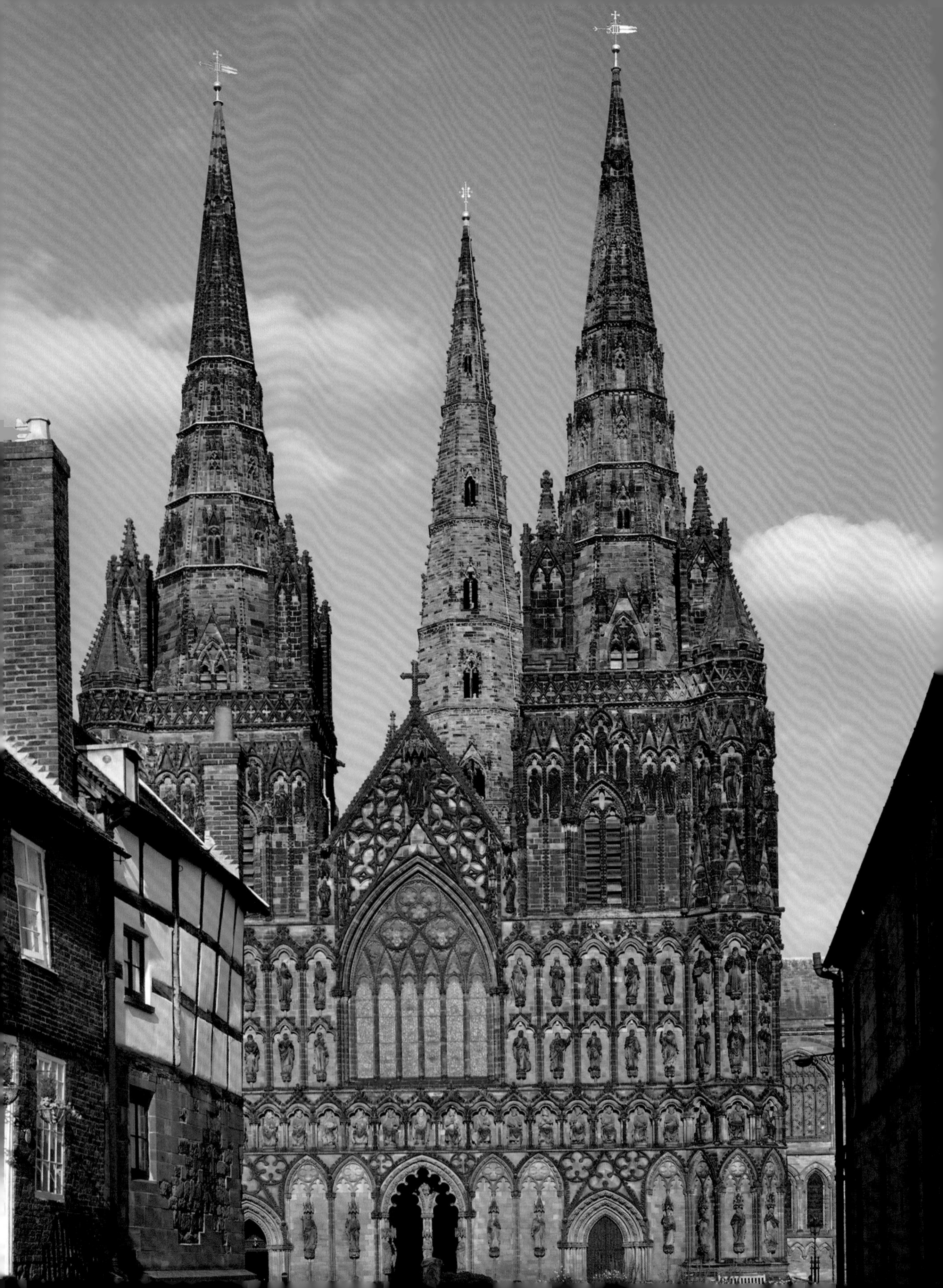

LICHFIELD

The Blessed Virgin Mary and St Chad

Ladies of the Vale steeples, Decorated west front, Scott restoration and screen, Belgian glass in Lady Chapel

Lichfield's three dark spires are the last such triplet to survive on any English cathedral. Dubbed the 'Ladies of the Vale', they rise over the Staffordshire plain as guardians of the unofficial boundary between southern England and the north. When seen across the nearby lake on a fine day they can look picturesque but, as we reach the close, they change character and gender. I have always regarded Lichfield as a pugnacious bruiser of a cathedral. It lurks like a fighter waiting for an opponent, despite the gentility of its grassy close. Without a softening sun, its sandstone can turn blood-red, almost sinister. Lichfield is 'gothic with attitude'. I am never easy in its presence.

The diocese might once have been a rival to Canterbury. In the late 8th century, Offa of Mercia persuaded the pope, briefly, to declare it England's second archbishopric. At the time, Northumbria was threatened by Vikings and Lichfield was home to the shrine of Mercia's patron saint, Chad, who converted that region to Christianity in the 7th century. The plan lapsed, however, and after the Conquest the cathedral went into decline, seeing its diocese shared uncomfortably, first with Chester in 1075, then with Coventry after 1102. The canons progressively rebuilt the old church over the 13th century. Then in 1296 Edward I's powerful treasurer, Walter Langton, was given the bishopric and, for thirty years, transformed it into his personal citadel.

Langton may have prospered under Edward I but was sworn enemy of his son, the effete Edward II, who charged him with patricide, adultery with his step-mother, bribery and communing with the Devil. (We might quote Gibbon, who wrote of an anti-pope that 'more serious charges were suppressed'.) In 1307 he was imprisoned though he was later acquitted. Under Langton, Lichfield was transformed from an episcopal backwater into the marvel we see today. A staggering £2000 was spent on a golden shrine for St Chad. Langton also transformed the cathedral's west front and Lady Chapel, and turned the close into a miniature castle, with walls, moat, gatehouses and a palace for himself.

All this almost vanished during the Civil War, which hit Lichfield harder than any other cathedral. The building was turned into a fortress and besieged three times. Shelling caused the central tower to collapse into the choir while Parliamentary troops occupied and wrecked the

Left
Decorated pugnacity: west front from the close

interior. The roof was ruined and furnishings and statues destroyed. Langton's encircling fortifications were demolished. At one point, the entire building was about to be pulled down, to be saved only by the Restoration. A new bishop, Hacket, with specific help from Charles II, set to and replaced the roofs and towers. The undertaking is vividly depicted in a window in the south choir aisle.

In 1788, Lichfield underwent what critics called 'ordeal by Wyatt'. James Wyatt arrived to carry out what might best be described as emergency repairs. The roof vaults were restored in wood and plaster, and statues were recast in cement, although the arrival of Belgian glass for the Lady Chapel must have lifted the chapter's spirits. By the 1840s, the cathedral was again a miserable place, empty and coated, so it was reported, 'in dead yellowing whitewash'. Rescue came with the arrival in 1856 of George Gilbert Scott, who set about restoration with characteristic thoroughness. The result is that little of what we see outside or inside is original, more a testament to Scott's talent as a restorer. Lichfield is not so much a medieval cathedral as a resurrected one.

The west front, by Scott after Langton, has been much criticised. It is in the form of a horizontal façade, a gallery of statuary, above which rises a central gable, flanked by two heavy towers surmounted by even heavier spires. The statues are most odd, as they have no plinths but seem to float on the surface of the wall. The balance between the façade and towers is certainly uncomfortable.

To Pevsner, Lichfield cannot make up its mind. If spires are 'meant to aspire, these aspire too little', while the portals are 'too small to join in as separate voices'. For his

Left
Victorian craftsmanship: the Skidmore screen

Left
Belgian glass in Lady Chapel

part, Alec Clifton-Taylor complains of the spires emerging from the towers in a messy cluster of pinnacles, with Scott's central window squeezed uncomfortably between them. As for the statues, they 'might pass as an advertisement for the local hairdresser'.

This is fair comment. The towers are indeed so muscle-bound they crush the life out of the west window. But to me, Lichfield's façade, with its rust-coloured walls, animated windows and Victorian statues, is among the most powerful works in the Decorated canon. By replacing the 113 statues (just five originals survive) with monarchs, saints, martyrs and bishops, Scott created a façade that is more authentically 'gothic' than the crumbling remains even of Exeter, Lincoln or Wells.

The remainder of the exterior is a rhythmic sequence of buttresses and windows. The east end culminates in a Lady Chapel with Decorated windows and polygonal apse. Outside the south transept is a row of bishops in lively conversation. On one corner stands Charles II, saviour of the cathedral but moved from pride of place on the west front by the Victorians. He shelters under a large 17th-century canopy like an umbrella, poorly dressed for bad weather.

The initial view of Lichfield's interior is that of a dark exotic forest, with the sunlit clearing of the Lady Chapel in the distance. Though the cathedral is not big, the uninterrupted view from west to east makes it seem so. The balance between horizontal and vertical line is perfect. Each nave pier is a cluster of shafts, rising to leafy capitals. The arcade spandrels contain giant cinquefoils. The triforium is ornamented, its arches crowded with dogtooth. The clerestory windows are curve-sided triangles containing three giant trefoils. Sandstone which outside looks a harsh red-black is inside a soft pink-grey.

The south transept has a Perpendicular window by C. E. Kempe, relating the so-called 'spread of the Church' to all corners of the Earth under Christ's dominion. Below are busts of two of Lichfield's famous sons, Samuel Johnson and David Garrick. From this point eastwards we are essentially in Scott's hands. Not only did he have to reroof the entire eastern arm of the cathedral, he had to re-create a Decorated presbytery.

Most masterful was his insertion of a new choir screen, framing yet not obscuring the choir from the nave. It is one of those made for him by the Midlands firm of Francis Skidmore in 1863, a supreme work of mid-Victorian art in which design and craftsmanship seem in complete harmony. Pevsner wrote, 'Let Salisbury and Hereford be vandals and remove

Left
Chantrey's Sleeping Children

Opposite
St Chad's Gospel: St Luke

their Scott-Skidmore screens, Lichfield must hold out until High Victorianism is at last fully appreciated in its best work.' It has done so. Similar superlatives apply to Scott's sedilia and high altar reredos and to his reproduction of medieval floor tiles. Scott also put statues back on the wall brackets, rare in a cathedral restoration.

The south choir aisle contains a curiosity, the St Chad's Head Chapel. Many shrines kept bits of their saint separate (as at Canterbury), to ease crowds and maximise revenue. Pilgrims would have reached St Chad's head last after passing his shrine. The skull was kept in a first-floor chapel and brought out onto the gallery on special occasions. It has long since vanished.

Various other relics of St Chad were rescued from iconoclasts at the Reformation and became peripatetic round Catholic houses until coming to rest in Birmingham's St Chad's cathedral. One, at least, of the bones has been archaeologically dated to the 7th century. The chapel was beautifully reordered by Kempe in the 19th century and has windows filled with musical angels. At the end of the south aisle is Francis Chantrey's 1817 depiction of two girls, The Sleeping Children, in the tear-jerking style beloved of Georgian visitors.

Lichfield's climax is Langton's Lady Chapel, its rounded walls and soaring windows recalling Paris's Sainte-Chapelle. The wall arcading is capped with nodding ogees. The 1895 altarpiece comes from Oberammergau and includes a shepherd in a Tyrolean hat. The chapel is dominated by its Belgian stained glass, rescued in 1803 by a local grandee, Sir Brooke Boothby, from Europe's monasteries sacked during Napoleon's campaigns.

The glass is from Herkenrode in the Belgian province of Limburg (where the Limburgish language is still spoken) and dates from *c*1530. The main east window looks almost medieval, the colours subdued and the composition simple, while the windows further west are quite different, baroque in colour and complexity. Adjacent are windows by Kempe, narrative and faintly Pre-Raphaelite. The whole group was restored and reinstated in 2015.

The chapter house is reached from the north transept down a corridor lined with stalls for the washing of pilgrims' feet (known as a pedilavium) on Maundy Thursday. It seems an elaborate installation for so infrequent a purpose though the corridor would have served also as a waiting room for those doing business with the canons within. The corridor and vaulted chapter house are Early Gothic of the 1240s. The foliage capitals, while full of

life, are rough compared with neighbouring Southwell's exquisite naturalism. They include a green man, green woman and boy bishop in an over-large mitre. Boy bishops were a popular medieval custom in which a choirboy was dressed as the bishop and performed, for a while, all episcopal rituals other than the Mass. It symbolised 'the mighty fallen and the humble raised up'.

Also in the chapter house are displayed Lichfield's two great treasures. The Lichfield Angel is a relief carving of remarkable vitality, found in 2003 under the nave. It is believed to come from the original stone shrine of St Chad (*c*800). Here too is the St Chad's Gospels, earlier even than the angel, a fragment of a bible in Latin but with some marginalia in old Welsh, and the first known text in that language. Anglo-Saxon objects from the Staffordshire hoard are usually also on show. A medieval wall painting rises over the double doorway.

The cathedral sits in the remains of Langton's once -fortified close. School, deanery, bishop's palace and diocesan offices form the boundary of what seems a contented town square. Lichfield is finally at peace.

Left
The Ladies of the Vale across the Minster Pool

LINCOLN

St Mary

Norman west façade, Dean's Eye window, 'crazy vault', Angel Choir, Wren library

Lincoln stands as one of my 'three graces', alongside Ely and Wells. It towers over the small county town at its feet, massive and aloof. Not yet fully restored, its wizened old stone gives it the appearance of an ageing aristocrat waiting for the world to respect its dignity.

The Saxon diocese of Lincoln stretched from the Humber across the east Midlands to the Thames. The reason was that, prior to the Conquest, it was under the sway of the Danelaw and thus vulnerable to Viking occupation. Its headquarters were safely in the south, at Dorchester-on-Thames. In 1072, when William faced rebellion along England's east coast, he ordered his bishops forward into defensible settlements, including Norwich, Durham and the then substantial settlement of Lincoln. A Benedictine monk, Remigius, was sent to build a new non-monastic cathedral on the hill. The diocese commanded – and profited from – no fewer than nine counties. Lincoln's chapter had a record fifty-eight canons with lucrative prebendary estates.

As with Norwich and Durham, Remigius's cathedral was sited for security next to the castle; indeed, its west front was built like a castle wall. This structure lasted barely a century since, in 1185, an earthquake left only a fragment of the west front standing. This disaster coincided with Henry II's post-Becket surge in piety, and with the arrival in 1186 of Lincoln's most distinctive personality, Hugh of Burgundy.

An eccentric Carthusian monk, Hugh embodied the revival of English monasticism under Henry, as well as the emergence of episcopal sanctity as an aid to commercial success. All 13th-century English saints were former bishops, and Hugh promptly styled himself a saint in waiting. According to his biographers, he chewed a relic of Mary Magdalene's arm, kissed lepers on the mouth and dreamed that 'a saint had reached into his bowels, withdrew something red and hot and threw it away', so that he 'never again desired sex'. He was duly canonised in 1220, twenty years after his death.

Hugh's rebuilding of Norman Lincoln in the Early Gothic style dictates the character of most of what we see today. The exterior is an extended variation on a lancet theme, with lancet windows, blind lancets, lancet arcades and lancet niches, as if the masons were exulting in their liberation from the romanesque past. The design is attributed

Left
West front with towers

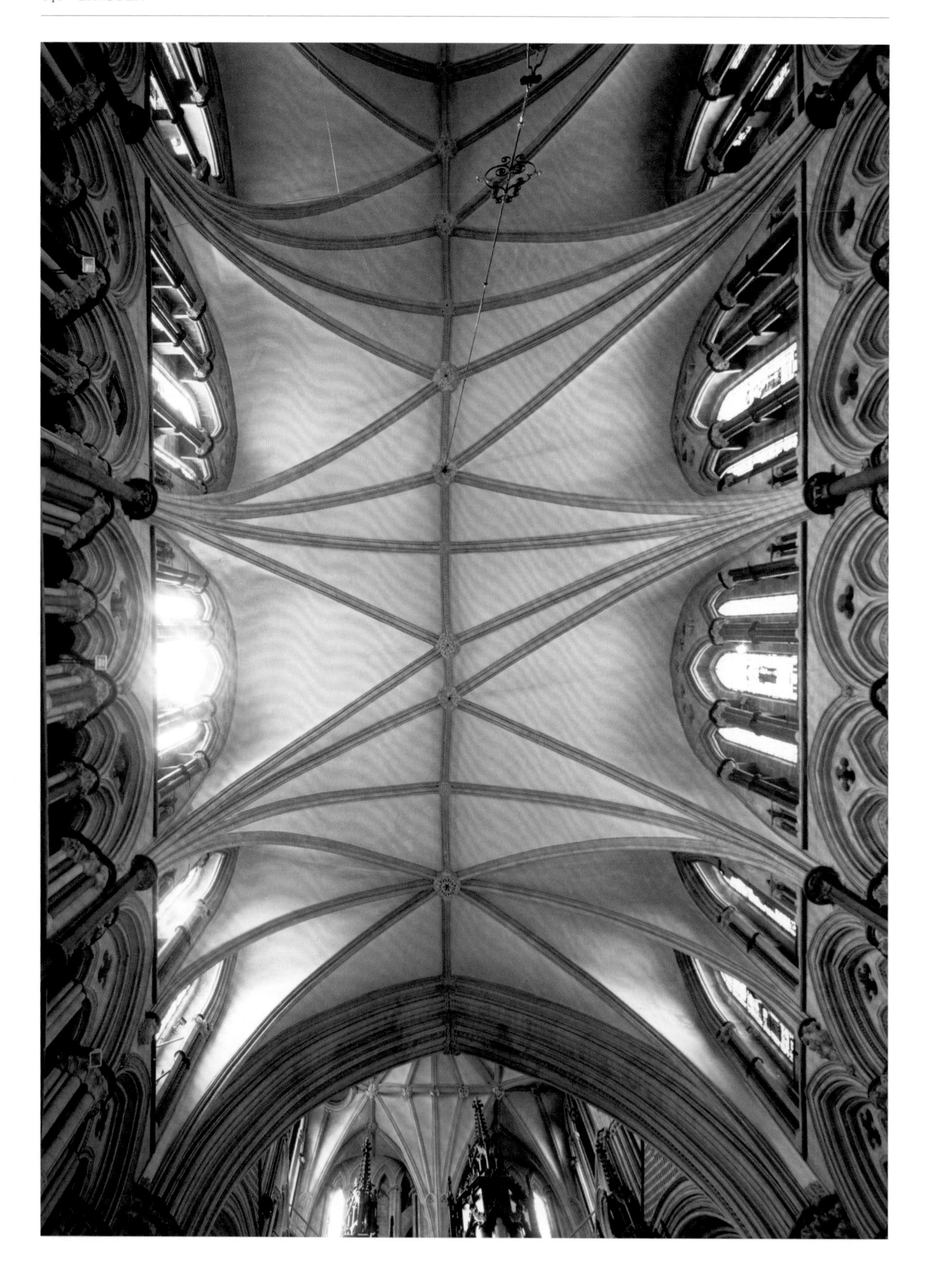

Left
The Crazy Vault

to Geoffrey de Noyers, once assumed to be French but now known to be from an established local family.

By the 1230s, the new cathedral was complete and ready to welcome pilgrims to Hugh's shrine. The enhanced diocesan revenues were soon able to pay for a new Decorated east end – the Angel Choir – begun in 1255, to which Hugh's shrine was moved in 1280, with Edward I and a reputed 230 knights in attendance. It was said that 'the gutters of the bishop's palace ran with wine for a week'. The central tower was rebuilt in 1307 and the two western towers half a century later. A former spire on the central tower, rising to 525ft, made Lincoln reputedly the tallest man-made structure in the world, taller than the great pyramid of Giza. It fell in a gale in 1549 and was never rebuilt.

I find the most satisfying initial view of Lincoln is not of the west front but from the lawn to the east, looking up at the exterior of the Angel Choir. The east window is here dominant, with spinning geometrical circles within circles. Every feature of the architecture is enriched almost to excess, with arcades, gargoyles, foliage and ballflower. As we step back, the outline of the choir recedes and the more severe mass of the Early Gothic cathedral takes over. Buttresses and chapels cling to the exterior like limpets, coated in lancet arcading.

To the right is the chapter house, its flying buttresses apparently intended for a larger structure. At the time of writing, much of Lincoln's stonework was unrestored, which is unusual for an English cathedral in the 21st century. Brown limestone remains etched with sooty black, while occasional patches of cleaned and restored stone are almost dazzling.

To the south of the Angel Choir, the Judgment Porch was, in its day, a Decorated masterpiece but is now a near ruin. Stiff-leaf bursts from mouldings, gargoyles start out of drains, crockets crawl restlessly up gables. Some carvings are decayed; some, such as the tympanum, are restored. On either side of the doorway are two Perpendicular chantries, while nestling against an adjacent buttress is a statue believed to be of Queen Margaret, Edward I's second wife, a beautiful study of 14th-century drapery. It is all a glorious mess.

Continuing westwards, we pass patches of restored walling to reach an over-sized porch, here called a galilee. As such, it must have had ceremonial significance in the Easter procession, although it may have been an entrance from Bishop Hugh's palace across the road. The galilee is lavish with lancet panels and Early Gothic dogtooth.

Opposite
The Angel Choir

We now reach Lincoln's signature, its west front. The five stepped Norman recesses, surviving from the earthquake, are like caverns hacked from a limestone cliff. They are heavy, almost brutal, and purportedly represent the gateways to Heaven. Only Peterborough has anything to compare. The central arch was later given a pointed top.

Round these arches rises a wall of Early Gothic blind arcading. The marriage of gothic surround to romanesque centrepiece fascinated the historian John Harvey. A French architect, he says, would have cleared the site and started again, but here 'clearly the old work was of such outstanding importance and interest that no one would allow its destruction'. Instead, we have an English compromise, the 'solid and massive Norman providing a foil for the light and airy gothic'.

The front is adorned with a jumble of Norman carving. The central doorway retains ancient pagan beakhead monsters chewing into the curve of the roll moulding. Surviving, too, are fragments of one of the best romanesque friezes in England, including a Last Supper, Noah building the ark, and Daniel in the lions' den. Some panels are eroded, some restored in white stone. The carving has been traced to similar work in Saint-Denis in France and Modena in Italy, evidence of the migratory nature of medieval masons.

Lincoln's nave is among the finest examples of the mature Early Gothic style. The arcades are still almost rounded, the Purbeck piers elegant, the windows edging towards Decorated but not yet with tracery. It lacks the vertical thrust of later gothic, deriving its beauty largely from its length – although here one longs to draw aside the organ above the pulpitum to gain the full advantage of distance. Lincoln's Victorian glass is much admired but here, by different hands in different windows, it can seem gloomy. The font is romanesque, of Tournai marble, with fine reliefs round the sides.

The pace quickens at the crossing. The crowded ribs of the nave vault suddenly dart in all directions, forming a cat's-cradle of intersections with carved bosses. The transepts are grand enough to be naves laid at right angles, overlooked by Lincoln's two great rose windows. The northern one has the Dean's Eye (1220), facing his residence, of four circles surrounded by sixteen smaller ones. They retain their medieval glass, filling the transept with soft blue light. In the south transept, the Bishop's Eye is later (1330), its rose formed into two ribbed leaves of spike tracery filled with kaleidoscopic fragments of medieval glass. The

two windows face each other defiantly over the crossing, majestic twins of the glazier's art.

The base of the transept walls introduces us to another signature of Hugh's time. The trefoil arcading over the wall benches is in two planes, an outer and an inner. The apex of each outer arch covers the pier of the inner one, a form of architectural syncopation. It is as if Hugh had told his masons to have some fun. The arcades are adorned with stiff-leaf capitals, dogtooth carving and faces in the spandrels. The effect is of baroque depth and movement, the walls seeming to undulate as we walk along the aisles.

Lincoln's pulpitum was built after an earlier one was destroyed in a collapse of the central tower in 1237. Its sumptuousness, said Pevsner, 'makes one understand how the Decorated style came to be called Decorated'. Eight tall niches beneath ogee arches flank a central portal. The surface of the west side is entirely covered in diapering, while the gables are thick with leaves and animals, like nature laid out on a quilt. The absence of statues is almost a relief.

To either side of the screen, the Early Gothic arches into the north and south choir aisles are dignified in comparison. Shafts of polished Purbeck carry blooming stiff-leaf capitals, supporting an arch moulding of deeply undercut foliage. Beyond the south portal is the Apprentices' Screen, apparently a display of carving-practice by young masons. Opposite lies the shrine of 'Little St Hugh', a child falsely said to have been killed by Lincoln Jews and later exploited by Edward I in his campaign of Jewish persecution. The cathedral makes no effort to conceal this notorious moment in its history. The ancient Jew's House down the hill below the cathedral is another relic of the time.

Lincoln's eastern arm comprises two building periods. The first is the Early Gothic choir planned and mostly executed by Hugh at the turn of the 13th century, the second is the Angel Choir, in which his shrine was to be displayed half a century later. The architecture of the choir is consistent with the nave, with rich arcades, elaborate triforium and clerestory lit by generous lancets. The choir stalls are surmounted by fiddly canopies and pinnacles, with misericords which are not easy to see. A handsome chandelier creates the aura of a comfortable chamber within a chamber.

This is still Hugh's church and his eccentricity takes flight in the bizarre choir vault. We can gaze at its asymmetric ribs for an hour and still not work out their pattern. Ribbed vaulting was in its infancy in the 1190s. Here the normal cross ribs of each bay rise to the central ridge and then go haywire, as if trying to jump into the next bay. Nothing

Opposite
Lincoln imp

Right
Adam and Eve

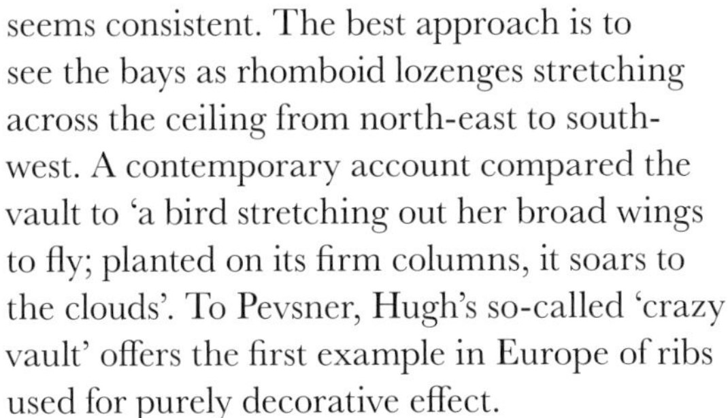

seems consistent. The best approach is to see the bays as rhomboid lozenges stretching across the ceiling from north-east to south-west. A contemporary account compared the vault to 'a bird stretching out her broad wings to fly; planted on its firm columns, it soars to the clouds'. To Pevsner, Hugh's so-called 'crazy vault' offers the first example in Europe of ribs used for purely decorative effect.

The sanctuary is flanked with screens and monuments, including that of John of Gaunt's wife, Katherine Swynford (d.1403), progenitor of the house of Lancaster and thus of the Tudor succession. She lies under a rich Perpendicular canopy. Opposite is a cathedral rarity, an Easter Sepulchre, usually a target for iconoclasts. It is composed of gables festooned with crockets, while beneath lie the sleeping sentries.

The eastern transepts both date from Hugh's church and are Early Gothic, tight, narrow and mysterious alcoves. Their lancets narrow to a sharp point, with dark Victorian glass adding to their privacy. The view from them out into the choir and its 'crazy vault' adds an exotic sense of disturbance.

The final movement in this architectural symphony is the Angel Choir, strictly a retrochoir. St Hugh's shrine survived the Reformation only as a battered gothic chest, but the surrounding hall is memorial enough. Designed as a place of public assembly, it is reminiscent of the Chapel of Nine Altars in Durham, its name deriving from the sculptures crowding the arcade spandrels.

The Angel Choir shares with Exeter and Lichfield the palm for a great Decorated interior. Every inch of wall space is enriched with carving. Piers are not just highlighted with Purbeck shafts but some are entirely composed of them. Thick bunches of foliage underpin vault brackets. Overlooking the chamber is a single, massive east window.

This is the land of Lincoln stiff-leaf, as if we were in the tropical house at Kew. Whorls of acanthus rise, dip and wave from capitals, so undercut as to be almost tearing free from their shafts. Ballflower crowds every arcade moulding. The clerestory seems buoyed up on cushions of light. The presiding angels are almost lost in the spandrels, but are superlative gothic carvings. A depiction of the Expulsion from Eden is full of mannerist gesture. In a spandrel of the north arcade is the Lincoln imp, turned to stone for throwing rocks at an angel.

The main east window has eight slender lights rising to a cluster of geometrical circles, Decorated tracery at its youngest and most subtle, with clear signs of the style's origins

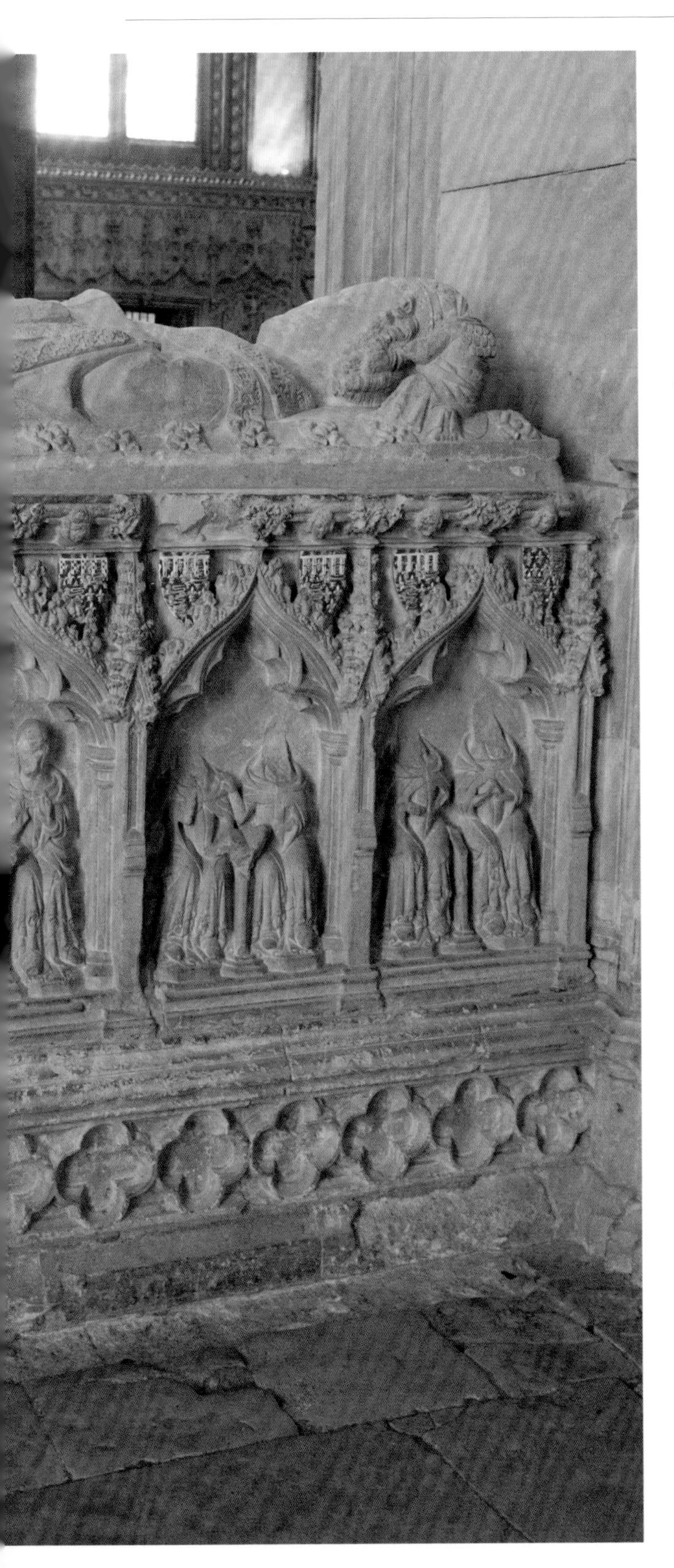

in the cathedrals of northern France. Its glass by Clayton & Bell complements the medieval fragments in adjacent windows. The dominant colour is blue, not garish but dark and cool, the only drawback being that it makes it hard to appreciate the roof bosses.

The Angel Choir is flanked by Perpendicular chantries and chapels lucky to survive the Reformation. The Russell Chantry next to the Judgment Porch has an interior painted in the 1950s by Duncan Grant and looks curiously fey. The adjacent Longland Chantry has tiny early Renaissance detailing visible in its west wall.

The north-east transept leads to the cloister and chapter house. The former is relatively small, Lincoln being a non-monastic cathedral, but with expansive Decorated tracery. Its north range was rebuilt by Christopher Wren in 1674 to house the cathedral library, and contains original book presses and old leather volumes. Of the original 109 chained volumes, 88 survive today: the guide briskly says, 'the chains worked'. The library is supported on Tuscan columns which shade tables outside the cathedral tea-rooms. To sit here on a sunny day and look up at the Dean's Eye window is a treasured cathedral experience.

The Early Gothic chapter house is supported by a central pier shafted in Purbeck marble. Stiff-leaf sprouts everywhere. The chamber is dominated by its stained glass, all by Clayton & Bell. Over the entrance hovers a lovely rose window. It is all a calming coda to a cathedral justly described by Ruskin as 'out and out the most precious piece of architecture in the British Isles'.

Left
St Hugh's tomb

LIVERPOOL

Church of Christ

20th-century gothic in dramatic setting, Dulverton Bridge

Liverpool's Anglican cathedral loves superlatives. It is the biggest church in England. It has the world's tallest tower and the longest footprint after St Peter's in Rome. Only Seville cathedral outranks it in gothic volume. Begun in 1902 and not finished until 1978, this great building is medieval in appearance, gestation and extravagance. Erected during a long period of decline in the city's fortunes, its rivalry with the Catholic cathedral along the road seemed to embody Christian waste and sectarianism. To some, it still does.

The new Anglican diocese was created in 1880 and the location of a new cathedral was challenging – a rocky quarry high above the River Mersey opposite the Georgian quarter around Rodney Street. As a result, the building's alignment had to be north–south rather than east–west. The competition judges were advised by two titans of late-Victorian architecture, R. Norman Shaw and G. F. Bodley, with heated debate over style. Committee minutes report a view that 'Gothic architecture produced a more devotional effect upon the mind than any other which human skill had invented.' Others regarded gothic as a 'worn-out flirtation in antiquarianism, now relegated to the limbo of art delusions'.

The committee rejected more than a hundred designs, including entries from Charles Rennie Mackintosh, Temple Moore and William Lethaby. Instead, it chose a gothic phantasmagoria by Giles Gilbert Scott, grandson of the great Sir George and only twenty-two at the time. This caused a sensation. The young man was said to have 'designed nothing but a pipe-rack'. Worse, he turned out to be a convert to Catholicism. Further, in an apparent act of blatant nepotism, Bodley was a relative of Scott and offered to be his partner and overseer. This was hardly an open competition.

The judges stuck with their decision, but the Scott/Bodley relationship proved fractious. Bodley left to design a not dissimilar cathedral in Washington DC, and his absences proved, said the young Scott, 'more of a farce than ever and … my patience is about exhausted'. When Bodley died suddenly in 1907, the committee was happy to leave Scott in sole charge and stayed loyal to him to the end. He died in 1960 with the building still not finished. It was a venture of medieval longevity.

Left
Celebration of space: Dulverton Bridge

Left
The cathedral from below

Work began in 1904 on the Lady Chapel, which was consecrated in 1910. Scott's design then began to alter, notably from two towers and two transepts to four transepts and a tower. Work proceeded from east to west, and was interrupted by two world wars. The west front was not completed until the 1970s, by when the city was in rapid decline and the 'hulk on the hill' seemed a financial and stylistic extravagance.

For all that, the cathedral's completion in 1978 marked a gesture of defiance. There is no doubt that, on a dark day, the sandstone edifice can seem grim, like Piranesi out of *Gormenghast*. But familiarity (and good lighting) has brought me round to this great work. Unlike Coventry and Guildford, Liverpool is not a gothic form in a modern idiom. Every sinew is gothic through and through, the creation of one style, one imagination and one building programme.

Close to, the exterior is massive, composed of chancel, transepts, buttressed walls and pinnacles. In the Lancashire rain, its dripping flanks might be those of a beached whale, waiting to be eased back into the Mersey. But the tower dominates the Liverpool skyline and is visible from the Peak District in the south-east round to Wales in the south-west. The cathedral gives no quarter. Over the (liturgical) west door is a statue of the Risen Christ, the final work of Elisabeth Frink. It stares austerely across the city, defying scepticism as to the cathedral's necessity.

Inside are all the features of a gothic church, fluted piers, lierne vaults and Decorated windows, exaggerated to the brink of excess. As Scott's plan evolved, it discarded a traditional nave and instead created a so-called Great Space separating two equal transepts in the heart of the building. To the west of the western transept is a stately bridge, looking east over the Great Space and west to where the nave should be, into a sunken well of just two bays. This Dulverton Bridge floats in air like something from a Tolkien castle, offering exhilarating views of the interior. The Well beyond is a sort of purgatory, used as a meeting area or annex. The Great Space is the real nave.

Not everyone is excited by Liverpool. To Alec Clifton-Taylor, the interior was bare and staid. As to its furnishings, 'neither inspiration nor sensibility seem to be much in evidence'. The building inevitably lacks the patina of age, which lends character to a gothic church. The use of the Well as an education centre – at least on my visits – seems a mess. Over it hangs a neon graffiti by Tracey Emin, 'I felt you and I knew you loved me'. It is a banal cliché for such a place. There are other moments of awkwardness. The ambulatory has curious 'nostrils' or openings to the sanctuary. The chancel aisles seem like tunnels.

Yet this is an awesome church. Scott, so long under the shadow of his grandfather, had the same gift of gothic imagination, the same mastery of proportion and drama. Liverpool cathedral is, above all, a celebration of arches, some round, some pointed, some low, some impossibly high, until the head spins with soaring and swooping arcs of stone. In the west wall, Scott inserted triple-lancet windows depicting the Benediction, with 200,000 pieces of glass crafted by Carl Edwards. To the east, the sanctuary reredos is massive, gilded and Perpendicular in style. The choir is spacious, with mural paintings over stalls of an Arthurian grandeur. The font of French marble has an apostle carved in relief on each of its twelve sides.

A different sensation is offered by the earlier Lady Chapel, to the liturgical south-east, which was clearly designed under Bodley's influence. It is Victorian in texture and richness, with high windows and flamboyant French vaults. Gargoyles gaze down from the triforium. The reredos is in filigree gothic, echoed in the brass lanterns. The altar has a Kneeling Madonna by Giovanni della Robbia.

When I last left the cathedral on a winter evening and looked down past the Oratory Chapel into the old quarry graveyard, some of my qualms returned. This is no place to be sad. But Liverpool shows that the noblest style to grace English architecture can be harnessed to any purpose and, with talent, turned to triumph.

LIVERPOOL RC

Christ the King

Modernist auditorium, Piper glass, art in side chapels, Lutyens crypt

The Irish population of Liverpool soared in the 1850s, driven by famine at home and drawn by the hope of work in the docks. The Catholic hierarchy decided on a new cathedral and in 1853 commissioned E. W. Pugin, son of Augustus Welby, for a design in the gothic style. It was never built.

Many years later, in 1928, the project was revived and a site acquired on Brownlow Hill, where the city's obsolete workhouse stood. Sir Edwin Lutyens, then at the height of his reputation, was commissioned to design a classical building that would contrast with Anglican gothic at the other end of Hope Street. Liverpool was imitating the style wars that had previously consumed Westminster. In both cases, the Catholics deployed classicism against the Protestants who, in their view, had hijacked the gothic of the Old Religion – not an issue that in the 1840s ever troubled Pugin.

Lutyens' megalomania was extraordinary even for an architect. He wanted his domed building to be the biggest church on Earth. It would mix Byzantium with Rome, romanesque with renaissance. It would not just outgun the Anglican cathedral but, for good measure, also St Peter's in Rome. Lutyens was a stranger to both cost and common sense. Though initial work on his huge crypt commenced in the 1930s, it was halted by the war in 1941. Five years later, the cost had risen to £27m, and Lutyens' bluff was called. Adrian Scott, yet another of the Scott clan, was summoned to finish the crypt, but the project collapsed under the weight of its bills.

Completion of a Catholic cathedral of some sort became a matter of sectarian pride. In 1960, Archbishop Heenan, the future cardinal of Westminster, launched a competition for a more modest structure to rest on Lutyens' crypt. It was to cost no more than £1m (the same as Coventry). The winner was Frederick Gibberd, with a design that was unmistakeably modern. Following the pronouncements of the Second Vatican Council, the altar would face the congregation, and allow worship 'in the round'. Its appearance was that of an inverted funnel, crowned by a spiky coronet and supported by boomerang-shaped struts. It could hardly have been less like the church down the road.

Left
Triumphal entry to 'Paddy's wigwam'

The new cathedral was consecrated in 1967 but, like many modernist

designs, it was more dramatic than practical. There were early problems with some of the materials used and almost all its surfaces had to be replaced. Decades of legal dispute followed, and it was not until 2003 that the finished building was delivered to an exhausted but elated diocese. It cost eight times its original estimate but at least that was cheaper than Lutyens.

The crown of Gibberd's cathedral sits spindly and unobtrusive on the Liverpool skyline. Resting on just half of Lutyens' crypt, it invited metaphors both derogatory and affectionate. It was 'Paddy's wigwam', a circus tent, a pagan temple, a decapitated space rocket. The exterior was helped by being clad in Portland stone rather than concrete, and looks clean and unstained to this day.

The new approach from Hope Street, up wide steps with flanking banners, is bold for an English public building, except that at the top there is a concrete wall directly over the entrance, as though willing visitors to turn back. Holes at the top contain the cathedral's bells and the wall is decorated with a giant semi-abstract relief of the three Calvary crucifixes (by William Mitchell). As Pevsner said, 'It might be the introduction to some cruel Mexican ritual.'

The inside is a coup de théâtre. Gibberd wanted the impact to be immediate. He duly created a single, immense space, crowned by a giant flue. The air is suffused with the blue light from the stained glass. The effect is supremely dramatic, with 2000 seats arranged in a circle, so all eyes are focused on the raised central altar. This is a simple slab of white marble over which hovers a slender crucifix by Elisabeth Frink. It honours Heenan's charge that all who enter 'should be arrested and held by the altar'.

Left
Interior: study in blue

Opposite
Lady Chapel statue
by Robert Brumby

The bishop's throne is positioned on a dais like that of a high priest about to perform Pevsner's ritual. Overhead, a baldacchino is suspended from the roof in a mass of tubes and struts, and above that is the great tower, entirely of glass, to designs from John Piper and made by Patrick Reyntiens. Once again, a modernist interior turns to this doughty duo to add warmth to space. Down below, the lectern is composed of two florid sea eagles by a local artist, Sean Rice, in 1995. He also made the fiercely metallic Way of the Cross statues.

As at Westminster's Catholic cathedral, Liverpool depends on its side chapels for more detailed visual appeal. Running round the circumference, they are the cathedral's defining feature. All are emphatically modern in idiom, but any bleakness is relieved by the presence of works of modern art and by ubiquitous coloured glass. The cathedral has its own studio which, with the addition of works by Rice, Peter Eugene Ball, Stephen Foster, Robin McGhie, Ceri Richards and Robert Brumby, turns the church into a gallery of modern religious art. Liverpool has none of the sentimental tweeness of many Catholic churches. The chapels' glass, each window different in shape, sends shafts of coloured light pouring into the auditorium.

A lift descends to Lutyens' crypt. This is a shock, as if Liverpool were intent on inverting Westminster, with a blackened vault beneath rather than above its nave. The subterranean chambers are heavy with Lutyens' thwarted grandiloquence. They comprise two halls and two chapels, used during the building of the cathedral and still in use today. A chamber of relics is guarded by a rolling stone, as if to Christ's tomb. Another hall should contain Lutyens' great model of his intended church, but this is in the Museum of Liverpool. It should come home.

MANCHESTER

St Mary, St Denys and St George

Holloway windows, Tudor choir stalls and misericords, Chetham statue

Manchester, a cathedral city? I find most people astonished. Yet the medieval church of St Mary, St Denys and St George on the banks of the River Irwell was, for centuries, one of the largest (and wealthiest) parish churches in the land. Evidence of an early Saxon church comes from the Angel Stone (*c*700), discovered in the wall of the old porch during 19th-century restoration. The present church was largely rebuilt in 1421 and a college of secular canons founded next door by Thomas de la Warre. In the 17th century, this college became Chetham's School and Library and is now a leading music academy. That this largely intact medieval enclave should have survived for five hundred years is remarkable. The church became a cathedral in 1847.

In those days, this part of the city was Victorian England at its most grim. To the west towards the Irwell was the neighbourhood that Engels described as containing 'unqualifiedly the most horrible dwellings which I have yet beheld'. It was here that Marx came to join him in 1845, to work in Chetham's Library and conceive his revolution. The district is now a tangle of car parks, railways and disused warehouses. It cries out for a new Marx and a new revolution.

The cathedral's exterior is of light brown Lancashire stone, an unfortunate material which soon looks dirty when polluted. It was more imposing as I first remember it, punctuating the view up Deansgate and coal-black with grime. The tower still has the air of a forbidding spinster aunt, wagging its finger at the awful Arndale Centre next door.

Manchester cathedral was so restored in 1882 that, to Alec Clifton-Taylor, it is so 'uncathedral-like' as to be no longer medieval. But the present building retains medieval fragments within and has the gothic style and appearance of its forebears. The exterior is rich Perpendicular, outlined with strong pinnacles and generous, if relentless, aisle and clerestory windows. The Victorian Basil Champneys designed the porch and many of the outbuildings. A beautiful Mother and Child with saints (1933) by Eric Gill presides over the Dean's entrance. Manchester cathedral is Perpendicular for all time.

The interior claims the widest nave in England (as does St Nicholas, Great Yarmouth). But this is no Chelmsford or Portsmouth, a parish church that needed to up its game to cathedral status. Manchester

Left
Fire Window in regimental chapel

Left
Chetham statue, detail

Opposite
Tudor carving in stalls

once boasted eight chantry chapels in its side aisles to soothe the medieval souls of rich Mancunians. Today, most of their screens are gone, so the chapel spaces merge into the nave. The restored stone is grey.

A German bomb in 1940 destroyed most of the north-east part of the cathedral and took out all the Victorian glass. Today, the west wall is dominated by five windows created by Antony Holloway from the 1970s to the 1990s. They depict the Creation, the Revelation, St George, St Mary and St Denys. On a sunny day, the glass fractures and splays light onto the floor in a welcome burst of colour. Even more dramatic is the Fire Window by Margaret Traherne (1966) in the Chapel of the Duke of Lancaster's Regiment, a burst of reds and yellows as if from a blazing furnace.

The roofs are of wood, the decoration growing richer as we turn to the choir and chancel. They date, as does much of the interior prior to restoration, from the patronage of the Lancastrian Stanley family.

Beneath lies the choir, Manchester's treasure. The Tudor choir stalls have canopies that display some of the finest medieval woodwork in England. John Harvey identifies their creator in 1505–9 as William Broomfleet from Yorkshire, who was also responsible for the stalls at Ripon. Thirty in number, they carry three tiers of canopy. One tier is of three-dimensional tabernacles, another a row of oriel windows looking inwards, and the top tier is a horizontal coping of arches and pendants.

Within the choir stalls, the desks are decorated with figures, foliage and shields while below are original misericords. Their themes are the familiar quarrelling couples, thieving foxes, fighting lions and men playing backgammon. It is hard to imagine the spirit of mischievous invention that must have presided over Broomfleet's workshop. His carvers were as meticulous as lace-makers, alert to the gothic tradition in their canopies yet also to the paradoxes of daily life in their misericords. The communion rail is another masterpiece, Georgian of 1750 with rococo swirls.

Over the chapter-house door and inside it are two semi-medieval compositions by the artist Carel Weight inserted in the gothic tracery, both in 1963: Christ and the People and The Transfiguration are in the narrative style of Weight's friend, Stanley Spencer. In the north aisle is an 1853 statue of the 17th-century benefactor of Chetham's School, Humphrey Chetham. It is a supreme work of Victorian art, naturalism without sentiment, showing a kindly man with a schoolboy at his feet, believed to be the son of the sculptor, William Theed.

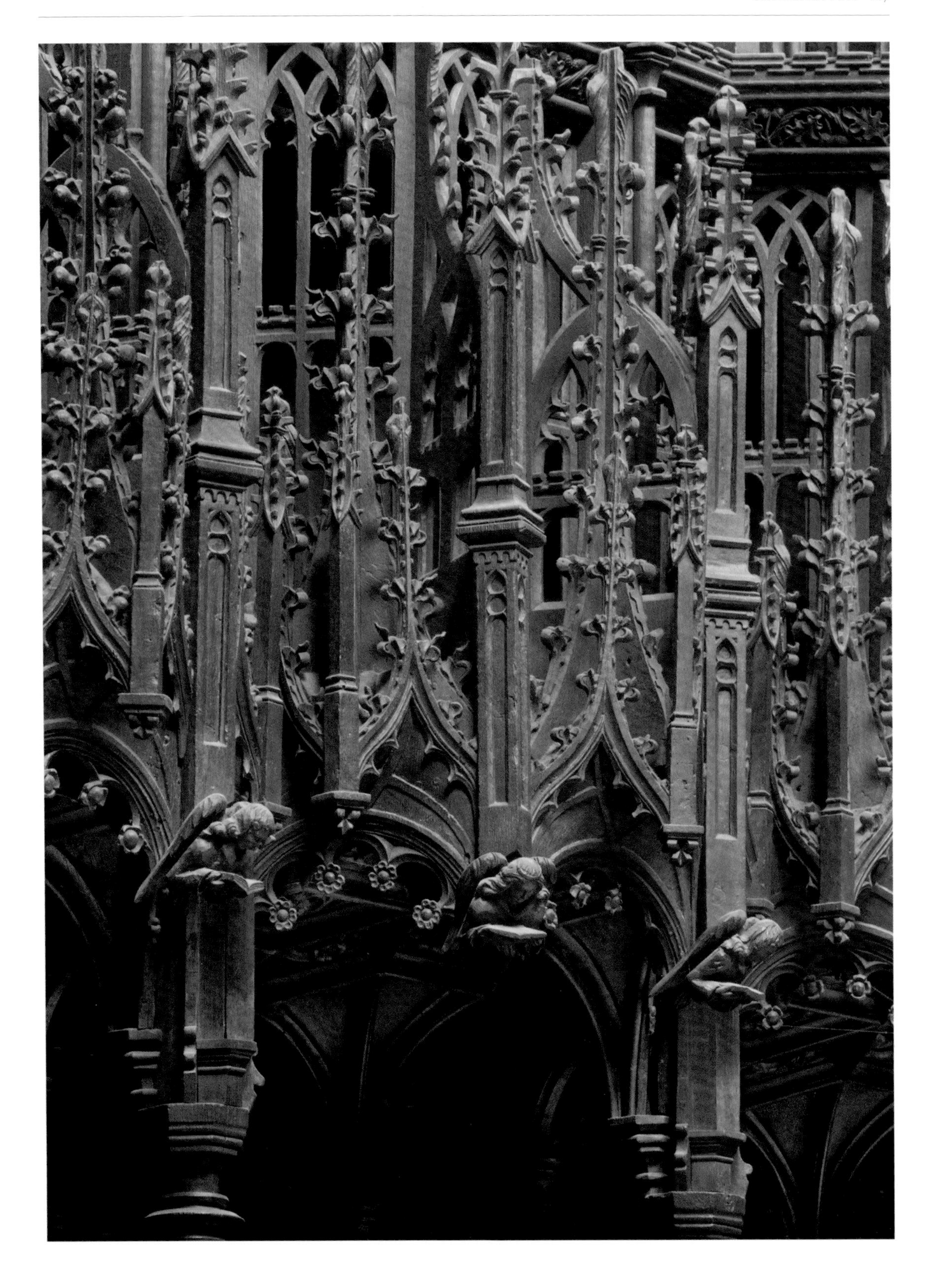

NEWCASTLE

St Nicholas

Wedding-cake steeple, neo-gothic chancel woodwork

Newcastle's parish church of St Nicholas, with its eccentric steeple and elegant crown, has graced the banks of the Tyne since the 15th century. A local chronicler wrote that it 'lifteth up a head of majesty high above the rest as a cypress tree above the low shrubs'. It was promoted to cathedral in 1882, when ecclesiastical Newcastle was allowed to emerge from the shadow of Durham. (It took academic Newcastle another eighty years to do likewise.)

The cathedral sits above the waterfront at the foot of what was in the 1830s Newcastle's new Regency suburb, Grainger Town. Named after its developer Richard Grainger, it was the handsomest urban development in Britain, as fine as Bath and Edinburgh. The destruction of much of it by Newcastle's boss T. Dan Smith in the 1960s, in search of his 'Brasilia of the North', was an architectural tragedy.

The church is modest in proportion and has no surrounding close, being hemmed in by busy streets. The exterior, in warm Northumberland stone, is cruciform, Perpendicular and heavily restored. The steeple, built in 1448, is a conventional tower up to its parapet, where the features of ts extraordinary crown start to emerge. Heavy buttresses become pinnacles which become much larger pinnacles and then four flying ogival ribs supporting a lantern. This lantern is a miniature steeple that roughly replicates the one below. It is a charming conceit, liberally coated in crockets.

Pevsner gives a possible origin for the design in the pre-Great Fire St Mary-le-Bow in London, but the only comparable example extant is the later St Giles in Edinburgh. During the Civil War, a Scots bombardment of the church was averted by the tactic of filling the tower with Scots prisoners. The exterior was largely rebuilt by George Gilbert Scott in 1872.

The cathedral nave is comfortably parochial rather than impressive. The short Perpendicular arcade has shallow moulded arches and piers with no capitals. A contrasting, highly ornamental font is situated at the west end. The crossing is spacious, the north transept filled by an enormous organ case of 1676, mostly by Renatus Harris. It previously stood over the choir screen and must have completely cut off the chancel. The original instrument, on which the Newcastle composer Charles

Left
The tower: 'a head of majesty'

Left
Laing window

Opposite
Victorian medievalism: the choir

Avison played in the 18th century, was rebuilt three times before it finally gave up the ghost in 2013 and awaits reconstruction.

Newcastle's chancel dates from the 1880s elevation to cathedral status. It was refurbished by a local architect, Robert Johnson, a master of late-Victorian Gothic revival. The choir, its stalls and surrounding screens were all crafted by Johnson to evoke the late-Perpendicular era, with the aid of a talented local carver, Ralph Hedley. I find the stalls are indistinguishable from those of the 15th century. Hedley even copied misericords from those in Carlisle and Exeter cathedrals. The canopy of the bishop's throne is an extravaganza, rising tier upon tier. The three-decker reredos is of alabaster. To the left of the altar, a medieval-style effigy of an Edwardian bishop lies with two angels strangely singing from a scroll over his shoes. Johnson's work at Newcastle merits a leading position in the story of 19th-century design.

The south transept contains an elaborate Jacobean monument of *c*1635 to Henry and Elizabeth Maddison, with Henry's parents kneeling behind him and his eldest son and daughter-in-law behind her. The remaining sixteen children have been tucked away below stairs. The elaborate pediment is presided over by Faith, Hope and Charity. In the north chancel aisle a 15th-century brass to the Thornton family is said to be the largest in England, the presiding couple standing on a base composed of their fourteen children.

Newcastle contains a large collection of Victorian and later glass. The windows in St George's Chapel celebrate two Tyneside shipping magnates, Andrew Laing and Charles Parsons, both whom died in 1931. Their products are illustrated in the panels below. These include Laing's *Mauretania*, holder for twenty-two years of the Blue Riband for the fastest Atlantic crossing, and Parsons's first turbine-driven yacht.

The west end has a Jesse window by Clayton & Bell. Other windows are by William Wailes, C. E. Kempe and Powell & Sons. The Ascension Chapel is overseen by a monumental work of cubist glass by Leonard Evetts (1962) celebrating the cathedral's survival of the war. The most charming windows are in the crypt off the north transept, small depictions of Tyneside life between the wars by Basil Barber (1932).

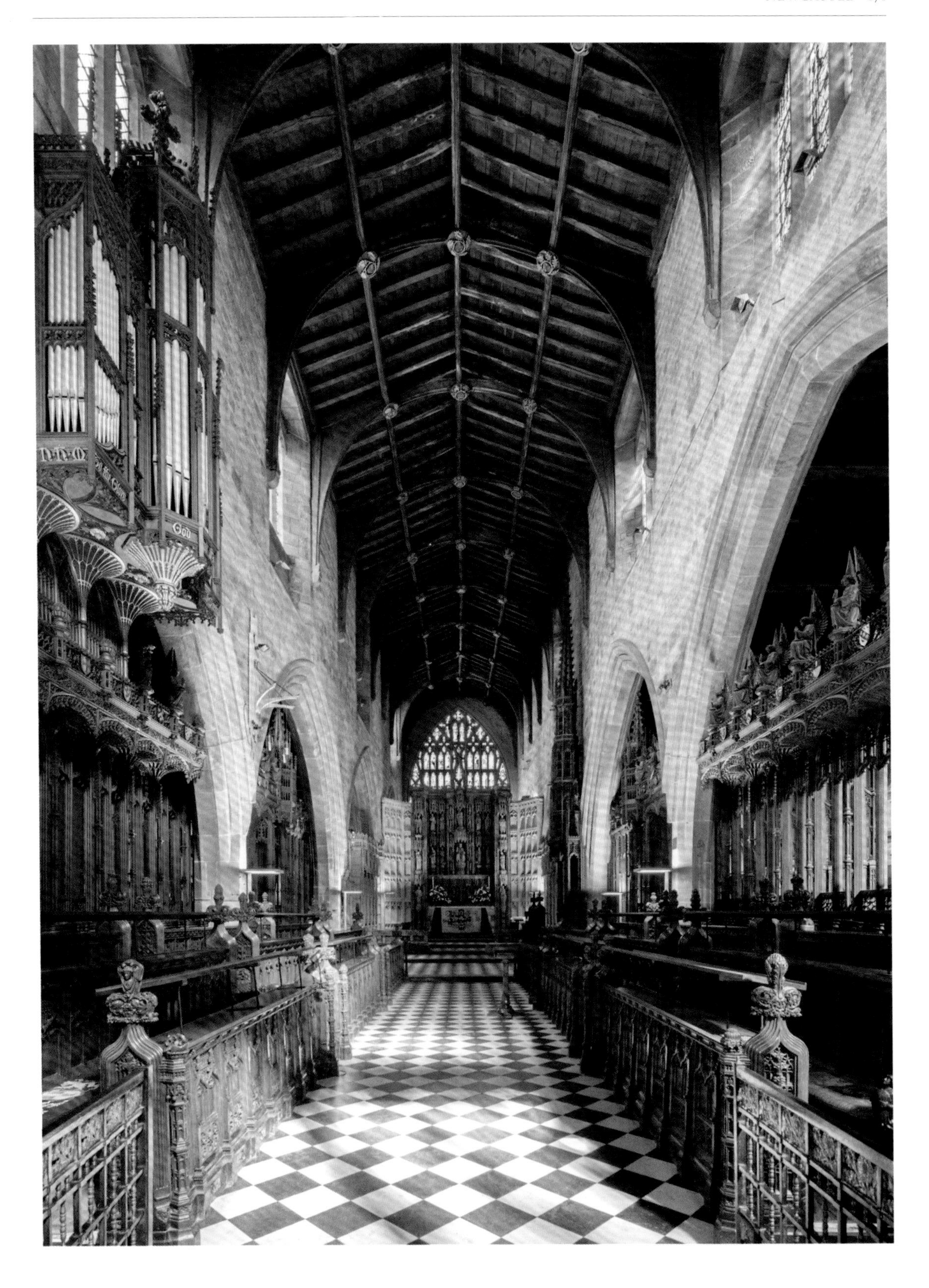

NEWCASTLE RC

St Mary

Pugin fittings, Wailes windows

★

Pugin's cathedral sits on a wide plinth opposite Newcastle's railway station, its slender spire visible from across the Tyne. A curving flight of steps rises beneath the east end, overlooked by a 21st-century statue of one of Newcastle's favourite sons, Cardinal Basil Hume. The cathedral is on the edge of Grainger Town, precious survivor of old Newcastle (*see* page 169).

St Mary's is one of the least altered of Pugin's Catholic Emancipation churches although the tower is a later addition. It was begun in 1842 at the expense, so it was said, of halfpennies donated by dockyard workers. Eight years later, it was converted into a cathedral for the new diocese of Hexham and Newcastle.

The interior displays Pugin's command of space and colour. The nave and chancel arcades are as one, with seven arches from end to end. There is no clerestory, just a steeply gabled wooden roof. This roof is painted in red and black, with beams and struts picked out in white spirals. From the west end, the effect is of a cascade of shooting stars. Spotlights pick out the angels on the corbel heads.

As with many Catholic cathedrals, some of the original fittings were removed under the reforms of the Second Vatican Council of 1962–5, leaving it almost nonconformist in its simplicity. The choir screen went in the 1980s. However, the parishioners firmly voted to have the rood cross restored and it is now left floating in air above the raised sanctuary space.

The furnishings are almost all by Pugin, notably the triple-gabled high altar, carved from Caen stone with carved relief panels, as well as a lectern and a bishop's throne, now officially renamed a chair. The east end is enlivened by vigorous repainting, mostly in maroon and green from Pugin's original pattern book. The modern floor tiles are based on medieval patterns.

Most of the stained glass is by Pugin or in his style, including a grand east window by the neo-medievalist William Wailes, here designing for his home town. A south-aisle window by Joseph Nuttgens (2006) celebrates Newcastle's shipyards and workers. In the west end of the cathedral, an organ gallery installed in 2013 looks jolly and most un-Puginian.

Left
The chancel: Pugin in austere guise

NORWICH

The Holy and Undivided Trinity

Norman nave, 1000 roof bosses, apsidal chapels, Despenser retable, Prior's Door

Paths lead through ancient gateways down wayward lanes to a passing river. An elegant steeple holds the eye. Norwich cathedral in its close forms the perfect adjunct to its city, still one of the finest such compositions in England.

It was not always so. The cathedral was founded after the Conquest by its first bishop, Herbert de Losinga, allegedly to atone for the sin of bribery by which he had secured the job. The Suffolk abbey of St Edmundsbury (*see* Bury St Edmunds) had already refused to host a new East Anglian diocese for the Normans, asserting its allegiance was to Rome rather than Normandy. Norwich took its place. This led to ongoing rivalry between the two churches, not least in the cost of rebuilding both of them.

The new cathedral was begun in 1109, downhill from the new castle. Losinga cared little for the locals, seizing and demolishing almost a third of the Anglo-Danish town for his project. He even charged townspeople to use their own market, which was just outside the new cathedral gate. The land that was acquired for the monastery led down to the River Wensum, where barges brought stone from quarries in Caen.

Losinga's ambitions were the equal of his crimes. 'Alms extinguish sin,' he announced boldly, 'as water does fire.' He spent lavishly. His nave was to be bigger than Canterbury and comparable in length to St Albans and Winchester. The tower was to be the highest of its day, while walls and gatehouses would keep the town at bay. The enterprise must have generated so much work for the people of Norwich as to leave little time for rebellion – although they still set the cloisters on fire in a riot in 1272.

Such was the size of Losinga's cathedral there was little need for the later expansion. Nor, since it enjoyed no saintly relics, did it need the retrochoir for pilgrims that replaced the eastern apse in most English cathedrals. Norwich therefore survives to this day little altered from its original plan. It has virtually no Early Gothic or Decorated elements. Only in the 15th century was it finally given a clerestory and stone vault, plus a new spire, the second-highest in England (after Salisbury). Norwich is best viewed as a box of Norman walls with a graceful Perpendicular lid.

The contrast between the walls and lid lends a distinctive personality

Left

The tower at night

Opposite
Norman presbytery with perpendicular 'lid'

Left
Football misericord

to the cathedral exterior. The nave from the south cloister shows at least five tiers of windows, like shelves in an architectural display case. The adjacent south transept might be the wall of a severe Norman palace. On the other hand, the tower is a gothic patchwork of vertical shafts, porthole tracery and intersecting arches.

The view from the east is quite different. Here all is Perpendicular fluidity. The transepts are dominant, the structure compact and the tower powerful. Flying buttresses over the presbytery billow like the rigging of a Wensum barge.

The exterior goes awry only with that English cathedral bugbear (*see* Introduction), the west front. This has been much restored over the centuries, most recently in the 1970s but, in my opinion, to no avail. Four clusters of attached shafts frame a characterless Perpendicular window. Possibly Tudor caps crown the corners. Three doorways look like nothing more than gaping holes. It is perhaps significant, as Pevsner points out, that this is one of the few cathedrals not restored by George Gilbert Scott. A redeeming feature is the good modern statue by David Holgate by the main entrance.

Norwich's nave interior restores its dignity. It is a masterpiece of counterpoint, between Norman arcades and gothic roof. Fourteen bays of silvery limestone undulate into the distance, the eye lifted by pier shafts that run from floor to roof. Only in a curious bay adjacent to the altar is the rhythm broken. Large Durham-style drum piers are thought to mark the sanctuary of Losinga's church, imitating St Peter's shrine in Rome.

Above the Norman arcade sits the Perpendicular vault which replaced the old wooden roof in the 1460s. Its spreading ribs are almost but not quite formed into the fans that would doubtless have graced it a generation later. The composition illustrates, as does all of Norwich, Pevsner's thesis that of all gothic styles, Perpendicular was the most in sympathy with Norman romanesque. The two styles share a visual clarity and simplicity of line.

Down the centre of the vault runs Norwich's gallery of over two hundred medieval bosses, among the thousand that adorn the whole cathedral. Many are reputedly taken from woodcuts in what were precursors of Luther's illustrated Bible imported from Germany at the time. The scenes are remarkably vivid, the depiction of Noah's ark being a favourite. There are wheeled mirrors, but the bosses are so distant they are best appreciated through binoculars.

Above
The Despenser retable

Left
Noah's ark

Opposite left
Noah plants a vine

Opposite right
Stonemason

In the centre of the nave is a gleaming copper dish acting as a font. Once used for boiling toffee, it was donated by the local Rowntree factory, perhaps forgetful of its Quaker roots. The west window intrudes loud Victorian glass, its elaborate Bible tableaux contrasting with the sculptural vernacular of the adjacent bosses.

Among the nave memorials is a curious vertical monument, incised onto a slab and known as 'the Skeleton'. It is to a cathedral mason, Thomas Gooding, who demanded to be shown standing upright, to give him a head start on his journey to Heaven. Next to it is a two-bay chantry memorial, apparently to two bishops, covered in extravagant Tudor shields and panelling. It was erected in the 1530s, before such structures were banned.

Norwich's organ is a superb instrument, but its location is controversial, above the pulpitum and three bays into the nave. Though a handsome design by Stephen Dykes Bower in 1950, it blocks what should be a dramatic view from nave to east end. It also means that the choir is located in the nave, like a panelled drawing-room lowered into the wrong place and detached from the sanctuary. The stalls are mostly 15th-century, although three misericords are modern replacements, one of them showing a Norwich City goalkeeper in action.

The crossing is thus east of the choir. The transepts on either side are uniformly Norman, with high triforiums, deep galleries and clerestory windows. The entire north wall of the north transept has windows with semi-abstract modern glass, by John Hayward and Keith New, which I find jarring in a Norman cathedral. In St Andrew's Chapel on the transept's east side is a poignant medieval Crucifixion, one of many paintings moved to the cathedral when a number of Norwich churches were closed in the 1980s.

This contrasts with a depiction of the same scene in the south transept, a florid Victorian imitation of a 16th-century Flemish Crucifixion. Beneath the window is the entrance to one of the few Early Gothic contributions to Norwich, the 13th-century chapel of St Catherine of Alexandria. It has a quotation from Eliot's *Four Quartets* in its arch moulding, 'At the still point of the turning world.' It contains the most serene of gothic vaults inside.

Norwich's majestic presbytery was effectively Losinga's throne room. Though Norman in plan and elevation, it was later gothicised with a lofty clerestory and vault. In pride of place is the throne, prominently (and uniquely) located

in the centre of the sanctuary, directly behind the high altar. It sits over a chamber intended to contain saintly relics, whose aura would infuse the episcopal posterior, relics that were never to materialise. The present throne is a replica, but the bishop still sits on it.

Only Canterbury and Westminster have apses comparable to Norwich, still surrounded by its original chapels and chantries. To one side of the sanctuary is the painted chantry of Bishop Goldwell (d.1499), who was responsible for much of the renewal of the cathedral in the 15th century. The face on his effigy was bashed by iconoclasts, and the niches are painfully empty of statues. A Cromwellian musket ball is lodged in the side.

The Jesus Chapel has its own modest apse, with a 15th-century Dutch triptych of the Adoration. A painting in the Bauchon Chapel is by the Georgian artist John Opie, rarely found far from his native Cornwall. Such work, so commonplace in Dutch or Italian places of worship, is sadly rare in an English church. Over the north ambulatory is the old treasury, now converted into a museum. Its walls are covered with a ghostly profusion of murals and graffiti.

The cathedral's greatest treasure is in St Luke's Chapel, the Despenser retable dating from the late 14th century. It comprises five panels vividly depicting the Crucifixion and Resurrection. It is believed to have been commissioned by Bishop le Despenser, known as the 'Fighting' Bishop of Norwich, to celebrate his suppression of local support for the Peasants' Revolt in 1381. The composition is of great elegance, characteristic of the artistic flowering of the reign of Richard II. The centurion at the foot of the Cross has the pose of a man in authority unnerved by the scene around him. The painting was disguised as the underside of a table-top until 1847, which may account for the damaged upper parts of the panels.

Norwich's cloisters were rebuilt over the course of the 13th and 14th centuries and are second in extent only to Salisbury's. The arcade openings are a gallery of medieval tracery, from swirling Decorated ogees to cusped Perpendicular panels. Some look almost oriental. The cloister's 394 bosses rival those of the nave – and are certainly more visible. Again, we see the carvers' talent at compressing stories into tiny triangles of stone: kings take counsel, the dead are buried, knights battle with monsters, bodies writhe in purgatory.

The cloister houses the celebrated Prior's Door, a unique work of English Decorated art. Four battered shafts on each side support

an arch broken by seven radiating figures, all in a state of colourful animation. They are crowned by alternating triangular and ogee arches, as though spinning in flames round a Catherine wheel. Christ presides over Moses, St John the Baptist, St Peter and the local saint, St Edmund, with attendant angels. It is a unique composition.

Set into the west side of the cloister and boldly visible across the close is Norwich's new visitor centre and refectory (known as the hostry) opened in 2010. Designed by Michael Hopkins on the site of the former pilgrims' quarters, its stone walls, slatted clerestory and grey sloping roofs echo the surfaces of the cathedral behind. Unlike most such additions, which are wisely unobtrusive, Hopkins' building is prominent and yet sympathetic in scale and materials. The interiors of the visitor centre and refectory echo the cathedral's arcades and vaults. Here, for once, is a modern church building that sings in harmony not discord with its surroundings.

Left
Prior's Door: Christ with saints

NORWICH RC

St John the Baptist

Emphatic architectural statement, Early Gothic arcades, Victorian glass

If Norwich's Roman Catholics wanted a riposte to the old cathedral seized from them at the Reformation, they could hardly have done better than St John's. Its tower dominates the hill on the west side of the city, rising above a mountain of masonry with a toughness more typical of the north country than the soft contours of East Anglia.

This is no hesitant Catholic Emancipation church of the 1840s. We are in the 1880s and under the patronage of the Catholic grandee, the 15th Duke of Norfolk, sponsor of large churches in Southwark, Sheffield and Arundel (*see* page 1). To commemorate his marriage in 1877, the thirty-year-old duke offered a church to Norwich 'bearing in mind the title that I hold'. It was deliberately located so as to look down on the city and Anglican cathedral. At the time, it was the largest Catholic church in England, and is still second only to Westminster. It became a cathedral in 1976.

The architect was George Gilbert Scott's son of the same name, a recent convert to Catholicism. When he became mentally ill, his brother, John Oldrid Scott, took over. The church was begun in 1884, by which time the gothic revival had spread its wings and acquired 'attitude', but the building is outwardly cold. The massing is heavy, the tower short and thick, the arms equally so. There is bullishness to it, as if Scott were showing off to prove himself to his father. As at Arundel, the duke's assertive Catholicism was on political display.

If the exterior is tough, even more so is the interior. Again, as if to stress distance from the Anglican cathedral, the church was in the one style almost completely absent from its rival, Early Gothic. The nave is ten bays long, the arcade composed of heavy cylindrical drum piers which are thick with black marble shafting. The arcade supports a triforium and clerestory and the nave is lit by lancets galore.

The crossing steps up a gear. Both transepts are aisled. Chapels shoot off at all angles, notably the 'sunken chapel' along the south flank of the nave. The stiff-leaf of the nave capitals acquires a dose of fertiliser. Leaves drip from every string course. The Walsingham Chapel has a virtual hanging garden on every capital. While the result is dark, even melancholy, it has a powerful unity. The duke makes his point.

Left
The nave: robust Early English revival

NOTTINGHAM RC

St Barnabas

Pugin chapel

★

Nottingham's Roman Catholic cathedral stands prominent on Derby Road, main route out of town from Maid Marian Way. The latter is a carriageway that devastated the south and west of the city centre in the 1960s, and in 2002 was voted one of Britain's five worst streets in a BBC poll. There have since been desperate attempts to prettify it, but the only cure would be reinstatement of its former self.

The cathedral is a much-altered work by A. W. N. Pugin notable for his miniature masterpiece, the Blessed Sacrament Chapel. The church was financed by the ubiquitous patron of post-Emancipation Catholic churches, the 16th Earl of Shrewsbury. Pugin promised 'the most perfect revival of a large parochial church that has been yet accomplished … a strict revival of catholic antiquity'. It opened in 1844 when the earl and Pugin were building Alton Towers and Cheadle church. What was at the time the biggest Catholic church in England became a cathedral in 1852. On its consecration, the guidebook assured readers that 'the joy and gratification of the occasion was not marred by the antagonistic activities of the Protestant Reformation Society'.

Although externally severe, the church clearly had episcopal ambitions from the start. It has an aisled nave, transepts and an ambulatory with retrochoir. The roof is open to the rafters and the east end is almost as large as the nave, with an enclosed sanctuary. The walls are a pleasing off-white and the floors emphatic red, white and black. Alteration both at the end of the 19th century and in the 1960s after the Second Vatican Council has robbed the interior of much of Pugin's distinctiveness and given it a somewhat monastic atmosphere. Pevsner is exceptionally critical, calling the alterations harsh and crude. 'The whole effect could hardly be farther from the enclosed richness Pugin intended.'

What does survive is the Blessed Sacrament Chapel off the south transept. Immaculately restored in 1933 by J. Alphege Pippet, the neo-gothic designer with Hardman & Co, it displays Pugin's bravura handling of colour. There is an elaborate altar and reredos beneath a gothic baldacchino. Every inch of the walls, arcades and roof timbers is stencilled and painted. The window, which is to Pugin's design, was hailed by Christopher Martin as 'majestic iconography and shimmering decoration in red, green and gold to rival Byzantium'.

Left
Pugin Lady Chapel

OXFORD

Christ Church

Norman nave, Tudor pendant vault, St Frideswide shrine, Burne-Jones windows

Given the splendour of its associated university, the seat of Oxford's bishopric is extraordinarily unobtrusive. It is the smallest medieval cathedral in England, lying hidden behind Oxford's grandest quadrangle, Tom Quad. Perhaps as a result, the cathedral has always seemed a jolly, welcoming place.

The 8th-century St Frideswide was canonised for spending three years hiding in a local wood to avoid the attentions of an insistent prince. When she emerged and found to her alarm that he was still waiting – she peers out from a hedge in a carving on her shrine – she had him struck blind by a thunderbolt. He then sensibly left her alone and she became a saint. An Augustinian priory grew up around her shrine, which was rebuilt by the Normans and continued to function as a priory throughout the Middle Ages. For reasons lost in time, it became a place of refuge to scholars fleeing Paris in the 12th century. The rest is history.

In 1524, Cardinal Wolsey sought to outdo his predecessor, William of Wykeham, in founding an Oxford college for students from the school he had also founded in his home town, Ipswich. He dissolved St Frideswide (a decade before Henry VIII's Dissolution) and put Cardinal College in its place. By the time of his fall from grace in 1529, Wolsey had built a hall and quadrangle, demolishing the end of the priory church in the process. He had intended to replace it entirely, but work stalled. In 1546, Henry declared the rump of the church a cathedral and named the college Christ Church, with the cathedral uniquely doubling as a college chapel.

The cathedral thus has a split personality – Oxford university gets no mention in its guidebook. An engaging but absurd archaism has it observing pre-railway solar time which, in Oxford, is five minutes behind London time and can be confusing for those attending services.

The cathedral entrance is sandwiched between Wolsey's Tom Quad and the priory's surviving cloister and chapter house. Only on the north-east side is the wall clear of attached buildings, but there it overlooks private college gardens. The cathedral's spire is visible from a distance, gothic above and Norman below. The Norman clerestory windows can also be glimpsed from the cloister.

Christ Church's interior comes as a shock. The college was home

Left
The chancel: Norman begets Perpendicular

to Lewis Carroll and the cathedral seems to have taken one of Alice's potions and shrunk. The old abbey lost four western bays of its nave to Tom Quad. What remains is a narrow chamber, and the five surviving bays are further reduced to three by an organ loft. In both nave and chancel, the seating is lateral, college fashion. This means that any extra congregation must sit in the aisles and transepts, with little sight of the altar.

The interior is intimate and can be seen in its entirety from the entrance. It is dominated by the 12th-century arcades to nave, chancel and transepts. The piers, which pre-date the university, are Norman and massive. Since they rise to the clerestory, the triforium has to be jammed within the arcades, supported by its own recessed arcades. This is most strange, like a Christian church slotted into an old Roman basilica. The composition is visually united by the clustered shafts of the crossing arches. The east wall was rebuilt by George Gilbert Scott, not his best work, with neo-Norman windows.

The capitals of the arcade piers are carved with crockets and water-leaf, with few signs of stiff-leaf, even though they date from the late 12th century on the threshold of gothic. Over the choir are human heads grimacing and gurning. Elsewhere are monsters, angels, fruit and flowers.

We now lift our eyes to Christ Church's most sensational feature, the chancel vault. It was created for the priory in the 1490s and was probably designed by Oxford's master architect, William Orchard, who had recently created the fan vault of the university's Divinity School.

Orchard's scheme is at first sight incomprehensible, rivalled in this only by the 'crazy vault' at Lincoln. The graceful rise of the stone ribs is interrupted by pendants, which seem to hang pointlessly in mid-air. Since each of the four chancel bays is laterally oblong, Orchard clearly decided to shorten them to squares by resting them on what are technically hammerbeams jutting out from the walls. From each hammerbeam he hung a pendant, supported only by the skill of the engineer. It is a beautiful architect's conceit.

Above, each rib forms a patchwork of liernes, with each lierne punctuated by greater and lesser bosses, the lesser ones dancing round the central ones, as round a maypole. The bosses portray, from east to west, the personalities of the church from Jesus to St Frideswide. To see them properly, you need to lie on a choir stall and view them with binoculars.

The ensemble is in honeyed Cotswold limestone, its crustaceous elements glorious

Opposite left
Burne-Jones: Liddell portrait

Opposite right
Saint on guard

when lit by the sun. As Alec Clifton-Taylor remarks, the renaissance may have begun seventy years earlier on the Continent, but here in Oxford, 'until the end, the gothic flame continued to burn as brightly as ever'. Christ Church vault was 'not only a tour de force of mason-craft but a superb work of art'.

The chief medieval addition to the Norman priory was the three chapels to the north of the chancel, in one of which stands Frideswide's shrine. They are coolly Early Gothic, with slender piers and arches and a dark, mysterious atmosphere. The shrine stands in the middle of the Latin Chapel – named for its defiant post-Reformation use of the Latin rite until 1861 – a canopied chest tomb in the Decorated style of *c*1290. The arch spandrels are filled with intricate but rather lifeless vegetation, in the midst of which we can see the saint spying on her tormentor. Catherine of Aragon came to the shrine in 1518, a curious venue in which to plead for a boy child. She, or at least Frideswide, was unsuccessful. The shrine was smashed to pieces at the Reformation but has since been meticulously reassembled, missing fragments replaced with carbon fibre.

Overlooking the shrine is a rare watching gallery, of stone below and wood above, used by monks guarding it against relic thieves. It is crowned by a forest of Perpendicular pinnacles.

Next to the Latin Chapel is the Lady Chapel, the two divided by a row of medieval monuments. That to Elizabeth of Montacute (d.1354) had its weepers' faces bashed off by iconoclasts, although they left Elizabeth's elaborate coiffure intact. Finally, between Lady Chapel and choir is a chapel in memory of Bishop Bell, who campaigned against the bombing of civilians in the Second World War. He is remembered in Chichester as well. Its altar is carved from a single block of oak. In the floor is inscribed Bell's courageous but unpopular war-time message, 'No nation, no church, no individual is guiltless.'

Oxford is excellently served by its stained glass. Along the north wall of the Latin Chapel are three 14th-century windows, much restored, depicting saints in architectural settings. The same chapel's east window is by Edward Burne-Jones, with a vigorous narrative of St Frideswide's supposed life story. It was made in 1858 when the artist was just twenty-five and before he had joined William Morris. The colours are loud and the narrative realistic, clearly pre-Pre-Raphaelite. The story culminates in a roundel showing the Ship of Souls conveying the saint to Heaven.

The east windows of the Lady and Bell chapels have Burne-Jones in his later mode, the design and figures being more formal.

Work by the same artist is in the Chapel of Remembrance, south of the choir, where St Catherine of Alexandria is said to be a portrait of Alice Liddell's sister, Edith, a lasting icon for Lewis Carroll.

Beyond lies the Lucy Chapel, lit by a Decorated window, in the upper lights of which is a rare surviving portrait/image of St Thomas à Becket. Most such icons were destroyed on the orders of Henry VIII. The north aisle is lit by a 17th-century window by the Dutch artist Abraham van Linge. It shows Jonah under a gourd tree contemplating the city of Nineveh in a Rubensesque landscape.

Steps from the south aisle lead down to the cloister, cowering beneath Wolsey's great hall and curtailed by the rear of Tom Quad. It is vaulted in part with stone liernes, and in part with the same liernes in wood, their bosses still uncarved. Surely a wealthy Christ Church donor can oblige.

Off the cloister stands the cathedral's final treasure, its chapter house. This is entered through an early Norman doorway, surrounded with zigzag. The chapter house is a perfect Early Gothic work of *c*1225. The windows are stepped lancets, lofty and symmetrical, with detached shafts, the vault rising from stiff-leaf capitals and tiny faces. The chamber deserves a better fate than as a gift shop.

Left
Frideswide's shrine with watching gallery beyond

PETERBOROUGH

St Peter, St Paul and St Andrew

Detached west front, retrochoir fan vault, Hedda Stone

★★★★

Peterborough has long been the poor relation of the great East Anglian cathedrals. It is buried in a new town of the 1960s, since bleakly expanded, with none of the suavity of its neighbours, Ely and Norwich. Yet it boasts two features second to none. Its west front is the most impressive medieval façade in England, and its retrochoir is a fan-vaulted delight.

The Saxon abbey joined with Ely as a centre of East Anglian resistance to the Normans, notably under Hereward the Wake in 1170. As a punishment, the town was garrisoned by Norman soldiers, for which the monks had to pay. The old abbey was rebuilt and when destroyed by fire in 1116, it was rebuilt again. This was in the late-Norman style of Ely and Norwich, with elegantly shafted piers, intersecting wall arcades and much zigzag. The west front was added in the 1220s.

Little else changed until the 16th century and the arrival of one of Peterborough's last abbots, Robert Kirkton, in 1509. Under him, Peterborough came to be regarded an exemplar of the need for Dissolution. A previous abbot had kept three mistresses in the town. A monk was caught stealing tomb jewels for his girlfriend. Kirkton himself infuriated the townspeople by enclosing their local cemetery and grazing land as a private deer park. He also built an ostentatious new retrochoir, hiring the leading Tudor architect, John Wastell, to design it.

Few abbeys were less mourned in their passing, but the abbey church appears to have survived the Reformation largely due to Henry VIII's guilt. His first wife, Catherine of Aragon (she is spelled Katharine on her tomb), died in 1536 at nearby Kimbolton Castle, rejected as queen by king and court and denied access even to her daughter, Mary. She was buried on Henry's orders in the nearest abbey possibly as a result. When he came to declare his new dioceses, he conferred the honour on undeserving Peterborough. The most intact of Norman cathedrals, it was again lucky in being restored in the 1880s by J. L. Pearson, George Gilbert Scott's equal in attention to scholarly detail.

Today's city of Peterborough is no beauty. But some ghost of its medieval past survives in a spacious grid of streets round the old parish church in the market square. This is a relic of the town founded by the

Left
West front: caverns of Early Gothic

Normans west of the abbey, after incorporating the earlier settlement in the abbey close. The abbey was in constant and furious dispute with its town, which it owned and taxed ruthlessly. Hence the embattled gatehouse that divides the close from the square, over which the towers of the cathedral loom enticingly.

The cathedral's west front is unlike any other. The original Norman abbey was to be completed by two west towers of which the northern one remains embedded behind the front, along with the base of a southern one. Whatever was intended was overtaken by Abbot Benedict's return from Canterbury in 1177, seven years after the murder of Becket. Like a souvenir hunter, he brought with him a Canterbury cathedral flagstone and other relics allegedly stained with Becket's blood. He is said to have lifted the stone when left alone in that cathedral one night.

Such treasure was clearly of great commercial potential, and merited an appropriate entrance. Benedict did not wait to demolish the existing west front but merely erected a new one in front of it. He also brought with him the new gothic style of Canterbury's east end. Peterborough demonstrates the transition to the pointed arch on what is essentially a Norman structure.

The result is a front of three cavernous recesses starting out from the west wall, as if carved from it rather than built up in front of it. On a dark evening, the effect is intensely dramatic, as if warning the visitor of some dire judgment within. Similar west fronts at Rheims and Amiens cathedrals are almost friendly in comparison.

That said, the architecture seems to have gone awry. The middle of the three recesses would normally be the biggest – as at Lincoln – but here it is the smallest

Left
Fan vault in Lady Chapel

and weakest. The central gable is also uncomfortably squeezed between the outer two. The twin towers on either side received non-matching spires. No less odd is that behind this gothic front we see the surviving tower of the earlier front, as if refusing to be left out of the picture.

The new façade thus looks rather uncomfortable. Doors and windows are not central to the arches while statues, some of them admirably restored, are crowded into the overhead spandrels. Then almost as an afterthought, the monks in the 14th century erected a porch with a Perpendicular upper chamber within the central arch. This was presumably to play some part in the Easter ritual, but also to welcome visitors.

None of this detracts from the personality of this structure. It is somehow both Norman and gothic, one of the set pieces of English architecture. The device of standing the entire façade one bay proud of the west wall, enabling shafts of daylight to penetrate within, conveys a sense of baroque depth that must have been intended.

Peterborough's interior offers a view that is almost completely Norman. The nave bays rise from shafted piers to a double-arched triforium with, above, a clerestory of three stepped arches. The nave was never vaulted, leaving us the earliest English cathedral ceiling, dating from *c*1250. Each lozenge panel contains an image, variously of a king, a monster, an animal playing a musical instrument and, in one panel, an architect with a set-square. It is like a glorious carpet in the air, albeit much repainted in the 19th century.

The former pulpitum, which survived into the 18th century, completely cut off the nave from the choir and presbytery. Its removal brought the choir, which is here positioned west of the crossing, firmly into the ceremony of the nave. Although the crossing has a 14th-century arch, it links what are the cathedral's four surviving Norman arms, north, east, south and west.

The north and south transepts are pure Norman, unaltered except in their window glass. They are three storeys high with original wooden roofs. The south transept has a watching gallery to guard what was, until the arrival of Becket's supposed blood, Peterborough's most holy relic, Oswald's arm. Acquired in 1000, it belonged originally to King (later Saint) Oswald, first Christian monarch of Northumbria (633–42) and much lauded as such by Bede. It vanished at the Reformation.

The cathedral's Norman character slightly dissipates in the presbytery. It retains its

Opposite
The Hedda Stone

Left
Pace/Roper crucifix

Norman arcades and apse, but they were later given gothic windows and vaults, the latter with painted ribs weaving blue and gold panels. Beneath stands a lavish if incongruous High Gothic Victorian baldacchino by J. L. Pearson, in pink marble. Pearson reordered and refurnished the entire sanctuary.

Peterborough lacks great monuments, but two Tudor queens are remembered in the sanctuary. One is the aforementioned Catherine of Aragon, granted dignity at last in death. She is the beneficiary still of an annual service of remembrance in the cathedral. Nearby is a memorial to another sad queen, Mary Queen of Scots. Her body rested here on its way from execution at Fotheringhay in 1587 to Westminster Abbey, long enough to be honoured with heraldic banners.

The choir aisles terminate to the east in tall Perpendicular arches, decorated with fleurons. Beyond lies Kirkton's retrochoir. In the most sumptuous late gothic, it was designed by John Wastell, architect of Canterbury's Bell Harry Tower and the fan vault of King's College, Cambridge. The screen openings between the sanctuary and retrochoir are triple-arched, each arch with filigree cusping. The retrochoir vault might be that of a Tudor hall. Its spreading fans open out as if to cool spectators on a hot day.

Against a wall rests the Hedda Stone of *c*800, with figures round its side. Its purpose is much debated but appears to be a memorial to Abbot Hedda and his monks carved after their slaughter by the Danes. It is thus a precious survival from East Anglia's Mercian past. However, this is complicated by the date of 870 carved on its end which, were it original, would have been in Roman numerals.

Over Peterborough's crossing hangs a vividly obtrusive rood, in bright red and gold. The cross is by George Pace (1975) and the crucifix itself is by Frank Roper. Of its sort, it is the most moving sculpture I know. Christ's face has the most intense poignancy.

PORTSMOUTH

St Thomas

Landmark tower, Buckingham memorial, della Robbia plaque

Portsmouth has the oddest of cathedrals. From the outside, it could be a lighthouse, a community centre or, from the west, a Roman gatehouse. A church was founded here in 1180 as a chapel of ease for the fishing settlement of Camber, honouring the recently martyred Thomas à Becket. As the harbour grew, so did the church. By the Civil War, it was important enough to be shelled by parliamentary forces over the water from Gosport. A direct hit destroyed the tower and the nave, forcing them to be rebuilt.

The fate of Portsmouth as a naval base has risen and fallen over time. Yet sheltering a hundred yards from the sea-wall at the town's seaward end is the old parish church, designated a cathedral in 1927. The result was the usual halting effort to make a silk purse from a sow's ear, completed in the 1990s.

The cathedral and its miniature close are an oasis of Portsmouth picturesque. The east end is medieval, the middle is the outcome of the 17th-century rebuilding and the west end is Charles Nicholson's 20th-century attempt at a cathedral upgrade. The jolliest feature is the tower lantern, long a landmark for sailors on the Solent. The exterior of the building is silvery white and, in spring, sits happily in a mass of crocuses.

A visit should be started at the east end, in the Early Gothic chancel of the medieval church, now relegated to a chapel. It is just two bays long, formed of fan arches containing two lesser arches linked by a Purbeck pier. In the aisle is a large memorial to George Villiers, Duke of Buckingham, close favourite of James I, on account of his being murdered in the town in 1628.

What is now Portsmouth's choir could be a City of London church by Christopher Wren. Built in 1693, it replaced the former nave with an arcade of three short bays set on octagonal bases, once the height of the former box pews. These bases give the arcade an elegant loftiness, while the exiled box pews survive in the aisles. Nicholson's modern nave to the west of the chancel suffers from a serious handicap in that the base of the tower cuts it adrift from the earlier parts of the church. Stylistically, the new nave is almost a pastiche of the choir. Its six pillars echo those of the choir, but with clunky bulbous capitals.

Left
'Wrenaissance' choir with nave behind

Mario's
Restaurant
27
Pizzeria
Ristorante
Italiano
01765 608 688

RIPON

St Peter and St Wilfrid

Early Gothic west front, art nouveau pulpit, Saxon crypt, Tudor choir stalls

It is tempting to suggest little has happened in Ripon since its abbot, Wilfrid, left for the Synod of Whitby in 664. Wilfrid's role at Whitby changed the English church. After a visit to Rome, he returned to persuade the synod that the Roman rite should prevail over the Ionan rite, then being championed by the monks of Lindisfarne. It was Anglo-Saxon England's first great yes to Europe. Wilfrid became bishop of York.

Wilfrid was a cantankerous, proud and political prelate, who was suspended from his living on three occasions. Eventually exiled from Northumbria, he sought relief in converting England's last pagans, who lived in Wessex (*see* Chichester), but he left behind crypts at Ripon and Hexham that remain the oldest intact places of worship in the land. He was later canonised, with a pilgrimage shrine at Ripon.

The Benedictine abbey languished over the centuries as a monastic outpost of York Minster. The archbishops owned its land, built themselves a palace and appointed secular canons. These canons, only one of whom was required to be resident, governed (and taxed) what was known as the Liberty of Riponshire, roughly the six adjacent parishes. The church was rebuilt piecemeal in the Norman, Early Gothic and Decorated periods. An ambitious rebuild of the nave after the collapse of the tower in 1450 was cut short by the Reformation, which Ripon was lucky to survive. The neighbouring and far more impressive abbey at Fountains was not so fortunate.

In 1836 Ripon became the first new diocese to be declared since the Reformation, in a nod towards the burgeoning population of industrial West Yorkshire. (Manchester had to wait another decade.) Even this seemed barely to disturb its rural slumber, though the interior and exterior were extensively restored by George Gilbert Scott in the 1860s. Not until 2000 did the church authorities think it appropriate to change the name of the see to 'Ripon and Leeds'.

Ripon's west front is England's most complete Early Gothic façade. This is no sculpture gallery or processional stage. It has not suffered from Perpendicular re-fenestration. Its façade, entirely of lancets, echoes the Five Sisters window in York Minster. Three portals are topped by two tiers of near-identical openings, three in each tower and five stepped

Left
Early Gothic poise: the west front

Left
Misericord of pig and bagpipes

Opposite
Henry Wilson's art nouveau

in the centre. The flanking towers have taller lancets, all perfectly proportioned. The only pity is that the towers are crowned with battlements where once there were spires.

The rest of the church's exterior includes a squat tower and transepts dating from its Norman period. Nave and east walls are heavily buttressed after numerous collapses. The Decorated east window is an enjoyable insertion, its tracery of seven lights rising to cusped circles, the central one pierced by a single lancet, as if to deflate it.

Inside, the view from the nave to the crossing shows immediately the impact of the Reformation in interrupting an ambitious rebuilding. The old Norman arch hovers uncomfortably over the crossing. A pier seems barely able to reach its arch. Shafts soar into nothingness. A blank tympanum faces the nave. All Scott could do in the 19th century was tidy up a bad job.

Ripon's pulpit is some compensation. Works of art nouveau are rare in English cathedrals, elbowed out by often insipid late-Victorian furnishings. This pulpit, by Henry Wilson in 1913, positively glows. It depicts in bronze Wilfrid's four northern or Midlands contemporaries, Chad, Cuthbert, Hilda and Etheldreda. In the south transept is a Joseph Nollekens memorial to William Weddell (d.1792) of nearby Newby Hall. It is in the form of a classical semi-rotunda as handsome as its owner's house.

Beneath the crossing lies Wilfrid's crypt of *c*670, the only substantial relic of Saxon architecture in an English cathedral. It is entered through a tunnel into what feels like a dug-out cave. Two tiny barrel-vaulted chambers carry traces of original plaster on walls and ceiling. There are niches for candles and relics. The space is so small it is hard to see how services other than individual prayers could have been held there.

A narrow recess in one wall, called St Wilfrid's Needle, was allegedly used to test women for virginity – presumably pregnancy – if their stomachs could fit the gap. It was rather more a test of credulity, but the ritual continued to be performed by local girls into the 20th century. The crypt is curious rather than atmospheric, having been diluted by artificial light. Such rough surfaces respond better to the flickering of candles.

Ripon's presbytery is blocked from the crossing by a Perpendicular pulpitum crowned by Scott's organ case. The niches are filled with early English kings and bishops, bravely inserted in the 1940s in full colour. The figures are certainly better than gaps, even if they look alarmingly like waxworks.

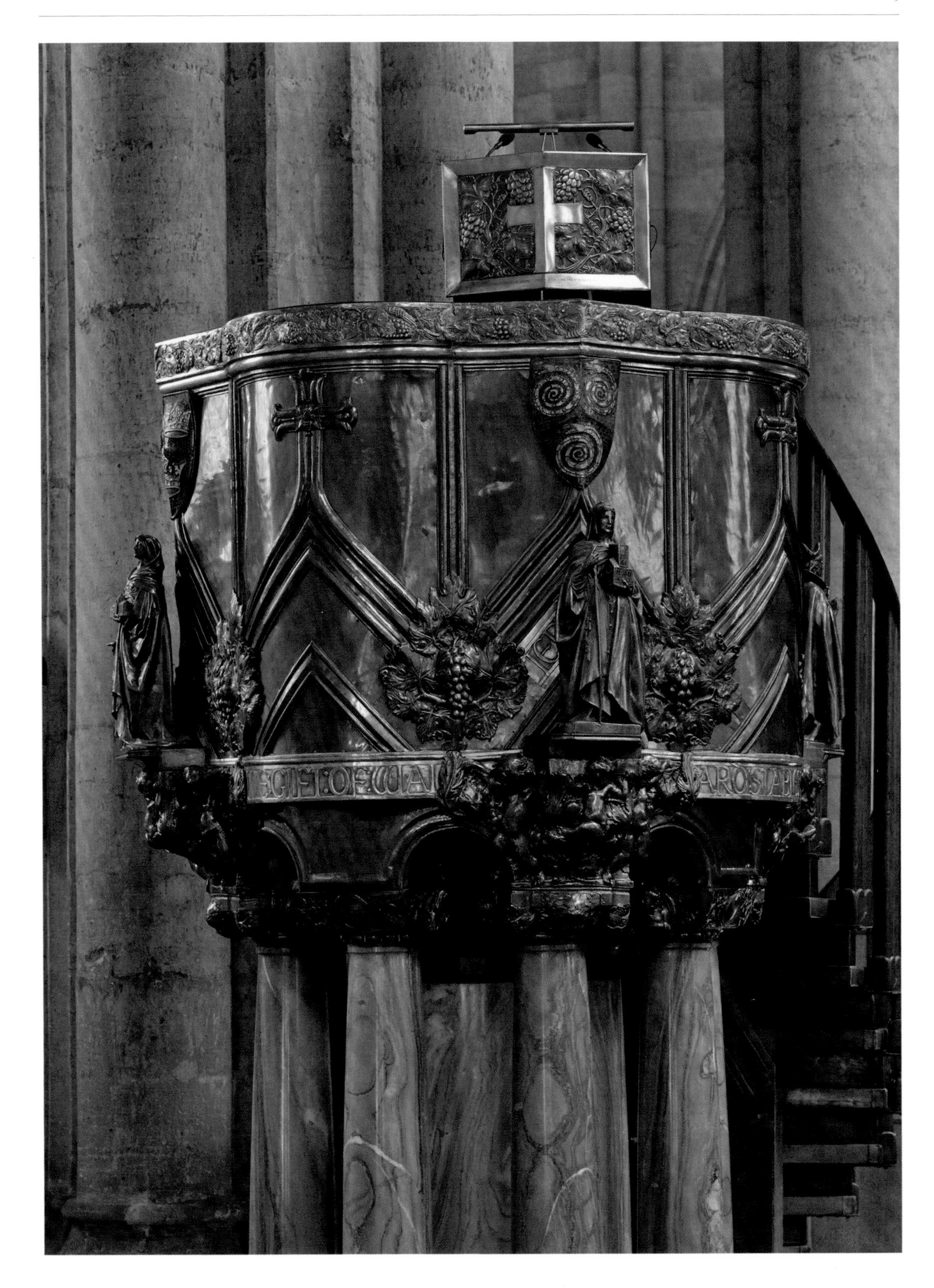

Seen from the choir side, the pulpitum and organ case rise up like the wall of a Tudor town house. The organ has a mechanical hand enabling the organist to beat time for the choir. Beneath are Ripon's magnificent choir stalls. They have been dated to 1489 and are attributed to the same carver, William Broomfleet, responsible for the stalls at Manchester. The canopies form a thicket of spindly pinnacles, while the misericords are open to view. This is late-medieval woodwork at its most accomplished. We see Samson at the gates of Gaza, Jonah and his whale, and a rabbit being chased by a monster down a hole; reputedly, this was the inspiration for Lewis Carroll's Wonderland. His father was a canon at Ripon, although his boyhood church was in Croft-on-Tees, which is filled with similar Wonderland references.

In the sanctuary, the high quality of Ripon's furnishings continues with three 14th-century sedilia with nodding ogees; some colour survives in the crevices. Above rises the Decorated east window, its circles like bubbles floating in the sky. The glass is by William Wailes (1856) and un-garish. Medieval roof bosses gaze down from above. The adjacent Chapel of the Holy Spirit has a modern metalwork screen by Leslie Durbin (1970), designer of the first one-pound coin. The screen is said to represent lightning bolts but looks more like razor wire.

Ripon's library south of the presbytery was a former Lady Chapel with pretty intersecting tracery in its window. The room now contains an exhibition of diocesan plate and other treasures. Among the items is the Ripon jewel, an exquisite Saxon ornament of amber and garnets found near the cathedral in 1976.

Left
The Broomfleet choir stalls

ROCHESTER

The Blessed Virgin Mary

Norman west front, wheel of fortune mural, Decorated doorway

'Old cathedral … earthy smell – pilgrims' feet wore away the old steps – little Saxon doors – confessionals like money-takers' boxes at theatres – queer customers those monks.' Mr Pickwick's loquacious guide to Rochester cathedral said it all. For Dickens' travellers, as for millions of others, the town was the first change of horses on the way to Canterbury. For Dickens himself, it was his home cathedral, near his house at Gad's Hill.

As we crest the hill on the road from London, we glimpse below us a Norman keep, bulky and sinister, crouching over an adjacent steeple like a cat waiting to pounce. The town is a sad place. The north Kent coast should be a natural wilderness or at least a picturesque suburb. Instead, it is a wasteland of half-used wharves, warehouses and refineries, dotted with random housing estates. But the old high street survives, as does the enclave round what remains the largest Norman keep in England.

Post-Conquest Rochester was a priory under the authority of Canterbury, not so much an offspring as an adopted orphan. Founded by St Augustine's first bishop, Justus, in 604, it was designated a cathedral but without land or other revenue to sustain that status. It was one of a handful of cathedrals (with Carlisle and Chichester) that were regarded as 'impoverished sees'. They were not popular appointments within the church.

Ten years after the Conquest, Archbishop Lanfranc realised the importance of the Medway crossing and granted Rochester to his chamberlain, Gundulf, who was to build castles both here and in London. A statue of him on the west front shows him holding a model of the Tower of London. Gundulf's battered north tower survives, as does some of his crypt, but the rest of the church was gutted by fire twice in the 12th century and subsequently rebuilt.

Throughout the Middle Ages, the bishops of Rochester, loyal to their Canterbury patrons, feuded with their priory monks over money, as did the monks with the townspeople. Partly as a result, the nave was never rebuilt, and the cathedral was often locked to keep out the locals. Relations deteriorated so much that a church was built next door for the town to use, and survives to this day. Meanwhile, the clergy spent freely on their own presbytery.

Left
Cathedral and castle over Medway

Left
Wheel of fortune

Opposite
Screen and organ case from west

The monks were aided by a familiar stroke of fortune. A Canterbury pilgrim, William of Perth, was murdered by his servant near the town in 1201, whereupon a local woman immediately declared herself cured of madness. Other miracles quickly followed. Rochester was already on the Becket pilgrimage trail. William of Perth was no Becket, but his shrine proved sufficiently profitable to finance a new east end. Other than a new tower in the 14th century, a Lady Chapel and a new west window, that was virtually an end to building at Rochester.

The west front is exceptional in England in being an almost intact survivor from the Norman period. The only sadness is the insertion of a Perpendicular window so large as to reduce the Norman work round it to what seems a picture frame. The front was restored by J. L. Pearson in the 1880s, guided by little more than a 1655 engraving. It is covered in blind arcading, with slim arches resting on elongated shafts. These arches are interspersed with a course of stone chains, adorned with corbels of human and beast heads.

Below survives an original Romanesque doorway of the sort to be found across Norman Europe but hardly anywhere in England. It is of five receding arches with elaborate motifs. Monsters dive in and out of leaves, capitals burst into flower. The doorway is flanked by etiolated statues, apparently of Solomon and the Queen of Sheba. In the tympanum is a Christ in Majesty. When Pepys visited in 1661, he reported that the doors had supposedly been covered in the skins of marauding Danes.

The initial view of Rochester's interior might be that of a modest opera house. Norman arcades lead to a raised altar platform on which sits the pulpitum, with organ above. It is an intimate space. The two eastern bays are gothic, the start of a rebuild that was never completed. The piers differ from each other, as if by different hands, one with no fewer than 18 shafts. Together they serve as a proscenium arch to the crossing 'stage'.

The pulpitum, by George Gilbert Scott, is in effect the stage's backdrop, lined with local worthies. For once, the organ pipes on top do not obstruct the view east but part to reveal a glimpse of the presbytery vault beyond. The pipes echo the shafts on the crossing arch.

Rochester's north transept was designed to admit pilgrims to William of Perth's shrine. It contains a modern fresco of Christ's baptism in the style of a modern Russian icon, by Sergei Fyodorov (2004). The opposite south transept was the entrance for the monks coming from the priory. It is flanked by an

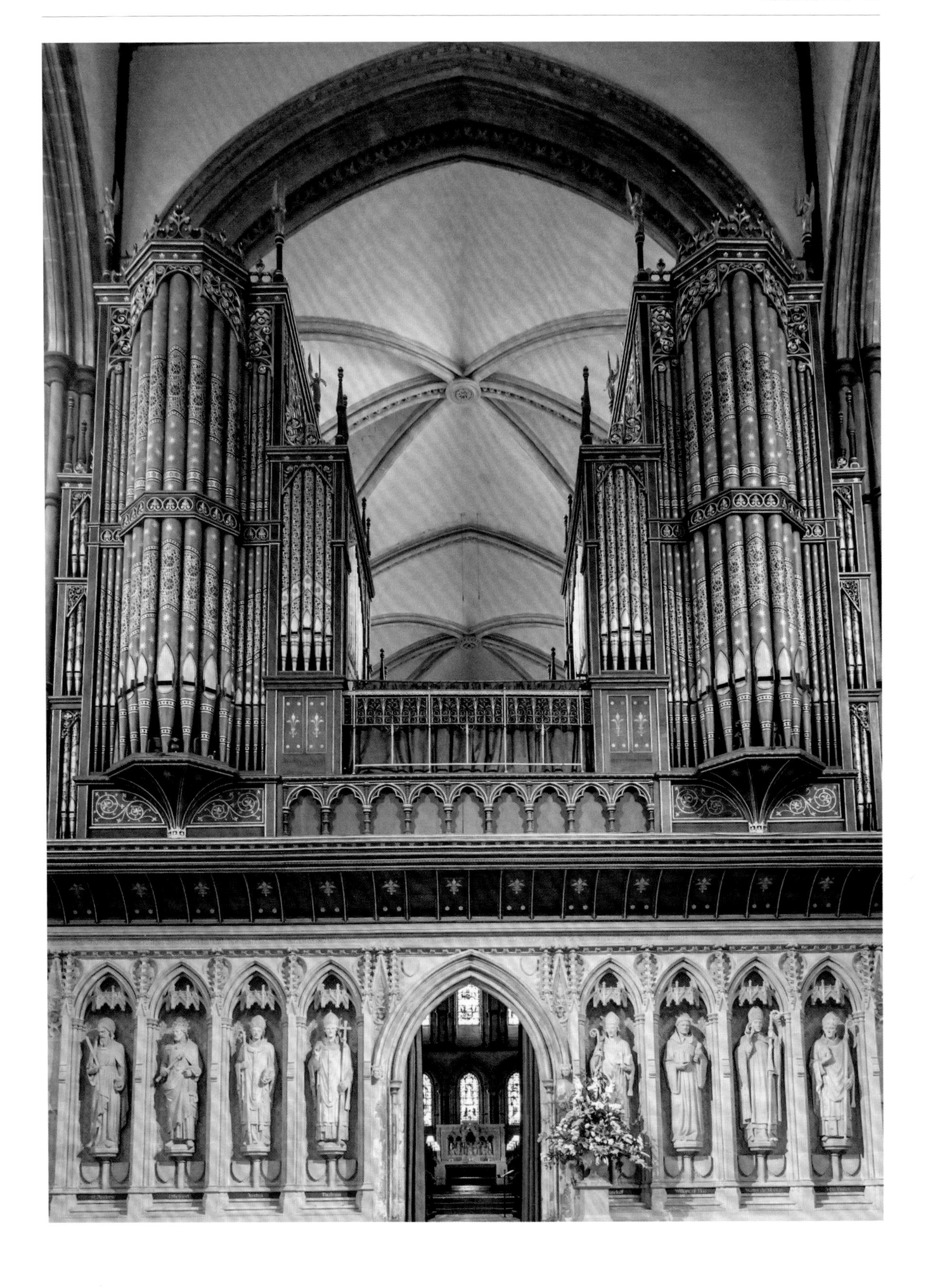

Opposite
Hamo doorway

unfinished Lady Chapel – an intended fan vault was not completed.

The choir is oddly enclosed by high walls, clearly to protect the monks from cold draughts. The stalls date from the 1220s and are among the earliest surviving in England (*see* Exeter), plain but rebuilt by Scott. The walls are painted with emblems of Edward III, who must have passed Rochester many times on his way to wage war in France. The choir's north wall displays a fragment of a 13th-century mural of a wheel of fortune. It has well-heeled individuals trying to scramble up the wheel, which Fortune turns back and forth. The topmost figure looks most unsteady.

Dark aisles flank the choir walls on either side, with the south aisle giving access to a crypt, parts of which survive from Gundulf's Norman church. The rest was rebuilt to support the new gothic east end, and claims to be second in size only to Canterbury.

Rochester's Early Gothic sanctuary offers a shift of gear from humble to sophisticated, reflecting the requirements of monks and pilgrims rather than the citizens of Rochester. Purbeck shafts rise to a smart clerestory and ribbed vault. Lancet windows, restored by Scott, are divided by detached pillars, arched and with dogtooth mouldings. The walls are a series of recesses, angles and planes. Daylight is orchestrated by architecture.

Rochester enjoyed brief celebrity in the 14th century under a monk turned bishop, Hamo de Hythe. His legacy was a new doorway to the chapter house (later a library) on the south side of the presbytery. This is a complex work of Decorated sculpture, built in 1343. An ogee arch covered in leaping crockets frames a band of figurative statues. The main ones are of Ecclesia and a blindfolded Synagoga, a favourite device of the time, representing the Christian church triumphing over Mosaic law.

Of the same period is the tomb of Bishop John of Sheppey on the north side of the presbytery. Unearthed from a wall in 1840, it retains its original colouring. Rochester is full of small bosses and corbels. One on the south-east pier of the choir is a corbel of entwined foliage with two green men peering out. The stone itself appears to sprout into life.

After the Dissolution, Rochester was lucky to retain cathedral status, but the monastery disappeared and the monks dispersed. The buildings were plundered for stone. The precinct is dotted with their ghostly remains, poking up in lawns, as outhouses or formal gardens. It was here that Henry VIII came incognito in January 1540 to glimpse his newly arrived bride, Anne of Cleves. He professed himself 'greatly disappointed', as later was she.

ST ALBANS

St Alban

Hilltop site, early Norman crossing and transepts, shrine of St Alban

St Albans is an ugly duckling of a cathedral. It squats on its hilltop above Roman Verulamium, grumpily apologising for not making more of its magnificent site. It was to this spot that Roman soldiers in AD 304 dragged England's first authentic martyr, St Alban, to execute him for converting to Christianity. The inevitable result was much spouting of springs and attracting of pilgrims. St Albans is plausibly the oldest known site of Christian worship in England.

A Benedictine abbey was founded in 793 in the time of Offa, and was revived after the Conquest in 1077 by Paul, bishop of Caen and nephew of Lanfranc of Canterbury. He summoned a Master Robert, who reputedly 'excelled all masons of his day', to build a nave even longer than that of his uncle. Robert was paid – or overpaid – so handsomely that he recanted his wealth on his deathbed and left it to the abbey.

The resulting church was an early manifestation of post-Conquest building mania, possibly based on an earlier Saxon building that had already been started. There are Saxon motifs in the walls. The shrine was later enhanced by the discovery of possible relics of St Amphibalus, reputedly responsible for Alban's conversion.

Then, in 1154, a local monk, Nicholas Breakspear, became the only English pope as Adrian IV. He duly promoted his old abbey as England's premier Benedictine monastery and centre of learning. St Albans was home to England's two most distinguished medieval historians, Matthew Paris and Thomas Walsingham. Its location, dominating the northern approaches to the capital, guaranteed its status, though it did not become a cathedral until 1877.

St Albans never enjoyed financial security. Like many abbeys, it was constantly at odds with its town, with the result that its nave and transepts were starved of funds for rebuilding, while money was spent on the monks' presbytery. The Black Death killed two-thirds of the hundred monks, and at the Dissolution St Albans did not merit cathedral status. The monastery buildings were demolished and the abbey church was sold to the town as a parish church for £400. The buildings steadily deteriorated. Significantly, there are few post-Reformation memorials.

In 1835, with ecclesiastical revival in the air, a new rector, Henry

Left
The crossing: early Norman simplicity

Left
Nave wall-painting

Opposite
Modern martyrs

Nicholson, took matters in hand. He charged non-parishioners for entry (though pilgrims to the shrine would have paid in the Middle Ages), and later appointed George Gilbert Scott to survey the fabric. Nicholson died before much work was done, and when Scott died in 1878 the restoration committee was taken over by a retired lawyer, Sir Edmund Beckett, later to be Lord Grimthorpe. He fancied himself an amateur architect.

In those days there was no control over the restoration of historic buildings, and the result of the Grimthorpe era was near disaster. Even the official guide calls the ensuing work 'Grim by name and grim by nature'. The peer took control by paying for everything himself, to a total of £130,000 or tens of millions in today's money.

Grimthorpe treated St Albans as his personal hobby. He refashioned the north and south transept windows, put battlements on the tower and built a new west front to his personal design. He even had himself sculpted as St Matthew (with wings) in the porch. Grimthorpe's changes were a stimulus for the founding of the Society for the Protection of Ancient Buildings by William Morris and others.

The cathedral is best approached up Fishpool Street from the Roman ruins, past medieval and Georgian buildings to reach an open meadow at the end of which sits the great church, looking rather lonely. The cathedral has no spacious close, rather an area of old gardens, flint walls and mostly Victorian diocesan buildings. The path round the south side of the church passes a modern chapter house – a charmless brick extension of 1981 by William Whitfield – before opening onto the hillside overlooking the valley of the River Ver. This view over the old monastic site to the Roman town is the abbey's best asset.

St Albans' nave is beaten for length only by Winchester, but length is no advantage. Master Robert's watchword was clearly speed rather than style. The southern nave wall might be that of an 11th-century barracks. As the site lacked local stone, such materials as lay round about were employed, mostly flint and rubble, but including Roman tiles from Verulamium. These had apparently to be 'de-paganised' by a priest for the purpose. Of the original building, only the tower, which has the appearance of a Norman keep, has some character, with window openings of paired (possibly Saxon) arches and decorated tympanums.

Grimthorpe's neo-gothic west front neither soars, nor does it spread. The blind arcades are plodding, the gables decorated with empty eye sockets and the porches deep and

unwelcoming. When it was first unveiled, the *Builder* magazine called it 'effective in a showy way, but totally devoid of refinement'. Pevsner said it was 'sombre … decidedly joyless … grim austerity'. A competition should surely be held for a replacement.

The first view of the interior is of a long, flat-roofed tunnel of plain arches, mostly Norman on the north side and gothic on the south. Rebuilding of the north began in the Early Gothic style but came to a halt at the third pier from the west end, which looks as if it is in splints. Then in 1323, five bays of the south arcade collapsed and the opportunity was taken to extend the gothic work the length of the south arcade, now in a contemporary Decorated style. Early Gothic dogtooth gives way to Decorated ballflower. We thus have the three styles of medieval architecture in just a few feet.

This may intrigue historians but it leaves the surviving Norman arches looking stark, as though openings had been punched through a wall. They are lucky to retain the most extensive medieval wall paintings in an English cathedral, other than Canterbury's crypt. Dating from the 13th to the 15th century, they have been carefully rescued from Reformation whitewash. The west-facing surfaces have crucifixions, the rest saints and biblical scenes, including a Doubting Thomas.

The view east down the cathedral is broken by two screens. The first is a pulpitum three bays into the nave, with behind it two jutting organ lofts, impeding the view. The pulpitum's niches have been filled with martyrs, from St Alban to the 20th century's Dietrich Bonhoeffer and Bishop Oscar Romero. By the sculptor Rory Young, they are unnervingly realistic. The hands 'took as long to carve as the faces'. They offer a welcome splash of colour.

Beyond this first screen, St Albans starts to show its personality. The great Norman crossing arches are decorated in stripes of black, red and white paint. On either side are the transepts, equally massive and plain. Only Winchester conveys the same unyielding directness of early Conquest architecture. Here, writes John Harvey, we are taken back to Christianity's earliest simplicities: 'The sombre gloom of cave-dwelling and cave-worship.'

Grimthorpe inserted dramatic, high lancets in the south transept; in the north, he opted for Decorated, with a rose window composed of random circles, like a poached egg pan. The window has been enlivened, but barely improved, by vivid stained glass.

A second Perpendicular screen of 1484 guards the presbytery, the niches here

Left
Alban's shrine with watching gallery

being filled with replacement saints beneath a crucifixion, the originals having been destroyed by iconoclasts. These carvings caused a bitter row between Grimthorpe, who hated images, and another local donor, Lord Aldenham, who had paid for them. Money talked and Aldenham won. Beneath the screen is an art nouveau reredos of Christ in a strange, acrobatic pose. It is an unfinished work by Alfred Gilbert, creator of Eros in Piccadilly.

On the left of the presbytery is the tiny Ramryge chantry, Perpendicular with a fan vault and dedicated to the so-called 'six stages of bereavement'. These are the five stages of grief – denial, anger, bargaining, depression and acceptance – to which the sculptor, Claudia Browne, added peace in her subtle Perspex statues (2008). It is a quiet, consoling place.

St Albans now enters the zone of medieval commerce. After the pilgrimage frenzy following Becket's murder in 1170, the east end was rebuilt to accommodate both St Alban's shrine and the relics of St Amphibalus. Matthew Paris helped with an imaginative biography of both, in effect a promotional guidebook. For a while, the abbey revenues were replenished.

The pilgrim route was along the north aisle, where there is now an exhibition of abbey history and of the 12th-century St Albans Psalter. Steps lead into the actual shrine chapel, where the faithful could kneel round a Purbeck marble base beneath the shrine. Diseased or wounded limbs would be thrust into its openings, candles lit and prayers for recovery recited. The base was destroyed in the Reformation and the stone used for walls sealing off the shrine area. When these were demolished in 1872, the fragments were found and reconstructed in a giant jigsaw puzzle.

The shrine chapel can justly claim to be the most complete such chamber in England, drawing pilgrims to this day. It is overlooked by a watching gallery, like a guardroom, from which priests on duty would check the behaviour of pilgrims and prevent theft of relics.

From here, three arches lead down into the last and loveliest part of the abbey, the Lady Chapel. Built in the early 14th century in the Decorated style, its window tracery is variegated and enriched with crockets, daggers, lozenges and trefoils. The botanical carvings beneath the vault springers include rose, ivy, pansy, poppy, buttercup and other flowers. From the Reformation to the 19th century, this chapel served as a schoolroom, and must have been a delightful place to study.

ST PAUL'S

St Paul

View across City, baroque exterior, military memorials, Gibbons choir stalls

★★★★

St Paul's has always been London's guardian angel. Its predecessor was the longest church in Europe, but was so badly damaged in the Great Fire of 1666 that it had to be entirely rebuilt. For a further three centuries, its baroque architecture made it the only English cathedral building not dating from the Middle Ages. In the Second World War, a famous photograph of St Paul's dome enveloped in the smoke of the Blitz symbolised Britain's resistance and eventual victory. As a small boy, I was later taken to see its battered roofs and bomb-damaged attics. We stumbled with torches over duckboards and gazed down into the nave through gaps in ceilings. I was overwhelmed by the place and remain under its spell.

That said, my responses to St Paul's have varied over the years. Its architectural majesty is undeniable but, in the long-standing rivalry with Westminster Abbey, I have tended to side with the abbey. St Paul's is a wigged and powdered master of ceremonies, imposing on the nation what seems a procession of ceremonies, memorials and oratorios. Westminster, as I remark in its entry below, is an old lady full of mischief and dotty anecdotes. I might have my funeral in St Paul's, but I would prefer my wedding in Westminster.

Originally founded in 604 by Bishop Mellitus of the East Saxons, the medieval cathedral was believed to be the fourth on the site. It was London's head and heart. The churchyard cross was a traditional place of assembly, a sanctuary where revelry, protest and sedition were half tolerated. To the north lay Paternoster Square, centre of publishing and book-selling. When the area went up in flames in the Great Fire, it took with it a national storehouse of medieval art, a library and a mausoleum of City history.

The old cathedral was already in terrible shape. The steeple had previously been taken down as dangerous. Inigo Jones had designed and built a new west front and nave interior. Christopher Wren, as surveyor, had already been discussing a new dome over the dilapidated crossing. This all came to a head. Two years after the fire, a royal proclamation from Charles II ordered a new cathedral, the cost to be met by a special tax on coal and wine. The authorities plunged into the usual debate over restoring the old design or replacing it with something new.

Left
Dome from the south over the Millennium Bridge

Previous spread
Wren's dome turned Victorian extravaganza

Left
The Great Model

Opposite
Wellington memorial

Wren had worked in both gothic and classical traditions, at Oxford's Tom Tower and Sheldonian Theatre respectively. Now he argued strongly that 'late calamities and fire had so weakened and defaced [the cathedral] … that scarce anything would at last be left of the old'. He was determined to have a classical building, whose 'beauty is from geometry'. He longed for London to have a Michelangelo dome, in the style of St Peter's in Rome.

The wrangling was intense, bringing Wren close to despair. His 1673 proposal, exhibited as 'the great model' in the cathedral Treasury, was for a cruciform building plus a portico. Further argument followed, with the traditionalists pressing for a conventional nave with transepts. The king finally ordered Wren to get on with it, making such adjustments 'as from time to time he should see proper'.

Initially the dome stretched upwards and was crowned with a strange, Hindu-like spire, but this was later reduced to the present half-orange. The nave and chancel were elongated and the transepts shortened, until the plan was essentially gothic, even if the building, as it emerged, became the embodiment of 'English baroque'.

St Paul's was the first cathedral in England by a named architect. Although started under Charles II in 1675, its finances were soon bogged down in ecclesiastical politics and it was not completed until 1711. The cost was a staggering £722,779, equivalent to some £1.5 billion today. By then Wren was seventy-nine although, unlike most cathedral architects, he at least lived to see his work completed. As an old man, he was hoisted by his son to the roof in a basket.

Of many ironies in the St Paul's saga, the oddest is that a building intended to sit at the hub of formally radiating avenues should instead remain crammed into what, even today, is a medieval street footprint. The reason is that, after the fire, the City fathers allowed the rebuilding of individual plots rather than slowly acquiring sites for Wren's radials. The only control was over street widths and building materials. Though the new cathedral was shorter than its forerunner, Wren's grandiosity was honoured. Until the second half of the 20th century, St Paul's dominated the London horizon, monarch of all it surveyed.

Since then, some distant views of the cathedral have been 'safeguarded', but the concept has become all but meaningless. The idea of a protected horizon, normal in other capitals of Europe, evaporated in London not with the Blitz but with uncontrolled

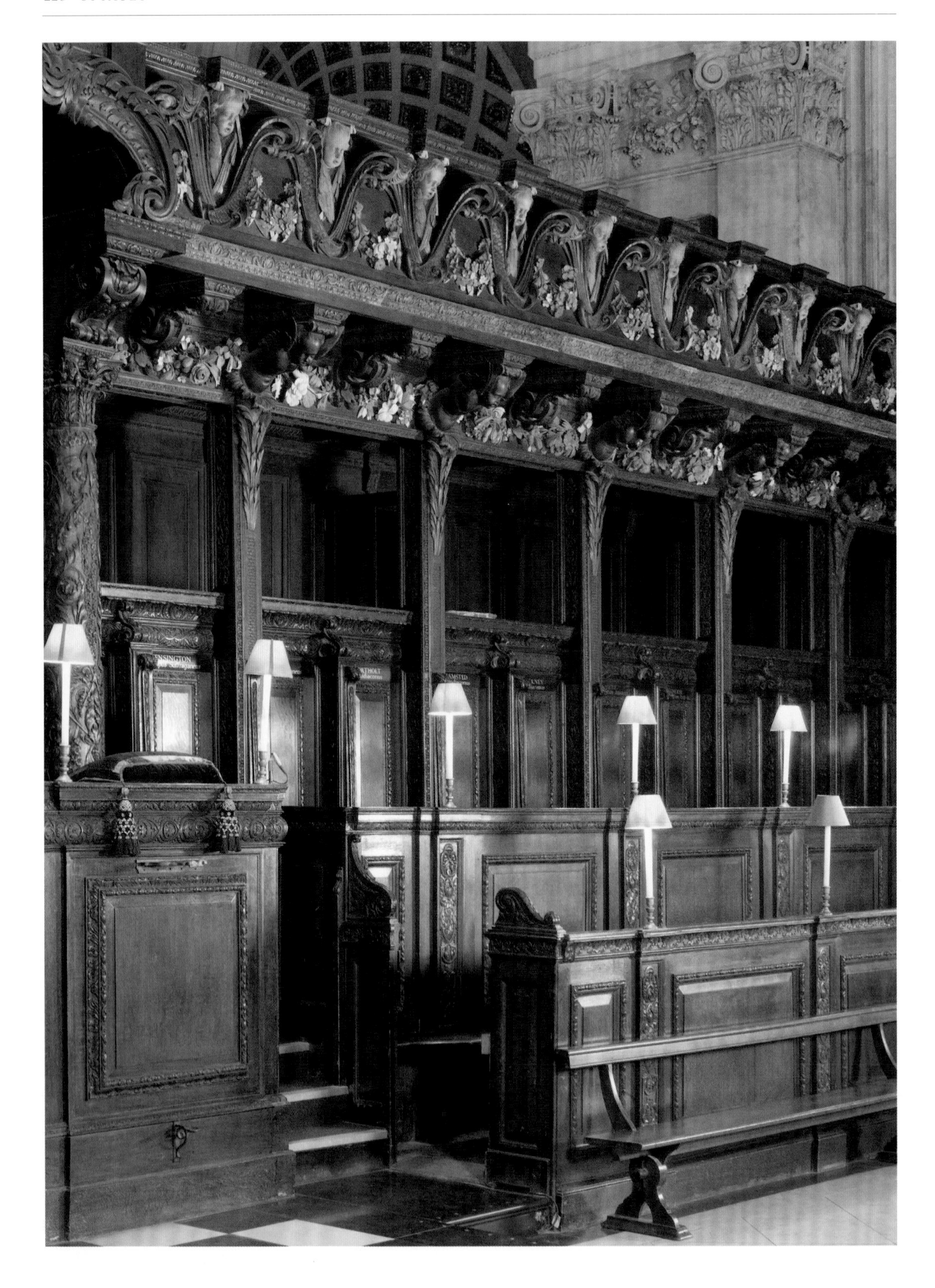

Left
The choir: Grinling Gibbons' virtuoso baroque

property speculation in the last quarter of the 20th century. The once-protected view from Waterloo Bridge is now of a gap-toothed grimace, with St Paul's overshadowed by towers behind and beside it. Parts of the exterior can be seen from the Millennium Bridge to the south and from the roof terrace of One New Change to the east. The famous oblique view up Ludgate Hill survives, while a second attempt at the post-war rebuilding of Paternoster Square has recovered the informal street pattern and brick façades immediately to the north.

Perhaps the best view is from the roof of Tate Modern across the river, from where St Paul's floats above the western City, free of immediate encroachment and with something of the bravura of Canaletto's 1747 depiction. From here, the towers and dome seem bigger-boned than the more restrained detail of the church porticos below. Whether Wren meant the porticos to be seen at street level and towers and dome from a distance is a matter of debate but they seem out of proportion.

Ever the perfectionist, Wren insisted on the purest of white Portland stone for St Paul's, much to the dismay of Bath stone salesmen who wanted London rebuilt 'in gold rather than silver'. By the 1960s, soot had turned white to black and pollution was damaging the surface. The prospect of cleaning was controversial. The critic Ian Nairn won support for the chiaroscuro effect of white etched on black on the cathedral's windward sides, deploring the blandness of cleaned stone. Others felt the sooty crust was falsifying the rhythm of London's most ornamented exterior. The cleaning progressed over the course of the 1970s.

St Paul's derives much of its grandeur from being set almost an entire storey high on a plinth. The steps up to the main entrance have become an endurance test for elderly VIPs, and for the coffin-carriers at state funerals. But the plinth lifted the cathedral above the surrounding rooftops. The exterior of the windows and doorways is a little-noticed gallery of classical motifs. Panels above the arches were carved by Grinling Gibbons and his studio. Swags, cherubs and foliage burst with life, draped over the tops of arches. Encompassing the first floor is a complete baroque frieze, culminating in Francis Bird's magnificent Conversion of St Paul in the pediment of the western portico.

The first impression of St Paul's interior is of the atrium of a vast, unmanageable palace. Wren offered London a sense of scale unequalled in English architecture. An arcade of four large bays with shallow saucer domes

BURIED THERE

Left
Art honours the artist: Randolph Caldecott plaque

strides from the west end to the crossing, and continues to the east in a crescendo of decorative splendour. Although officially the focus of the diocese of London, St Paul's image is not that of a diocesan headquarters. Nor does it boast a saintly shrine to draw the pious on pilgrimage. Its purpose is to celebrate that most secular of institutions, the nation state. It is a place, as Paul Johnson put it, to be 'filled and warmed by ceremonies, in which sovereign and high priest are coadjutors, and society is present in corporeal form, each in its ranks, lay and hieratic'.

The nave is lined with memorials to the great and, usually, good. Here is Alfred Stevens' 1857 monument to the Duke of Wellington, lying dignified and, according to Pevsner, 'without vulgarity or bathos of excessive earnestness'. In the north aisle are effigies of Lord Kitchener, Gordon of Khartoum and the artist Lord Leighton. A child asked in my hearing, 'Why are there so many old men asleep?' We expect Handel at any moment to sit down at the great organ, as he so often did, and blast the air with *Zadok the Priest.*

The crossing is St Paul's climax. It compares with York for size and with Ely for vertical excitement. Ever the mathematician, Wren saw it as an overlap of circular and rectangular planes, creating a contrast of darkness and light. As at Ely, the curvature of the dome deceives the eye as it reaches its distant lantern. Its swirling circles are echoed in the marble floor below. The dome is painted with copies of James Thornhill's original monochrome murals, after Raphael, of the life of St Paul. In the triangular spaces below them are mosaics of prophets by Stevens and G. F. Watts. These decorations give St Paul's a Victorian overlay which spoils much of Wren's original simplicity of line.

The transepts continue the theme of national mausoleum, crowded with military and political heroes (and an occasional heroine). While military heroes are given dramatic poses, set about with cherubs and encomiums, the writer Samuel Johnson is left in solitary contemplation. A chapel in the north transept contains Holman Hunt's portrait of Jesus as the Light of the World, the artist's own copy of the original in Oxford. Boosted by world-wide sales of a steel-engraving, this version acquired great spiritual appeal as it toured the world in 1905, to be seen by millions.

For all this, I find myself in agreement with those, such as Alec Clifton-Taylor, who find St Paul's 'easier to admire than to like'. It is a venue for the grand occasion, as the guide puts it, 'to express joy, gratitude and sorrow', to

Left
John Donne in death

welcome home victorious generals, dead and alive. Yet its memorials seem poles apart from Westminster's valhalla. Statues are rarely of artists and poets, rather of soldiers, statesmen and governors. They die in battle and/or ascend to Heaven, attended by nymphs and corpulent cherubs. They offer little emotional or spiritual appeal, more the illustration of a national narrative. Aisles are peopled by those whom the state defined as great, but into whose minds and souls we gain no access.

East of the crossing lies the presbytery, its vault decorated in 1900 after Queen Victoria had complained that the place was 'dull, dingy and undevotional'. The artist William Richmond was commissioned to cover it with mosaics, in accordance with Wren's original intention. He was as good as his command, filling the ceiling and the apse beyond with soft colours. The scenes represent the Song of Creation, combining the formalism of a Byzantine mosaic with the flourish of art nouveau. Giant angels hold up the rim of each dome as if it were a magnificent dish.

Below lies Wren's choir, a baroque answer to the ingenuity of the 15th-century wood carvers. The removal of the screen in 1861 opened the chancel to the rest of the cathedral, allowing the choir stalls to form a visual guard of honour to the baldacchino beyond. The carving of choir and organ loft is by Grinling Gibbons, combining the stateliness of space with the intimacy of a country house overmantel. Gibbons was paid one pound for each of the sixty-six cherub heads, a handsome reward. The baroque canopy of the bishop's throne is indigestible in its richness.

Beyond stands the baldacchino, not by Wren but by Stephen Dykes Bower in 1958, replacing Wren's altarpiece which was destroyed in the war. Normally a 'neo-goth', Dykes Bower displays a versatility in the baroque style that Wren would have appreciated. Flanking the sanctuary in the north choir aisle are gates of 1700, by the Frenchman Jean Tijou, the ironwork a glorious tangle of rococo ornament. Nearby is a late work by Henry Moore, a charming Mother and Child (1983).

The south choir aisle is oddly lined with ornamental frontispieces, like a row of private tombs. Opposite them stands a macabre shrouded statue of the poet and dean of St Paul's, John Donne, supposedly designed by himself and carved by Nicholas Stone in 1631. It was the only monument to survive the Great Fire. More controversial, at the east end of the aisle is a plasma screen by the artist Bill Viola depicting 'martyrs'. Actors are shown tortured by the elements of earth, air, fire and water to 'represent the darkest hour of the martyr's passage through death into the light'. It forms a grim distraction.

More of St Paul's interior is inaccessible except on special tours. This hinterland is part of its personality, a warren of studios, corridors and attics. The triforium floor houses a library designed by Wren, with woodwork by Gibbons' contemporary Jonathan Maine. It has the smell of ancient volumes. In the treasury stands Wren's great model, looking strangely unlike the final product. The south-west tower contains Wren's tribute to Inigo Jones' 'geometrical' staircase in Greenwich, a spiral cantilever rising the full height of the nave.

The crypt of St Paul's covers almost the same floor space as the cathedral above. Now a clutter of visitor facilities, it has at its core the shrine of Admiral Lord Nelson, reached after passing a screen erected in memory of Sir Winston Churchill (who wished to be buried near his birthplace at Blenheim). Nelson lies in a simple coffin made from the timbers of a defeated French ship. It sits on top of a marble sarcophagus originally made for Cardinal Wolsey but unused after his fall from grace. It had long awaited a celebrity of suitable distinction. Wellington's memorial is in the nave above, but his tomb is in the crypt, an imposing granite coffin. Other memorials are less militaristic, to Reynolds, Turner, Millais, William Blake and Florence Nightingale, among others. Wren himself is buried in a south aisle outside the Chapel of St Faith (also known as the OBE Chapel). Inside the chapel to the right is a moving art nouveau statue of a girl holding a plaque in honour of the illustrator Randolph Caldecott. It makes a fittingly subdued coda to this grandiloquent place.

SALISBURY

The Blessed Virgin Mary

Constable setting with steeple, Early Gothic interior, Audley chantry, chapter house carvings

★★★★

To most Britons, Salisbury embodies the ideal of the English cathedral. Rising elegantly over its close or across the everlasting water meadow, it is regularly voted the nation's favourite view, adorning a million jigsaw puzzles and biscuit tins. When John Constable, custodian of the Salisbury vision, first caught sight of its spire he recalled it 'darted up into the sky like a needle', its silver stone seeming to sparkle. He worshipped it for the rest of his life, and the world said amen.

Although gothic is a symmetrical style, its appeal at Salisbury lies in picturesque informality. Although the cathedral is rare in being – apart from its steeple – the product of one time, one mind and one style, it has always been part and parcel of its close. This expanse of grass surrounding the cathedral, within an amphitheatre of trees, allows views of the building unobstructed from every angle. The mostly Georgian brick of the canons' houses is a foil for the cathedral's medieval stone. Red pays tribute to white against a backdrop of green.

Constable was to depict these views some three hundred times, balancing the steeple with the elms of the close or with a passing storm cloud or rainbow. Horizontal answered vertical. Everything was somehow in the correct place. Such conversation between architecture and nature has always appealed to the English eye. Constable made it the quintessence of Englishness.

In 1219, Abbot Richard Poore petitioned Rome to move his seat from its cramped quarters two miles north at Old Sarum down to the junction of the Avon and Nadder rivers. England had emerged from the papal interdict on King John into what became the long and pious reign of Henry III. Poore was a deft diplomat. He was regent for the young king and was later sent to pacify feuding Durham. Pope Honorius III replied to his request, through a topographically alert secretary, 'Let us spread joyfully to the plains, where the valley abounds in corn, the fields are beautiful and there is freedom from oppression.' Planning notices today are not what they were. We can only imagine Old Sarum, its castle, cathedral and palace rising cheek by jowl on what is now just a grassy mound, an English Carcassonne.

A field was duly selected and Salisbury's canons were invited to choose plots for their houses round its circumference. The new church

Left
Darting into the sky like a needle

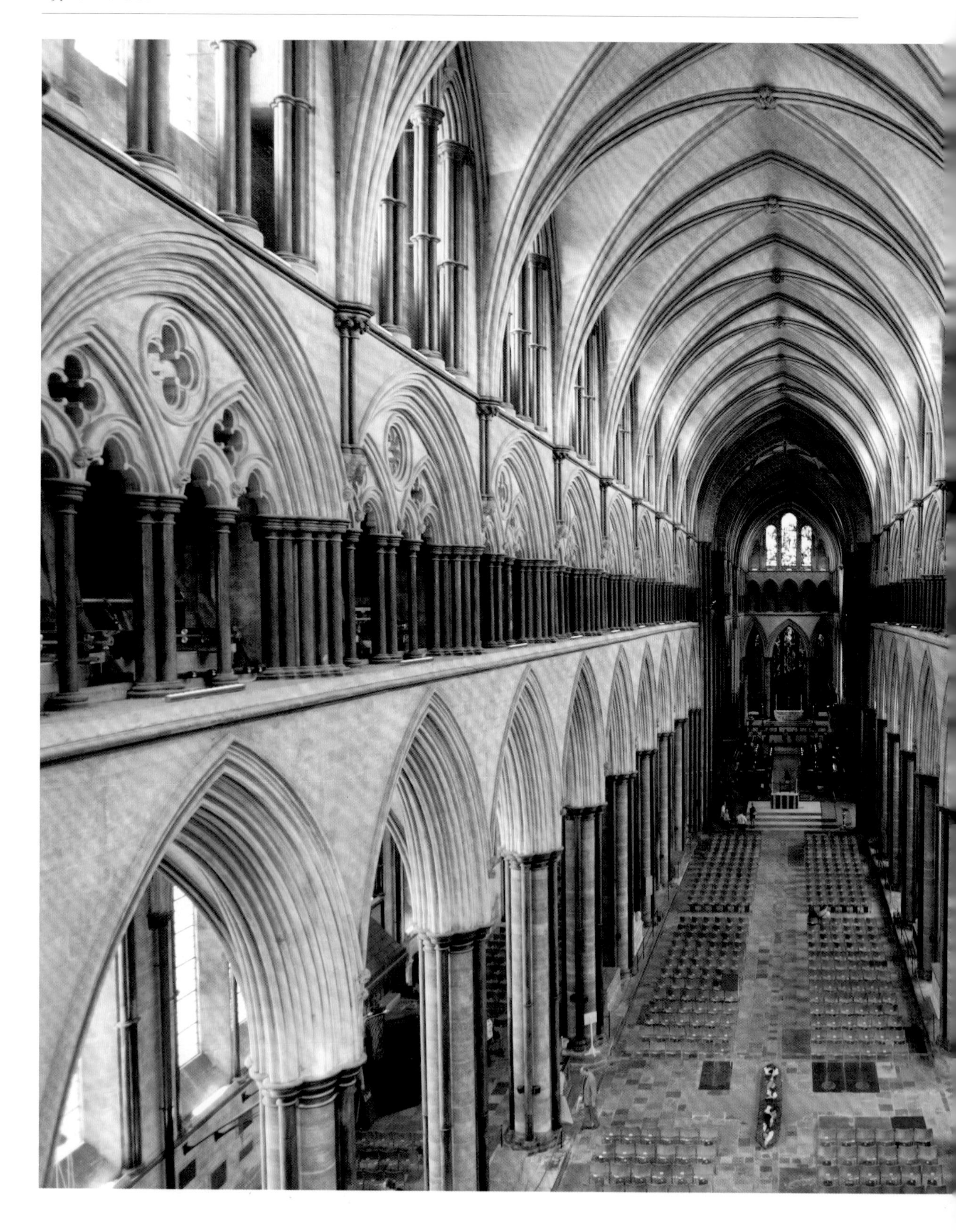

is attributed to a former official of the royal works, Elias of Dereham, described in documents as 'artifex', with Nicholas of Ely as master mason. They built fast and at great cost. Henry III gave almost half the 1443 oaks required for the building, plus a large ruby. The fifty canons were taxed at 23 per cent of income. Indulgences were shamelessly sold.

The first stone was laid in 1220 and the eastern chapels were consecrated by 1225. The style is a mature Early Gothic. Nave walls have flying buttresses. The windows are lancets throughout, with some early plate tracery. Every corner is square. The finished cathedral, albeit with a crossing merely capped, was consecrated in 1258. Poore wrote a new liturgy, The Sarum Rite, to govern the cathedral's (Catholic) ritual, which three centuries later was to form the basis of Cranmer's (Protestant) Book of Common Prayer.

The steeple was not added until a century later, in 1334, with a structure over 400ft high to a design by Master Richard of Farleigh. Of him we know only that he worked at Bath, Pershore and Reading. Designing at the height of the Decorated era, he emphasised verticality, deploying minimal buttresses, slender bell-openings and pinnacles hugging the base of the spire, as if architecture could lift his steeple into the sky. To its most effusive admirer, Olive Cook, it was 'the supreme emotive evocation of a power beyond the material and earthly'. It had 'the sparkle, purity and delightful ornamentation which transport us in the highest flights of Mozart's genius'. The building below must have seemed dull indeed before it acquired its steeple.

There are many 'best views' of Salisbury. I prefer to see it obliquely, such that rectangles become triangles of light and shade. From the north-east, we can see a hierarchy of walls,

Left
Purbeck perspectives: nave from west end

roofs and turrets in a series of planes, placing the spire on what might be seen as a Cubist plinth. The most popular views are at an angle from the west, with steeple and west front cresting a wave of trees, especially across the water meadow.

For all this magnificence, Salisbury's architecture has long troubled its critics. Few challenge the splendour of its setting and steeple, but even those lovers of all things medieval, the Victorians, had their doubts, especially about the interior. John Ruskin found Salisbury 'profound and gloomy … the savageness of northern gothic'. Henry James called it a 'blonde beauty', but banal. Even the anodyne 1880s Bells guidebook by Gleeson White declares it 'faultily faultless, icily regular, splendidly null'. We arrive exhilarated but leave with a puzzled frown.

Salisbury's problems start when we turn from the tower to details of the exterior. The porch clamped to the north wall seems far too big. The west front, however often Constable painted it, lacks a compositional theme, either vertical or horizontal. The eye is led nowhere. The design pieces together gables, turrets, panels and lancets yielding, as Alec Clifton-Taylor says, 'a sad travesty of a great prototype: a miscellany of small motifs which are nowhere co-ordinated. The large statues are all Victorian, and a very poor, insipid lot they are.' To Pevsner it is simply 'a headache … perversely unbeautiful … stunted'.

There is no denying the placid elegance of Salisbury's interior. There are ten bays of nave and ten bays of choir and presbytery, each with the same arcading of Purbeck marble piers. Above is a richly moulded triforium and clerestory. The view east culminates in three simple arches, wide in the centre and narrow on each side, with a hint of the Lady Chapel visible beyond. The transepts are equally calm, the lancet windows in the north transept retaining their original grisaille glass. Both sets of transepts had to be strengthened with bracing arches in the 14th century when the steeple was constructed. The main crossing is supported by ornamented bridges, and the east transepts have strainer arches, miniatures of Wells's 'scissors'.

That said, the interior has the vice of its virtue in that the purity of its Early Gothic lacks variety. The west end has no relationship to the side walls. The vault is tedious. The plethora of Purbeck comes to seem not so much smart as 'bling'. The piers have few carved capitals or corbels – presumably a matter of cost – depriving them of the gothic quality of distinctive craftsmanship. It is as

Opposite
Prisoners of conscience in Trinity Chapel

if everything came off a 13th-century production line.

Some of this coldness can be blamed on James Wyatt's decision in the 1780s to declutter the interior. Almost all the cathedral's medieval glass was removed and thrown into a ditch, a comment on Georgian aesthetics as much as an act of vandalism. Matters were not improved by the insertion of an east window, in the style of Michelangelo, high above the presbytery. It was not the sort of diversity Salisbury needed.

Wyatt can be less criticised for removing the stone pulpitum to clear the view down the nave to the presbytery. Part of it survives in the north-east transept where its finely carved niches, alive with trefoils, heads and so-called 'agitated stiff-leaf', demonstrate an artistry that the nave lacks. In the pulpitum's central niche is Laurence Whistler's revolving prism of Salisbury's steeple, made in memory of his brother Rex.

Salisbury makes some amends in its retrochoir. Here scale diminishes, piers grow slender and the atmosphere is of a forest glade, the contemplative calm of Early Gothic at its best. Even so, this calm was disrupted in 1980 by the dark blue east windows of the Trinity Chapel, by Gabriel and Jacques Loire, commemorating 'prisoners of conscience'. A window, like a building, can be beautiful in itself yet lose that beauty to its context. Prisoners are here seen peering gloomily from prisons of blue. Is this how they would wish to be remembered?

If I seem unfair on Salisbury, it has certainly been much improved by modern interior lighting, inside and out, an anachronistic blessing for many cathedrals. Two windows by Edward Burne-Jones in the south aisle are welcome. The south-east transept has a 1262 tomb of Bishop Bridport, a Decorated masterpiece with stiff-leaf carving and scenes from the bishop's life. In the north-east transept is a much-rubbed brass to Bishop Wyville (d.1375), in which he looks out from a fantasy castle.

The Perpendicular chantry to Bishop Audley (d.1524), Salisbury's principal treasure, stands in the north choir. It was built at the climax of Tudor gothic, a doll's-house chapel with a fan vault, painted and gilded and with the roses and pomegranates of Henry VIII and Catherine of Aragon.

The cathedral was not monastic, so its cloisters were largely a matter of form. They remain the biggest in England and the earliest to survive intact. The arcade tracery is based on large cinquefoils, marking the arrival here of the Decorated style in the 1270s. In the

Left
Chapter house carved head

Opposite
Chapter house vault

garth stand two glorious cedars; it is an idyllic spot in which to take tea and contemplate the great steeple overhead.

Off the cloister is the chapter house, one of many to emerge towards the end of the 13th century, taking their cue from Henry III's polygonal chamber at Westminster. A central pier rises past large windows with cusped tracery to a complex vault. The pier is so slender that Daniel Defoe, on his travels, alleged that it moved when he leaned on it. Don't try it.

The chapter house masons seemed released from the asceticism of the main cathedral. The heads carved above the canons' seats are to portraiture what Southwell's carvings are to botany. There are male and female heads, bearded and beardless, smiling and frowning. The guide suggests that they depict actual people. One has his tongue out, another is leering. A three-faced head by the dean's seat depicts the Trinity or, to other authorities, Prudence as memory, intelligence and foresight. The chapter house displays the cathedral's treasured copy of Magna Carta.

Few of the medieval canons' houses survive round the close, but their Tudor, Jacobean and Georgian replacements respect the one-time English genius for townscape. It is a casual distribution of buildings softened by nature, rus in urbe or country in town. Unlike the austere environs of most continental cathedrals, Salisbury's close suggests a comfortable, secularised clergy at peace with the world – or at least with themselves. There is not a house, tree or shrub in Salisbury Close one would want to move.

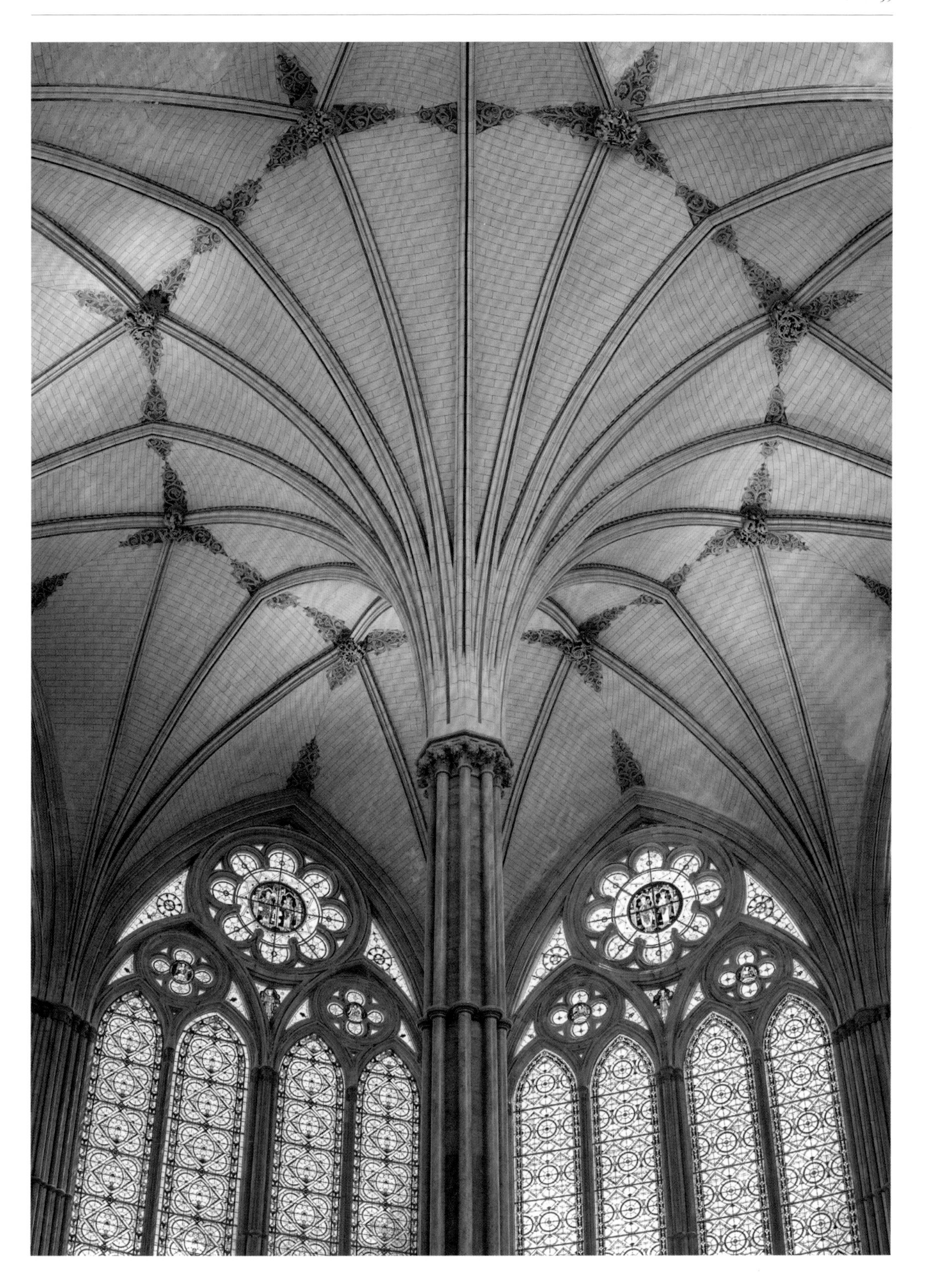

SHEFFIELD

St Peter and St Paul

Modern lantern, Shrewsbury Chapel, Webb glass

Sheffield is no place for nostalgics. As old cities were surrounded with moats and walls, modern ones hide behind bleak ring roads and shopping centres. Sheffield is one such. Its cathedral is therefore best approached up Paradise Street into Campo Lane. Here we can still catch a breath of the Victorian city, of steep lanes, pleasing contours, and older houses and commercial buildings. They seem to have drawn protection from their proximity to Sheffield's medieval parish church.

This church had Norman origins – of which a few stones are cemented into the chancel – and was rebuilt in the 13th and 15th centuries. It was made the cathedral for south Yorkshire in 1914. The requisite expansion led to an almost panicky series of changes of mind. The first idea was to reorient the church north–south, to a 1918 design by Charles Nicholson that was abandoned after the Second World War. A west end by Arthur Bailey was built instead in the 1960s, with glass by Amber Hiscott, installed in 1998. The result is enjoyably chaotic.

From the south, we can still appreciate the original church with its solid Yorkshire profile, medieval tower, transept and chancel. The new extension is to the west in a half-hearted gothic revivalism with a lantern tower. Concrete buttresses rise to slab-like pinnacles, more military than ecclesiastical. The later entrance porch is jollier.

The western extension dominates the entry into the interior. The inside of the lantern has stark angularity. Wooden pendants droop beneath it, apparently representing the Crown of Thorns but looking more like a trapped daddy-long-legs. It is rescued, as so often with modernist churches, by coloured glass. Hiscott's is certainly vivid. The west end has a steel font by Brian Fell, a rare but welcome evocation of Sheffield's once most-prominent industry.

Moving east, we enter the original nave and the medieval embrace of the 15th-century church's Perpendicular arcades, embossed ceilings and spacious aisles. The chancel follows without interruption, still with its original stalls and misericords. The modern gothic throne is by Nicholson of 1914. Above in the rafters is a flight of realistic golden angels flapping their wings in the dark.

North of the chancel is the shambolic result of the mind changes of the 20th century. The Shrewsbury Chapel of the Talbot family contains the

Left
'Daddy-long-legs' lantern with abstract glass

tomb of the 4th Earl of Shrewsbury (d.1538) in exquisite alabaster, lying with his two wives and devoted dog. The style is still medieval. The tomb of the 6th Earl (d.1590), one of Bess of Hardwick's many husbands, lies opposite and is renaissance. The Talbots were Roman Catholics but such was the family's status that their chapel, most unusually, was retained and declared a Catholic 'zone' within the Anglican church. It was surrounded by a firm wooden screen to prevent cross-contamination, a bizarre feature removed in the 1930s.

St Katharine's Chapel opposite has a set of Tudor sedilia and a window by Christopher Webb, dedicated to the role of women in the Christian story. St George's Chapel was to be the new sanctuary of Nicholson's church and is now an over-large regimental chapel with banners. A screen of swords and bayonets forms a somewhat grim screen to the aisle. Old St George's Chapel is flanked by the former Shrewsbury screen and has a ceiling of bright red and white roses. Another excellent window by Webb shows six Sheffield worthies displaying suitable machismo.

Down steps to the north, we reach the Chapel of the Holy Spirit, Nicholson's intended Lady Chapel. It is an austere space, enlivened by Ninian Comper stalls with vivid blue canopies. The window is again by Webb. Opposite the entrance to the chapel is the small crypt, an intimate space with, hidden in a corner, a brilliant window by Keith New (1966) made of tiny tubes of coloured Perspex. But in Sheffield, of all places, I would like more steel. The guidebook has the best photographs of any cathedral I know, by Ian Spooner.

Left
Tudor piety: tomb of the 4th Earl of Shrewsbury

SOUTHWARK

St Saviour and St Mary Overie

Chaucer and Shakespeare memorials, Pugin tabernacle, Early Gothic retrochoir

★★

Southwark is a frigate among cathedrals. It lurks grey and slightly menacing in its Thames-side inlet, as if waiting to sneak out and bombard the encircling cruisers of capitalism. I first visited it with John Betjeman in the 1970s, and he refused point blank to enter because, he assured me, its sole occupants were some Irish drunks round the porch who would 'unquestionably assault us'. In retrospect, I can see its very survival as something of a miracle. Just 100 yards from the east end are the bleak footings of The Shard and the London Bridge approach.

Yet Southwark has come to define the area around it, offering a sanctuary of older buildings and informality amid the commercial slabs and towers. It cowers beneath a swirling knot of railway bridges, heading for Cannon Street, Blackfriars and Charing Cross stations. Under and around the arches is the ancient covered Borough Market, today a food emporium crowded with bankers seeking relief from toil in steaming vats of paella and tagine, mountains of cheese and a daily hog roast. The scene is not so much medieval as movie set, but testifies to the necessity of preserving such oases in modern urban deserts.

The Augustinian priory of St Mary Overie – 'over the river' – was founded in the 9th century. It was rebuilt by the Normans in the 12th century, with fragments of this work surviving in the fabric of the nave and transept. To this was added a hospital dedicated to St Thomas à Becket, later moved to its present site across the river from the Houses of Parliament. The monastery clung on throughout the Middle Ages. Since it was outside the jurisdiction of the City of London, it developed as a lawless district, of prostitutes, theatres, the Clink prison and cheap lodgings for pilgrims heading for Canterbury. Monks were forbidden to leave their quarters unaccompanied.

After the Dissolution, the priory served as a local parish church but declined into ruin. The Early Gothic east end was restored in the 1820s by a local architect, George Gwilt, narrowly avoiding demolition for a new London Bridge approach. The nave was completely rebuilt in the 1830s, yielding what A. W. N. Pugin called 'as vile a preaching place as ever disgraced the 19th century'. This, in turn, was replaced by Sir Arthur Blomfield in the 1890s with suposedly a copy of the former nave. Southwark was finally designated a cathedral in 1905. Then in the

Left
Choir screen, Perpendicular with 20th-century statues

Left
Hamlet window

Opposite
Chaucer's pilgrims set off for Canterbury

Second World War the Blitz blasted the south wall and removed its windows.

Inside, Blomfield's nave may have the hard edges of Victorian masonry, but it is at least based on pictures of the earlier church, replicating its alternating round and square piers and Early Gothic vault. Southwark's interior is chiefly of interest for its memorials, many attempting to link it with more distinguished residents of the borough than can have attended its services. Thus the south aisle can boast Henry McCarthy's 1912 alabaster monument to Shakespeare, whom Southwark is certainly entitled to claim. He is recumbent with the cathedral depicted behind.

The north aisle has a window to Chaucer in honour of his Canterbury pilgrims, who are shown setting off on horseback from the nearby Tabard Inn. Here too is a much repainted effigy of the poet John Gower, who died in 1408. He lies with his head resting uncomfortably on a pile of his books. Pride of place in the north transept goes to Nicholas Stone's 1626 sculpture of a lawyer, William Austin, based on 'the allegory of the heavenly harvest'. Two farm maidens relax from their labour in sunhats amid golden corn, a welcome surprise in urban Southwark.

Off the north transept is the Harvard Chapel, dedicated to the founder of the American university, John Harvard, born in Southwark and baptised in the cathedral in 1607. Its treasure is a gothic tabernacle by Pugin, a jewel-studded masterpiece designed for the 1851 Exhibition and kept until 1971 in Pugin's church in Ramsgate.

Southwark's sanctuary is dominated by a restored Perpendicular screen of 1520. Its statues, by Thomas Nicholls from 1905, are of saints, bishops and others linked, however distantly, to the diocese. They contrive to include Augustine of Hippo, Margaret of Antioch, Becket and Jesus.

Behind this screen we reach a calmer Southwark, the much restored Early Gothic retrochoir of 1215. Its piers form a shady glade of vaults, protecting Ninian Comper's four eastern altars installed in 1930, each with its own triple-lancet windows. The altars are dedicated to causes of 20th-century moment, such as the war dead of the local OXO factory and gas works, and those afflicted with AIDS.

The site of the old cloister south of the cathedral has been rebuilt with vestries and other diocesan offices. The Millennium refectory wing, by Richard Griffiths and Ptolemy Dean, was opened in 2002. It is a discreet addition, from which there is a pleasant stroll to the riverside. It is a momentary staying of London's hand of greed.

SOUTHWELL

The Blessed Virgin Mary

Norman nave, chapter house stiff-leaf, pulpitum carvings, Reyntiens window

★★★★

Southwell Minster holds a unique position in the canon of English cathedrals. At the end of the 13th century, the old Norman minster received a chapter house that was not so much a building as a cascade of leaves of stone. They floated down from some celestial forest to sprout, tangle and droop from its walls. They were carved at an exultant moment in the history of English art, in the reigns of Edwards I and II, by unknown craftsmen at whose talent we can only marvel.

The old Nottinghamshire minster was a country seat and perquisite (like Ripon) of the archbishops of York. They used it primarily for hunting, leaving it endowed in the charge of a 'college' of lay canons, living off local rents and tithes. Few of these ever lived in Southwell and their limited duties were left to local deputies or vicars. Southwell was an ecclesiastical rotten borough. Since these colleges were not monasteries, they were mostly untouched by the Reformation. Not until the 1840s was Southwell college formally abolished and its revenues seized for the church. Then in 1884 the minster found a new purpose as a cathedral for the industrial towns of Nottingham and Derby. It lost half its see to Derby in 1927.

Long inertia left the old building little touched by time. It retains its three Norman towers, two of them with the conical spires once common to Norman churches. The imposing west front is pure Norman, apart from the customary Perpendicular window. Doorways and windows are thick with zigzag, giving it a slightly jazzy appearance. To Alec Clifton-Taylor, it has a 'gawky, homespun quality which is not unlikeable'.

The nave interior comes as a shock. It was begun in 1108, with arcades, triforium and clerestory that are strangely out of proportion. The triforium lacks the usual subsidiary double arches within each bay, with the result that the nave arcades seem to gallop towards the crossing like carthorses. The eye is not drawn to any vault, just a Victorian recreation of a Norman wooden roof.

The nave is presided over by two modern works of art. A Christ in Majesty by Peter Eugene Ball (1987) gazes down from the crossing arch, brassy, bold and a match for the heavy architecture round it. The west end is dominated by a window from John Piper's long-term collaborator Patrick Reyntiens (1996). It shows Reyntiens as a major artist in his own

Left
Norman west front

Opposite
'Wondrous sculpture': chapter house portal

right. Each panel is filled with angels in soft golds on a blue background, with none of the shouting of so much modern glass.

Southwell never needed to rebuild its transepts, which remain Norman. The crossing arches are big and uniform. Some carry subtle Norman carved capitals comparable with those in Canterbury's crypt. They depict the Annunciation, the Entry into Jerusalem, the Last Supper and other biblical scenes. Pevsner found them, for their date, 'among the most important examples of such capitals in England'. They are superb but extremely hard to see.

In a wall of the north transept is a Saxon tympanum, said to depict St Michael and King David, an echo from a past even more distant than the capitals. Otherwise, Southwell is poor in furnishings and memorials. This was no civic church or aristocratic mausoleum, and was much bashed about in the Civil War.

An exception is the tomb of the Tudor archbishop of York, Edwin Sandys (d.1588), a leading figure in the English Reformation. Vice-Chancellor of Cambridge, he fled into exile in Switzerland under Mary I but returned to high office (and marriage) under Elizabeth. Sandys was a keen reformer and co-translator of the Elizabethan Bishops' Bible. He lies in prayer with his nine children on the tomb chest, all made of that most beautiful stone, Nottingham alabaster.

The east end of the cathedral was in effect the private chapel of Southwell's few resident clergy. It was rebuilt after 1240 by the then archbishop of York, Walter de Gray, financed by indulgence sales. Its style is the most elegant Early Gothic. The arcade piers are delicately clustered into shafts and the east wall lined with two tiers of four lancets. Most of the shafts carry foliage capitals, an architectural feature that was to emerge as Southwell's especial glory.

The portrayal of leaves in 'stiff' or stylised form evolved from Norman motifs known as water-leaf and crocket, echoes in turn of classicism's Corinthian capitals. Gothic masons took the motif far beyond the ancient form of the acanthus leaf. Each column would erupt in leaf clusters, their stalks seeming to grow from the column itself. Initially stiff, the leaves later become lively or 'wind-blown', deeply incised and undercut, as if about to wave free and fall to the woodland floor. The vegetation was often populated with animals, birds and green men. From the late 12th to the early 14th century, such decoration was to adorn capitals, corbels and niches across not just England but much of northern Europe. The gothic imagination seemed to drift out

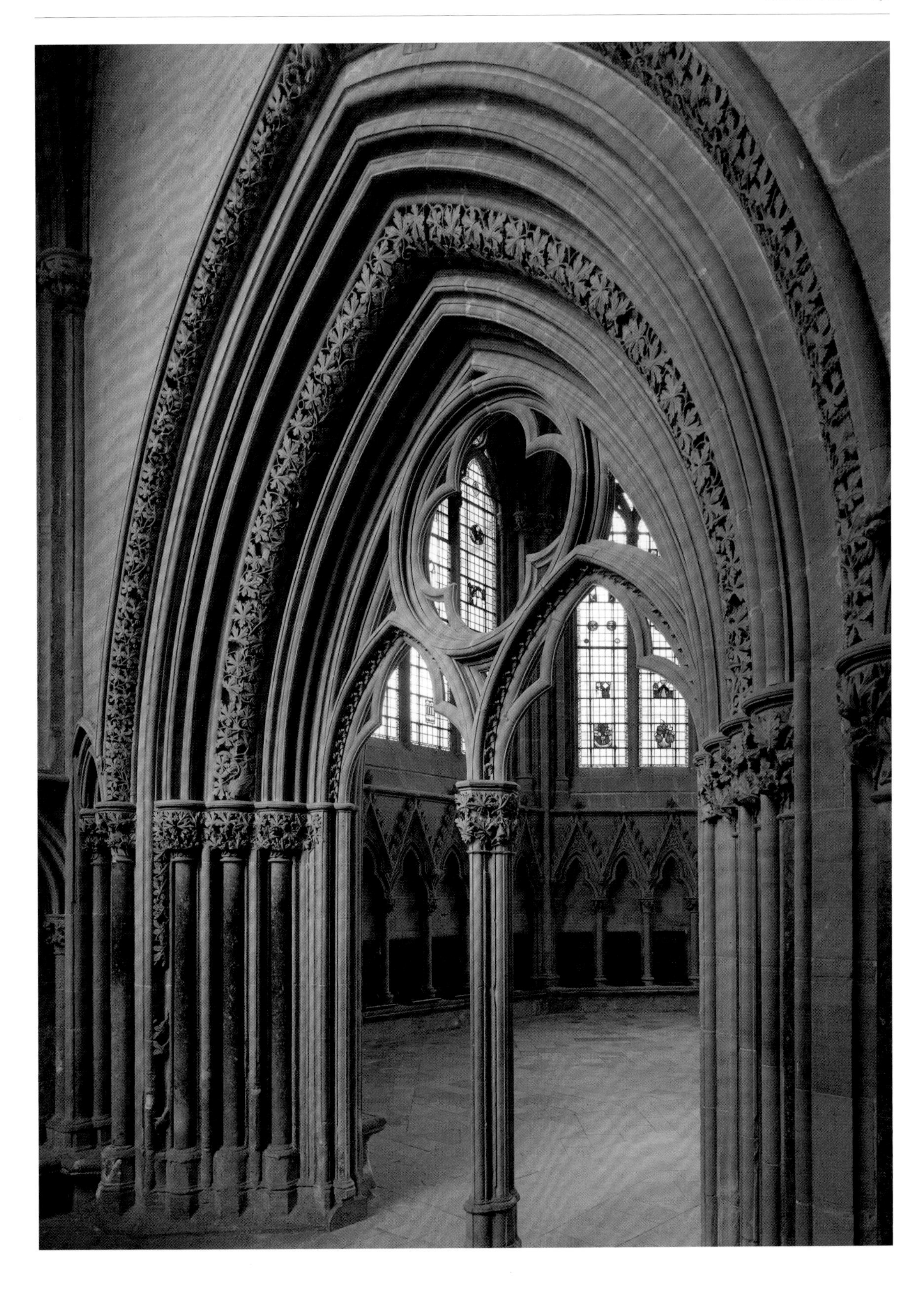

Previous spread
Stiff-leaf on portal capitals

Left
Lacework in stone on pulpitum stalls

Opposite
Chapter house heads

of churches to the trees and hedgerows of the countryside.

Southwell's leaves are exceptional, meticulous portrayals of nature. Only Rheims is their rival. The carvers rarely depicted the simpler leaves, such as beech, willow or lime. They chose instead the complex patterns of oak, maple, hawthorn, hop and vine. They cannot, as some have suggested, merely have been cataloguing the 'fruits of the fields'. They were harnessing botany to the cause of aesthetics.

To appreciate the evolution of this carving at Southwell, we should ignore the pulpitum which is of a later date, and return down the north choir aisle to the earlier chapter house (1290–1300). It is reached through a portal marked enticingly by a single band of entwined leaves. This gives onto a passage lined with blind arcading, where tenants would presumably sit awaiting judgment from the chapter. At the end is a vestibule lit by a large Decorated window.

From here, a second portal – an arch over two lesser arches – leads into the chapter house itself. The outer arch has two bands of foliage on polished Purbeck jambs. Each of the inner arches contains a trefoil, supporting a single quatrefoil and divided by a slender pier. The capital of this pier is crowned with a garland of buttercup leaves, a work of superb proportion and charm. Pevsner guessed that this capital was the work of the master carver, 'the caprice of an artist who knew very clearly how far he could go … He must show his mastery by breaking rules, or at least questioning them.'

The chapter house was commissioned for the thirty-six canons to sit in conclave. Since there was no dean or bishop and the canons were almost all absent, this must have been more a matter of form than substance. The chamber, an octagon, is unusual in having no central support, and is thus a smaller version of the earlier York chapter house. As at York, the vault is carried on a splay of ribs, here sixteen rising to a central star burst and boss. The seats beneath are each crowned by a tall Decorated gable, the seat backs giving the names of local villages whose tithes supported the relevant canon.

The profusion of vegetation adorning this interior so delighted Pevsner that he wrote a book in its honour, *The Leaves of Southwell.* He pointed out that a capital or corbel is a natural stop, 'a halt, a junction … a moment of leisure for looking at ornament'. In Southwell, it was as if nature were running riot over the surface of the building, yet it was a riot disciplined by architecture. To Pevsner, these leaves were a manifestation, 'one of the purest symbols

surviving in Britain of Western thought, our thought, in its loftiest mood'. They had significance as a source of food, herbs and magic, while evoking the spirit of St Francis, of Brother Sun and 'our Sister, Mother Earth who … bringeth forth divers fruit and bright flowers and herbs.'

A dozen species of growth have been identified by botanists, the most popular being maple (36 leaves), oak (28), hawthorn (20), potentilla (20), vine (18), ivy (12) and hop (8). They are followed by buttercup, wild apple, wild rose, geranium and wormwood. Where leaves are mixed with animal or human faces, it is noticeable that more attention has been paid to the veins of the leaves than to details of the faces. As Olive Cook puts it, 'this is not the naturalism of the botanical draughtsman, content with fidelity to nature; it is the sculptor's sense of wonder'.

Who were these men? Scholars have compared the work with York, Southwell's mother house, and with Rheims, whose leaves are nearest to Southwell in style, though more formal. Scholars have detected from the style just three carvers at work, so was it a local master who inspired these craftsmen, or did some passing band of masons carry out the work? All we can see is that when the central boss came to be inserted, sometime after 1300, the style changes. The leaves are tighter knit, with an artificial surface undulation. There is a sudden loss of exhilaration.

We should now return to the pulpitum in the main church, completed by 1340. The façade to the nave is formed of five arches, the central three larger and with spreading cinquefoil tracery. They glow richly amid the romanesque simplicity of the crossing. Behind them, the pulpitum's interior bay has a rare vault of 'flying ribs'.

The pulpitum's façade to the choir is quite different, an eruption of Decorated design. Two storeys of five nodding ogees flank a central sweeping ogee within a triangle. The bays are encrusted with foliage so delicate we can hardly believe it is of stone; it looks like the lace collar of an overdressed cardinal. The transom above carries minuscule heads of priests and laymen. John Harvey claims to have counted 'over 50 carved heads of appreciable size … over 200 large-leaved crockets and some 100 foliated capitals or finials'.

We leave Southwell blinking into the daylight. I am glad this is no bustling cathedral city, but rather a somnolent country town. For a moment in history, it played host to a burst of genius. A corner of Nottinghamshire was seized by a collective magic.

TRURO

St Mary

Pearson gothic revival, Clayton & Bell glass, Cornish chapel

Truro cathedral is a French tourist lost in Cornwall – speaking barely a word of English. It was begun by a dynamic bishop, Edward Benson, in 1877 after the old see of Exeter was divided in two. As chancellor of Lincoln, he had been infused with a love of gothic revival, and duly staged a competition for his new church in that style. He chose the consultant architect at Lincoln, J. L. Pearson. A scholar of French gothic, Pearson was also a keen evangelical. Of a church he asked, not is it beautiful, but 'does it send you to your knees'. Benson was his ideal client. Accused of having 'drained Cornwall of money' to build his cathedral, Benson replied, 'Yes, but not of zeal.'

Pearson had to sweep away houses and streets in central Truro to squeeze his work into its cramped quarters. With some sensitivity, he wanted to retain one aisle of the old St Mary's parish church on the edge of the site as a Lady Chapel. This was despite Benson's desire for no 'tinkering up rotten stones'. Pearson produced a scholarly exercise in French early gothic, claiming improbably that such a style responded to ancient links between Cornwall and Brittany – links that far pre-dated the gothic era.

The building shows no trace of Cornish culture or tradition. Nor is there any sign of the dominant English styles of the day, of art nouveau or the emerging Arts and Crafts movement. Nor more regrettably does Truro display the decorative dynamism Pearson brought to his masterpiece, St Augustine's Kilburn in London. It is really rather dull.

Seen from the west, the cathedral exterior is imposing, with three towers and high windows. To the south-east, the remains of St Mary's church cling to the side of the chancel, like a van crushed by a passing juggernaut. Its homely Cornish granite is overwhelmed by Pearson's looming lancets.

Inside, the lines of the gothic nave and chancel march eastwards with monastic discipline, softened by sunlight during the day and careful lighting at night. If Benson was hoping for an echo of his old cathedral at Lincoln, says Pevsner, Pearson seems to have neglected 'the lovable irregularities of Lincoln'. Instead, Truro rather evokes the cold perfection of Salisbury. English cathedrals do not warm to regularity.

Left
Pearson's austere gothic

That said, there is a dignity to the design that comes with the

customary features of French architecture. The arcades are sharply pointed, and the four-arched triforium and ribbed vaults have dogtooth adornment. The machined Victorian edges are relentless, though they may soften with age.

The choir and sanctuary are richly traditional, the bishop's throne a splendid construction of Victorian woodwork. The reredos is an elaborate work in Bath stone by a little-known specialist in late-Victorian church carving, Nathaniel Hitch. Truro's glass is perhaps its greatest pleasure, a complete programme by Clayton & Bell, with that firm's confident ability to convey a united composition in a medieval style. The east windows are a blaze of reds and blues.

To the north is a chapter house by John Taylor. Its concrete structure dates from 1967, a time of nadir in English architecture. It makes Pearson seem as cosy as a Tudor snuggery. But if Tudor is our preference, we can always return down the south aisle to St Mary's Chapel, relic of the old parish church. Its modest dimensions, wagon roof and Perpendicular windows smile a friendly welcome, back home to Cornwall.

Left
Exterior: France lands in Cornwall

WAKEFIELD

All Saints

Scott rebuild of medieval church, Kempe windows, Pearson retrochoir

Wakefield's former parish church was never a shrinking violet. It sat overlooking the centre of the market town, as now it presides over the wreckage bequeathed Wakefield by its post-war planners. The church and its handsome Perpendicular steeple – the highest in Yorkshire – were rebuilt by George Gilbert Scott between 1858 and 1874; his son John Oldrid Scott was also involved. Their respect for the existing fabric makes it near impossible to disentangle the 15th century from the 19th. A new east end was built after the church was elevated to cathedral in 1888. It was designed by J. L. Pearson and his firm, and was completed in 1904.

Pearson spared the church the episcopal 'modernisation' visited on Blackburn and Bradford. Its interior is dominated by handsome Early Gothic arcades, flanked by later aisles and a friendly wooden roof. Some medieval bosses were reused in the latter. The more recent renovation was extensive and successful, rendering the nave light and warm, its grey-pink stone lit by candelabra. On the floor is a labyrinth, lately fashionable as an 'aid to contemplation'. The west window is an over-crowded Last Judgment by Hardman & Co. Beneath are jarring metal doors, reminiscent of an airport security zone.

The glory of Wakefield is an almost complete set of windows by the fringe Pre-Raphaelite C. E. Kempe. The Old Testament is depicted on the north side, the New Testament with added saints on the south. As at Bradford, it is the uniformity of the whole that gives these windows impact.

The choir is guarded by a Jacobean rood screen of the 1630s, with tapering pilasters and carved figures, an artisan mannerism taken from Flemish patterns. The modern rood is by Ninian Comper, in his 1950s saccharine mode. The choir itself is a church within a church, cosy and enclosed, with chunky medieval stalls and a royal blue ceiling above a gilded reredos.

Behind lies Pearson's retrochoir, transept and St Mark's Chapel conveying more of the dignity of a cathedral. They reflect Pearson's studious high gothic, at the time of his Truro cathedral, with four slender piers rising to a lierne vault. The chapel is lit by large Decorated windows depicting northern saints, apparently one of Kempe's last works.

Left
West entrance with contemplative labyrinth

WELLS

St Andrew

Sculpted west front, crossing scissor arches,
Romanesque capitals, chapter house stairs and vault

★★★★★

I first caught sight of Wells from the Mendip escarpment as I looked out over the Somerset Levels in a storm. Rain was falling but, in the distance, a glancing sun was lighting the tower on Glastonbury Tor. At my feet lurked the three towers of Wells, dark and faintly menacing. It was a truly medieval view.

Wells is a happy cathedral. With Ely and Lincoln, it is one of my 'three graces' and, on a good visit, I am inclined to hand it the palm. It is also a complex, challenging building, a variation on a gothic theme. Wells offers intellectual stimulus as well as aesthetic delight.

St Andrew's spring at the foot of the Mendip Hills was long a place of Christian worship and its water still trickles amiably down the main street. Throughout the Saxon era into the Conquest, the minster – which had been raised to cathedral status in 909 – competed with its neighbours at Glastonbury and Bath. The Normans formally established the bishop's seat in the bigger town of Bath. Only with the arrival of Reginald de Bohun as bishop in 1174 was it decided to build a cathedral on a new site north of the old minster.

Reginald was thirty-four and had been a friend of both Becket and Henry II. He was a much-travelled Norman, eager to take advantage of Henry's post-Becket rapprochement with the Roman church. The new building in the gothic style coincided with William of Sens' work at Canterbury. It began, as was customary, with an eastern Lady Chapel, and gathered pace under Reginald's ambitious successor, Jocelin of Wells, counsellor to kings John and Henry III. The work was financed by Jocelin, who renounced supremacy over Glastonbury in return for much of Glastonbury's land. To him we owe the bulk of the cathedral we see today, including the celebrated west front. The new building was consecrated in 1239.

Shortly after Jocelin's death in 1242, the pope restored Wells' status and made his successor bishop of Bath and Wells, a title retained to this day. Wells was never a monastery and the chapter of fifty-four canons was the second-largest in the country after Lincoln. Over the course of a century of rebuilding, they were able to call on the finest builders of the age, including Thomas of Witney, William Joy – the two men also worked at Exeter – and William Winford, architect of Winchester, who

Left
West front at dusk

contributed the west towers. Wells might have been a small settlement, but its church was a national church led by men with national aspirations.

The cathedral, like so many others, was frequently at odds with its townspeople, resentful of its exclusivity and wealth. The chapter had to erect protective walls and gatehouses round its enclave, which still has a gently embattled feel. Vicars' Close, the longest medieval street in England, was built to keep the clergy aloof from outsiders. Jocelin also built himself a palace, fortified by walls, gates and a moat, which survives today despite all attempts to convert it into a hotel.

Every approach to Wells begins with the west front, one of England's most celebrated gothic façades. A rectangular structure twice as wide as it is high, it carries a gallery of medieval statuary. Four tiers of niches, with more in the central gable, contain some four hundred statues, each on a theme from the Bible or from the history of the Church. Its silvery limestone comes alive at dusk as the sun pierces every crevice and turns silver into gold.

The front has never been free of controversy. Most critics are exultant. To Alec Clifton-Taylor, 'The composition has a beautiful logic, and is quite unlike any other … one of the great sights of England'. To Olive Cook, it is 'a great Te Deum of sculptured praise … a stupendous reredos in which architecture and imagery conspire to expound the systematic theology of the early gothic period'.

Pevsner will have none of this. To him, the front is out of balance. Winford's towers, added almost two centuries after Jocelin's front, clash with the proportions of the façade. The six lumbering buttresses seem intended for much bigger towers, but end in what amount to stumps. Some of the niches are too big for their contents, others too small. The statues are either invisible or 'weird and gaunt'. Barely a quarter of them survive in a remotely recognisable state, and just twenty, on the north side of the north tower, are of distinction.

While I always marvel at Wells' front, I can see Pevsner's point, especially about the statues. I climbed the scaffolding during restoration and found them near meaningless. Iconoclasts had toppled or beheaded the lower ones, and time has done as much damage to the rest. They are gothic only in outline and posture, in the fold of a garment or the angle of an arm. On the less eroded north side, only the 'Four Marys' still manage to convey the power of medieval sculpture.

Hence the understandable debate in the 1970s when restoration led to the insertion of copies, notably of the Madonna's head in the

Opposite
Inadmissible insertion: replacement Madonna in west front

Following spread
The great scissor arch: masterpiece or intrusion?

tympanum over the west door. Other new statues by David Wynne and Derek Carr are excellent. But such was the outcry from fundamentalists that further replacement ceased. Only angels, niche surrounds and spandrels were allowed to be re-carved. Thus some niches are original, some are modern copies. Some earlier copies are now softened by erosion, while some are mere lumps of eroded stone, often in new frames. The work is an aesthetic hodge-podge.

We should try to capture, at least in the mind's eye, the original purpose of this front. Its principal moment would have been the Easter ritual. The front would have been draped in banners. Choirs would have gathered in its gables, where holes have been found through which trumpets were played. John Harvey reminds us that these façades were triumphs of painting as much as carving: 'Every statue was painted and gilt, and at its completion must have presented a dazzling sight, only comparable to the brilliance of the Parthenon in its first state.' What we see today is thus not a medieval façade, but really the ruin of one, a battlefield across which feuding scholars have fought each other to a draw. The best hope now is that lighting technology can help us by projecting images onto the west front of what was meant to be.

The rest of the exterior is largely Jocelin's church. The north porch is an Early Gothic masterpiece, and was once the principal entrance. It has shafted arches with chevron decoration. The capitals carry some of the finest stiff-leaf in the cathedral, including a portrayal of the martyrdom of King Edmund. The porch interior is a tour de force of arcading, vaulting and carving. In the attic above is a rare surviving tracing floor where the medieval architects plotted their dimensions for the stonemasons.

Today the cathedral is entered not through the north porch but from the south, through an electronic glass door from the visitor centre. The centre itself is admirably discreet, in the form of a semi-cloister with slate-hung roof and water garden designed by Martin Stancliffe (2008). It is an exemplary insertion.

The nave at Wells is initially a challenge. The main arcades are considered the apogee of Early Gothic design. Perfectly proportioned, the pier shafts and arch mouldings stress the play of light and shade. They convey a visual fluidity that is characteristic of the gothic style. On the other hand, the triforium pays scant attention to the arcade bays and, as Clifton-Taylor says, 'for some unaccountable reason … hurries along in an unbroken line of small

lancets' as if impatient to reach the choir. This emphasis on the horizontal foreshortens the nave, when perhaps it most needs lengthening.

This is relevant as the arcade runs bang into Wells' celebrated signature, the massive strainer or 'scissor' arches closing the nave to the east. They were inserted in the 1330s, a century after the nave was completed, to underpin the new crossing tower when it showed signs of cracking. The designer was William Joy, who is thought to have perished of the Black Death in 1348. Backed by a giant organ case, the arches fill three sides of the crossing, filtering the view through to the presbytery. They rise from floor to ceiling without bases or capitals, defining two criss-crossing ogees. They present two round 'eyes' gazing down on the congregation below.

The effect is controversial. Where Ely's crossing draws the cathedral into a glorious unity, Wells splits itself in two. But what a split. Some visitors may agree with Clifton-Taylor that the arches are 'a grotesque intrusion' but, to Pevsner, they are 'no punches pulled' Decorated. They may have originated as medieval engineering at its most promiscuous, but they appear today as works of immense decorative force. They bend, soar and swoop. They shift planes like raptors in flight. Only a fiddly modern rood group perched on the nave arch spoils their cleanliness of line. Above the crossing vault is a Perpendicular fan vault of 1480. Wells' ceilings throughout carry restored stencils depicting a medieval Persian 'tree of life'.

The nave contains one stylistic curiosity, a renaissance pulpit emerging from a gothic chantry. The chantry was endowed by a canon, Dr Sugar (d.1489), in high Perpendicular gothic. After the Reformation, Bishop Knight (d.1547) made it the access to his new pulpit, now in a renaissance style. Knight, who was a Protestant adviser to Henry VIII, thus produced probably the first classical pulpit in England, rising symbolically from a gothic base.

Wells' transepts and aisles contain superbly carved medieval capitals. They date from the mid-13th century, half a century before the botanically precise work at Southwell, and earlier too than York's chapter house and Lincoln's Angel Choir. They display, says Harvey, 'the highest quality of workmanship … linked to a charming and genial humour'. Whereas the carvers of the west front seemed bound to the liturgy, here they were released to ponder the delights, fears and imaginings of domestic life. We have to wonder if they were the same craftsmen.

We see a farmer chasing a fox that has stolen

Opposite and left
Transept scenes from medieval life

his goose; a cobbler bangs at a shoe; a man takes a thorn from his foot; four separate reliefs round one pillar depict boys stealing fruit from a tree, then being caught and chastised. A man displaying his toothache is so realistic that an adjacent bishop's tomb was long credited with power to cure toothache in general. There are some two hundred such scenes, a brilliant tableau of medieval England.

The north transept contains the Wells clock, dating from 1390. On the quarter hour, jousting knights knock each other over and the Quarter Jack kicks his heels. The original mechanism is sadly in London's Science Museum, while in 2010 electricity supplanted hand-winding.

In the south transept is St Calixtus's Chapel containing the alabaster tomb of Thomas Boleyn, great-uncle of Anne. On one side is a rare relief of the Annunciation of the Virgin of the Lilies that escaped the iconoclasts. The transept gives access to Wells' chained library and muniment room, which fills the east gallery of the cloister. Although some books are medieval, the library mostly dates from the 17th century. During the Commonwealth, it was given to the local parish church for use as a lending library, but was returned (intact?) on the Restoration. The room is a serene retreat and open to visitors.

Wells' eastern arm might be a different cathedral. The choir survives from Jocelin's time, but was given a Perpendicular refresher by Joy in the 14th century. The overall proportions, the piers and aisles retain the rhythm of the nave, but the choir has a curious stone grille inserted between the arcade and clerestory. The effect is of a chamber within a chamber.

The throne is spare and Perpendicular, probably also by Joy but altered, as was the whole choir, by Anthony Salvin in the 1840s. The latter's pulpitum stalls are a virtuoso display of Decorated revival. Their most prominent feature is the colourful embroidered seat backs, produced during the Second World War by a hundred local ladies (and seven men). Overhead is Joy's lierne vault, a white and gold canopy that would do credit to a Regency ballroom. It barely recognises ridge or bay, as if the gothic era were already passing into the night.

Lining the choir aisles to both north and south are effigies of Saxon bishops. These were carved in the 13th century as a political gesture, asserting Wells' historic supremacy over Glastonbury and Bath. Most of the other tombs and memorials were moved into the cloister by the Victorians, leaving the interior mainly to bishops. The tomb of the 14th-

Opposite
Pieces of eight: the Lady Chapel vault

century Bishop Harewell is of alabaster and carries his rebus of two hares drinking at a ribbon of water. The tomb of Bishop Bekynton (d.1465) is surrounded by a railing, the devil having a reputed dread of iron; his cadaver lies below.

All eyes now turn east. Towering over the sanctuary is the Jesse east window (*c*1340), the finest of the genre in England. Supposedly an echo of the west front, it tells the story of the House of David, emerging from the side of the sleeping Jesse to climax with the figure of Christ at its summit. The window is sparing of the familiar reds and blues of most medieval glass, stressing greens and golds instead. Long known as the 'golden window', it was saved from iconoclasts by its lofty position and, more recently, from bombs by being dismantled and stored during the war.

There is no reredos below the east window but something more precious, three elegant arches giving a view through to the retrochoir and Lady Chapel. This part of the cathedral was rebuilt in the 1320s to serve as a processional route and venue for a possible saint's shrine. Sadly none of Wells' candidates – or at least their lobbyists – passed muster in Rome. Instead, we have what I regard as the loveliest gothic space in any English cathedral. The retrochoir and chapel form a single inter-related space. It was designed by Thomas of Witney, surely the finest architect to emerge from the great burst of Decorated invention at the turn of the 14th century. He was reputedly fascinated by geometry.

The retrochoir piers are like clusters of bamboos, their Purbeck shafts refracting light and shade and drawing the eye into the Lady Chapel. The chapel's plan is an ovoid octagon, formed of two overlaid circles of differing diameters. The chapel roof replicates this shape, in the form of a burst of lierne stars inside larger stars, as if each junction were releasing a golden spark. The lierne pattern in the top half of the vault (opposite) does not match the bottom.

Cook compares the impact of this vault to that of the 16th-century baroque: it 'reminds us, despite the difference of idiom, of the affinity between the two great architectural expressions of the same faith'. Pevsner sees a similar parallel. He reflects that 'the sensitive visitor is at once thrown into a pleasing confusion ... as intricate and thrilling as German rococo space'. To leave the eye to roam over this chamber 'is like penetrating a piece of complicated polyphonic music'.

The Lady Chapel is lit by five large windows, each filled with reticulated tracery (like fish-net). Four have original glass, while the eastern

Opposite
Chapter house – or forest of palms

one of 1845 is by the Victorian medievalist Thomas Willement. Ribs, capitals and bosses have all been coloured, though why repainting is acceptable in a chapel but not in the rest of the interior is a mystery.

We should now look back from the Lady Chapel across the retrochoir westwards down the length of the cathedral. We have a vision of curving stone and glancing light, of visual depths and infinite complexities. Clifton-Taylor found it simply 'one of the most subtle and entrancing architectural prospects in England'.

Nor is Wells finished. Its final offering lies past two renaissance tombs off the north transept. An ancient door hangs on elaborate 13th-century hinges, their ironwork flowing uninhibited across the woodwork. Beyond, a long flight of steps is guarded by a corbel depicting a monk who is cheerfully killing a dragon while holding up the building. Gothic masons could never resist a joke.

The steps led originally to a right-handed curve into the chapter house, but were later extended upwards to link with the Chain Gate Bridge to Vicars' Close (*see* page x). This dividing of ways has given rise to many metaphors. It is a stairway to Heaven, passing by a diversion to worldly pleasures. It is a choice between the path of prayer and that of ecclesiastical politics. Above all, the junction emphasises options, the freedom of the will. It is surely the finest stair in England.

Taking the right-hand turn, we enter a chapter house to rival even Southwell's. It dates from the early 1300s and has as its centrepiece a single 'palm tree' pier, from whose trunk radiate no fewer than thirty-two ribs. These fan out to fill the entire octagonal vault. The side walls push up rival ribs, clustered in groups of nine that meet the central ribs in a girdle of liernes and bosses. At this point they appear to join hands and dance, as though round a maypole. The glass is mostly clear, a few medieval fragments dappling the stone.

The stalls below are each capped by a trefoil and a gable. Their corbels form a gallery of divines, presumably canons; some stern, some laughing, one even sticking out his tongue. These surely are portraits of men who once climbed these steps and filled these stalls. Like the earlier carvings of the transept capitals, they convey an impression of a 14th-century cathedral that is far from the stern hierarchy of Reformation history. These are clearly individuals, devout perhaps, but sorrowing, ridiculing, arguing and laughing. They are men who saw their great church not just as a place of prayer but as a mirror of the entire community of medieval England.

WESTMINSTER ABBEY

St Peter
Hawksmoor west front, Poets' Corner, Edward the Confessor shrine, Henry VII chapel, Tudor/Stuart tombs

★★★★★

Westminster Abbey is a royal peculiar. It thus lies outside the jurisdiction of its diocese and the monarch is its head. Its site is that chosen for a Benedictine monastery, founded in *c*1040, on Thorney Island on a long bend of the River Thames, deliberately apart from the plagues, dirt and discord of the City of London. The 'west minster' soon attracted palaces, courts, parliament and government. It remains chapel royal to England's ruling class.

The abbey is a most eccentric place. It has no triumphal approach, no avenue, parade or grand entrance, none of the grandeur of Notre-Dame in Paris or St Peter's in Rome. Its entrance is tucked away in a forecourt called the Sanctuary, where carriages must manoeuvre to deliver worshippers, however important, to the door. The site embraces a warren of former monastic buildings. Although the monastery has gone, its school remains, cohabiting with Church House, the headquarters of the Church of England.

The founder of the present abbey, Edward the Confessor, was half Norman and spent his early life in France. His building was begun in the 1040s as an emphatically Norman structure, based on the abbey of Jumièges, whose abbot became Edward's archbishop. It had three eastern apses and two west towers. The stone was imported from Caen, as were the French masons who worked it. Thus it was the Confessor, not the Conqueror, who brought Norman culture, law and language to England, well before 1066. He instituted the writing of English laws in French.

William I chose Westminster for his coronation, rather than the Saxon capital of Winchester, to emphasise his legitimacy from Edward. He was crowned by a Saxon archbishop, Ealdred, but the formal cries of acclamation were taken by troops stationed outside the abbey as cries of rebellion and outbuildings were set ablaze in the confusion. The coronation became a riot.

Every monarch since William has been crowned at Westminster. When Elizabeth I entered it in 1559, to be greeted by her sister Mary's Catholic monks chanting and carrying candles, she shouted, 'Away with these torches, for we see very well.' It was here in 1821 that George IV shut out his estranged wife, Caroline, as she sought to assert her

Left
West front: Hawksmoor's 'mongrel gothic'

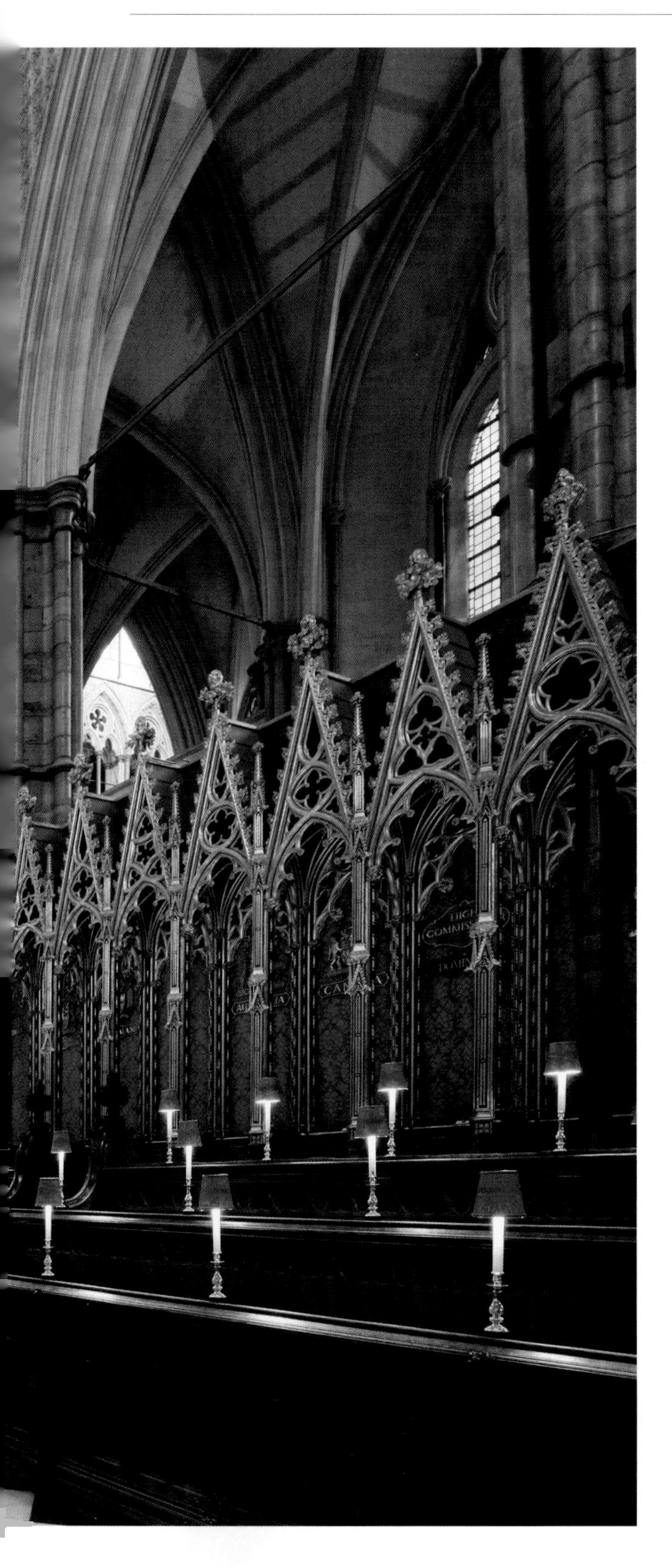

rights as queen. It was here in 1997, during the tense memorial service for Princess Diana, that applause from the crowd outside at Lord Spencer's perceived criticism of the Establishment reached the shocked congregation inside. Westminster has always generated political electricity.

Fragments of Edward the Confessor's creation survive, mostly buried in Westminster's monastic outbuildings. What we see today is a 13th-century rebuild by Edward's pious successor, Henry III, as a shrine to his hero. Henry had an assertively French wife, Eleanor of Provence, and, like Edward, he turned to France for inspiration, to the abbeys of Amiens and Rheims, importing as his architect Master Henry of Reynes. It is ironic that both England's most politically charged medieval churches, Canterbury and Westminster, owe their inspiration to the great enemy, France.

Henry's new abbey was built at his own expense – and with donations extorted from courtiers – over forty years from 1245. It marked the arrival in England of Decorated gothic, defined by tall roofs, elaborate arcades and, most noticeable, the appearance of bar tracery in the windows. By the time of Westminster's completion at the end of Henry's reign, the then staggering sum of £45,000 had been spent on it (assessed as roughly £9bn today).

What is remarkable is how little the abbey has changed since then. Its outline remains embarrassed by the lack of any crossing tower, merely an ugly cap. The most substantial addition was Henry VII's Chapel in the 16th century, followed in the 18th by Hawksmoor's peculiar west towers. From then on, many hands have embellished Henry's work, notably

Left
Choir looking towards sanctuary

the ubiquitous George Gilbert Scott, but the Westminster we see today is essentially Henry III's.

The exterior is unspectacular. Most visitors enter the abbey through Scott's austerely restored north transept onto Parliament Square. This is not beautiful. Four giant buttresses stick out from its façade, flanking a central rose window, crouching over the square like a cyclopean spider. East of the transept rises Henry VII's Chapel facing the Palace of Westminster. This burst of Tudor panels, turrets and pinnacles was to be the last spectacular throw of English Perpendicular before the arrival in England (indeed inside the chapel) of the European renaissance.

To the right, the eye is led by a phalanx of buttresses towards the sanctuary, where the west front is so familiar as to obscure its mongrel style. The bottom portion of the façade contains a fragment of Henry's original church. Above, it becomes Perpendicular with a gable and west window, and above them are Hawksmoor's towers, which were not completed until 1745.

Both Hawksmoor and his predecessor as Westminster surveyor, Christopher Wren, had agreed that these new towers should be gothic. It was the style, said Hawksmoor with characteristic directness, for all 'antient durable publick buildings … instead of erecting new, fantasticall, perishable trash'. Yet at Westminster, his towers are a stylistic mix. Their gothic fenestration is punctuated by classical cornices and by the most emphatic baroque clock openings. Hawksmoor's inconsistency has become one of Westminster's delights.

The interior of the abbey is in two parts. The first, to the west, is the familiar ceremonial church, the other to the east is a national mausoleum. Of the first function, Pevsner writes, 'Nowhere else in Europe can the sacred and continuing rites of kingship be so well comprehended from a physical setting.' The second part takes the form of a gallery of some 450 memorials. The assemblage is astonishing. Tombs, monuments, memorials cram every inch of space. They lurk and they soar, some quiet, some thoughtful, some absurdly ostentatious. At times, the abbey seems like a mason's yard, with tombs tossed this way and that.

This has had its detractors. John Ruskin deplored 'the ignoble incoherent fillings of the aisles'. William Morris called the monuments 'the most hideous specimens of false art that can be found in the whole world'. There were constant calls for an alternative national pantheon to free the abbey from such

Opposite
Henry III

Left
Richard II and Anne of Bohemia

indignities. All have been ignored.

To me, this element of the chaotic is what makes Westminster so appealing. There is artistry in every corner, a gigantic, cacophonous, very un-British exhibition of egotism. Compared with pompous St Paul's, Westminster is a batty old woman cackling over her mementos in the nation's attic.

Those lucky enough to enter the abbey from the west door do so as if gliding onto the floor of a ballroom. Purbeck piers line the central space, with pools of silent darkness in the aisles behind. Chandeliers drop like diamonds over the short nave. Overhead rises a roof of golden bosses, lit by a generous clerestory.

The nave is unusual in its shortness and in its ratio of width to height. At 1:3 it is narrower than any other English medieval cathedral (though the proportion is common in France). The effect is of a shimmering canyon, drawing the eye eastwards to the unseen rituals of statehood beyond. The nave is brought to an abrupt halt by the pulpitum. This shortening was intended by Henry III to increase the ceremonial space in the crossing beyond, but it renders the space patently inadequate for grand ceremonials, which is why St Paul's has to be used for many official functions.

The pulpitum is a composite work of gothic revival, dating from the 17th century but essentially Victorian. It is one bay deep with a fan vault below and orchestra gallery above. Embedded in its west façade are masterpieces by J. M. Rysbrack and William Kent. One is of Sir Isaac Newton, crowded with putti interfering with his experiments, the other is of a Georgian secretary of state, Earl Stanhope, whose fame was more transient.

The choir beyond leads into the central crossing, Henry's stage-set for the ceremonies of kingship. To north and south are aisled transepts, dominated by large rose windows. The south transept has four tiers of arcading rising to a rose that fills the gable. Buried in its wall are stairs leading to the old monastic quarters. Medieval sculptures can be seen in the arch spandrels, some with their original colouring.

The architecture of Westminster's crossing is overwhelmed by its congregation not of the living but of the dead. To the south lies Poets' Corner, spilling over into most of the transept. Here are all the masters of sculpture on parade: le Sueur, Stone, Nollekens, Roubiliac, Rysbrack, Scheemakers, Cheere, Flaxman and Westmacott. It is as if sculpture mattered more than poetry. Chaucer is seriously underplayed, but at least Shakespeare gets his due. At Westminster, no lights are hidden under bushels although more recent poets are

Opposite
Chantry of Henry V raised over entry to Henry VII's Chapel

relegated to plaques.

The eccentricity of the crossing is best characterised by the Nightingale monument (1761) in the east aisle of the north transept. Lady Elizabeth Nightingale, whose right to lie in the abbey is obscure, was struck by lightning on a walk and died of shock. Roubiliac depicts death emerging from a vault to hurl his arrow at the fainting lady, defended by her desperate husband. John Wesley wrote of this work that 'here indeed the marble seems to speak'. Canning, Gladstone and Disraeli look on in mute horror.

The crossing leads eastwards up steps to the sanctuary. Here begins the business part of the abbey. This is the venue for coronations, royal weddings, funerals and memorial services, the space shifting from public to semi-private, from expansive to enclosed. The abbey becomes in effect a royal family chapel. Even Elizabeth II requested in 1953 that cameras be averted from her 'sacred anointment' as queen, on the grounds that this (surely) public moment was private to her.

Overlooking the sanctuary is perhaps Scott's greatest work as a master of the gothic revival, the Westminster reredos. It is of alabaster, marble, cedar and porphyry, studded with jewels and framing a mosaic of the Last Supper by Antonio Salviati. In front is the much earlier medieval pavement laid down in 1268 by the Italian Odoricus in a style known as Cosmati. It is said to depict the universe. The sedilia are not of stone but of wood, apparently to ease their removal during coronations.

The abbey now becomes more private still. Beyond the sanctuary lies the refetory of the shrine of Edward the Confessor. It is the emotional and spiritual core of the abbey, encircled with tombs and chantries mostly of Plantagenet monarchs. The place is dark and claustrophobic, the holy of holies of Plantagenet England.

Edward's coffin was much abused in the Reformation and is now replaced by a simple renaissance box on the original 13th-century pedestal. This is of Purbeck marble inlaid with precious stones. In an oval round the shrine lie tombs, like wagons drawn close to defy any challenge to their claim to the Confessor's throne. Each is the finest exemplar of the art of its day. Much debate has gone into how far the effigies on top of the tombs are true to life. Their vitality and variety make it hard to believe they are not.

We now proceed round the abbey's eastern arm in a clockwise direction, from north to south, including Henry VII's Chapel. The north curve of the oval includes Henry III himself in bronze, serene, effete, with dress

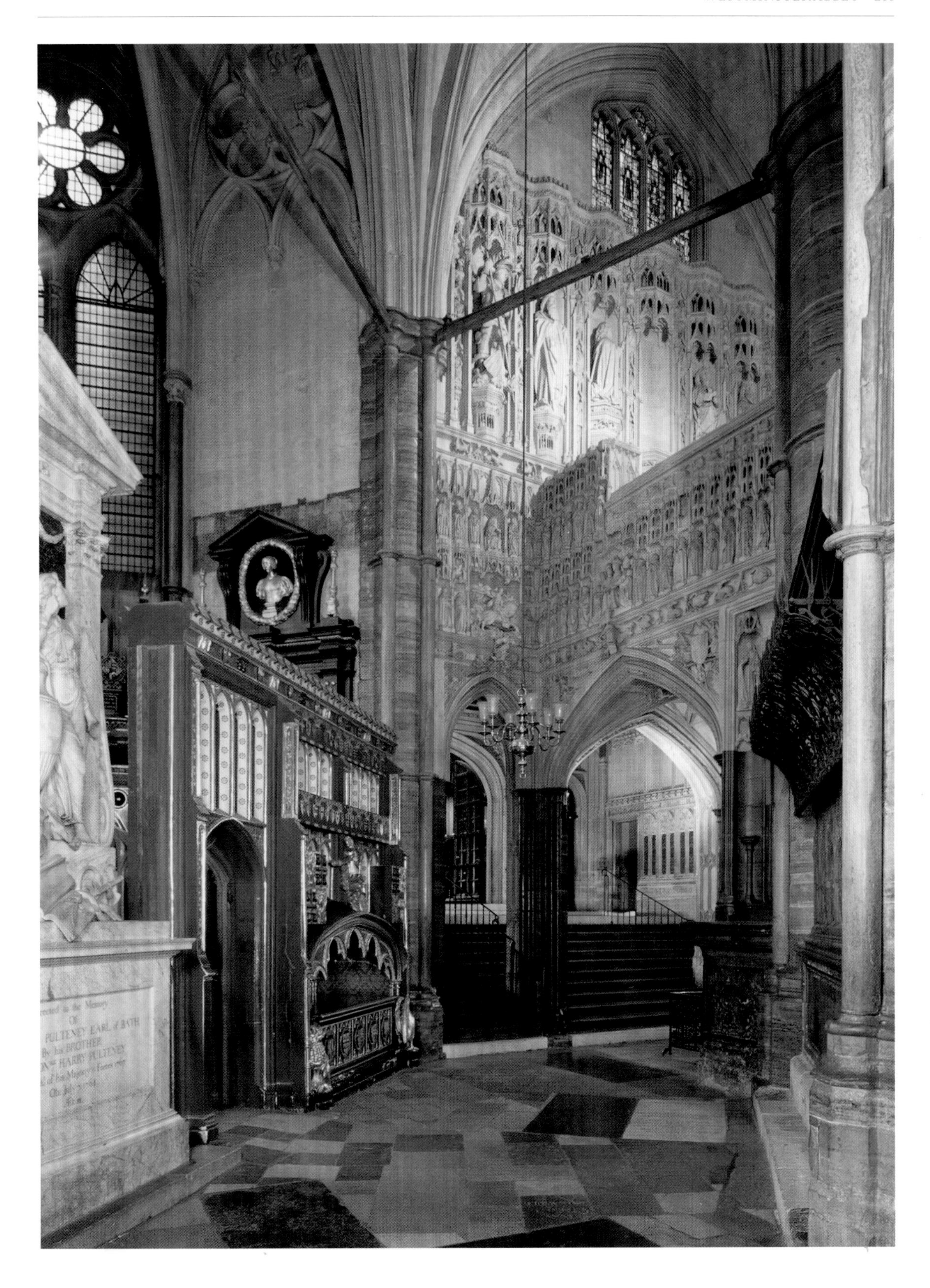
OF
PULTENEY EARL of BATH
By his BROTHER
HARRY PULTENEY

Left
Tudor magnificence:
Henry VII Chapel

flowing free. Edward I's tomb carries no decoration or effigy, just the single inscription to him as 'hammer of the Scots'. Nothing so evokes raw Plantagenet power as this cold memorial. His adored wife, Eleanor of Castile, lies more sensitive in gilded bronze.

Outside the refetory, the north ambulatory is crammed with monuments. Courtiers and lesser royals jostle with aristocrats and soldiers. The Chapel of St John the Baptist contains the biggest tomb in the abbey, of Lord Hunsdon (1596) and his wife, a 36ft-high façade, as of a renaissance villa. The shambles of memorabilia is enjoyable for those with a sense of humour. The statues are like film stars at a premiere, furious at finding themselves herded into a group photograph.

Overlooking the refetory is the elevated chantry of Henry V, towering over its eastern apex. The early death of the young monarch in 1422 caused a memorial crisis. There had supposedly been no room at the abbey for his father, the usurper of Richard II's throne, Henry IV, who was buried with his wife at Canterbury. But before departing for Agincourt in 1415, Henry V ensured this was rectified by planning his own tomb, to face Edward the Confessor and dispel any air of illegitimacy.

The coffin was duly squeezed in east–west, with a miniature chantry raised into the space overhead. This has to be reached by two turret staircases and is festooned with late-gothic motifs, niches, plinths and tracery. Its reredos is a display of 15th-century sculpture, missing only the Trinity in the central niche. The vault beneath displays Henry's emblems and coats of arms, making a dramatic entrance to Henry VII's Chapel beyond.

No such reticence afflicted Henry VII. His chapel, located east of the original outer wall of the abbey, was intended first as a Lady Chapel and then as a shrine to Henry VI, whom Henry VII hoped to have canonised as a saint in resolution of the Wars of the Roses. When this strategy failed, the chapel became his own memorial, with a stipulation that 10,000 masses be said for his soul. It went on to become the mausoleum of his Tudor and Stuart descendants.

The chapel is one of the most ethereal chambers in England. Begun in 1503, it was probably designed by the royal master mason, William Vertue. The walls are composed almost entirely of Perpendicular windows, supported on the thinnest of wall piers. Above is not so much a fan vault as an umbrella vault, divided by ribs encrusted with crockets. The pendants, more delicate even than those in Oxford cathedral, seem to float in space, their

Left
Elizabeth I

Opposite
Final repose: the Little Cloister

honeyed stone defying reason and gravity alike. Vertue, with his brother Robert, was author of similar but heavier vaults at Bath Abbey and St George's Chapel, Windsor.

The chapel walls are filled with statues, over a hundred in all, some of saints and kings, some of tiny animals and heraldic symbols pinned to the insides of arches. It is a gallery of history, religion and mythology at the climax of medieval England.

Then comes the conundrum. In the centre of the chapel lies the tomb of the Lancastrian Henry VII and his wife, Elizabeth of York, a marriage whose symbolism was intended to mark an emphatic end to the Roses Wars. Whether intentionally or not, the tomb also symbolised a cultural transition. For it is not gothic but Italian renaissance.

Designed by an Italian craftsman, Pietro Torrigiano, the tomb is in gilded bronze and lies on an ornate renaissance chest. The king lies in prayer next to his wife, his faced lined with care, his garments a swirl of opulence. Pevsner sees in it 'a gentleness and tenderness and a unison of life-likeness with sheer beauty of modelling unprecedented in England'. Yet it seems odd to celebrate this most English of moments in an imported style.

The chapel's choir stalls are original, as are the misericords. The stall canopies are more military than devout, carrying the helms and swords of the Order of the Bath. Above hang colourful banners of the Order's members. Only the east windows jar, dedicated to the RAF in a discordant bright blue.

The chapel is flanked by secret aisles, burial chambers of the Tudor and Stuart dynasts. In the north aisle is Elizabeth I, buried with her sister, Mary I, who gets no effigy. She lies in prayer, handsome rather than ostentatious, beneath a baroque canopy. Beyond her, against the west wall, is the 'innocents' corner', for royal children who died in infancy. It supposedly includes the recovered bones of the murdered 'princes in the tower'.

In the south aisle is the monument to Henry VII's mother, the redoubtable Lady Margaret Beaufort, with gothic headdress, again by Torrigiano. Also in this aisle is Mary Queen of Scots in a more flamboyant baroque style than her nemesis Elizabeth. Scottish thistles adorn the coffering. She is accompanied by the Stuarts, Charles II, Mary II (and William) and Anne. Around them are arrayed their courtiers, including Buckingham, Lennox, Albemarle. This astonishing array of royalty is, in my experience, little visited except by foreign tourists. The English prefer their history in books and films.

Back in the south ambulatory, the south

curve contains Edward III with a long beard, his troublesome children depicted as bronze weepers round the base. His Queen Philippa has a realistic middle-aged face. Finally is the tomb of the unfortunate Richard II and his wife Anne of Bohemia. His face is uncannily like the portrait of him hanging at the west end of the nave. The effigies of the couple seem to consummate late-medieval beauty, cushioned in royal wealth and attended by lions, harts, eagles and leopards. St Edmund's Chapel has tombs from the 13th to the 17th century and two superb brasses.

Westminster's monastic outbuildings are chiefly remarkable for having survived the succeeding waves of development that have swept past them across the modern city. The Great Cloister was built in the 13th and 14th centuries. It forms a spacious antechamber to Henry III's chapter house, begun in 1246. Its double-arched portal leads to a majestic chamber. The vault rises from a 'palm tree' pillar, its ribs soaring and then dipping between the windows. The building was entirely reconstructed by Scott and is regarded as his most masterly restoration. The floor retains its medieval tiles, and the panels behind the seats have traces of medieval paintings.

Beyond the Great Cloister, a maze of passages and alleys leads to the Little Cloister, my favourite spot in the abbey. Here within just a hundred yards of Parliament Square, we might be in a corner of some rural cathedral close. It is a place of quiet repose, with only a tinkling fountain to disturb the birdsong.

WESTMINSTER RC

The Most Precious Blood, St Mary, St Joseph and St Peter
Italianate exterior, marble veneering, Gill reliefs, Arts and Crafts chapel

★★★

Westminster cathedral has always suffered from not being Westminster Abbey. It is a half-Italian, half-Byzantine immigrant, housed at the other end of Victoria Street. The tall bell-tower is elegant, but the church at its feet is a jumble of Mediterranean motifs bulldozed into a heap. It is protected from behind by the redbrick ramparts of the archbishop's palace, diocesan offices and an enclave of stately mansion flats.

The cathedral was begun by Cardinal Vaughan in 1895 after his predecessor, Cardinal Manning, had stalled on the project for years, wondering if such money should rather go to schools and the poor. In commissioning the architect J. F. Bentley, Vaughan was insistent it should be different from the abbey down the road. 'Not the abbey' became something of an obsession, like the later stylistic rivalry between Liverpool's cathedrals. As it was, the basilica form offered a simple, large volume for worship, and also meant that interior decoration could easily be left to later.

The campanile is italianate, of brick with white stone bands rising to a colonnaded lantern. It is what a London tower should be, a proper architectural statement, not just a tall thing. Until recently, it shared prominence with Big Ben on the Westminster skyline, but is now lost amid tawdry towers. The west façade below is more reminiscent of Byzantium, crowded with buttressed turrets, strange arches and an over-elaborate tympanum above the west door. Bentley originally proposed a second tower to balance the first, which might have helped.

The cathedral's interior is altogether different. This is one of London's finest indoor spaces. Bentley composed a nave of three domed bays, followed by a larger domed crossing over the sanctuary. In the air above hovers a gigantic 30ft cross in bright red and gold. The upper two-thirds of the cathedral are unfinished, and peer out of the gloom in blackened brickwork. It is astonishingly grim, like some Piranesian prison. Even the clerestory windows are prison-like. Bentley intended this upper part of the building to be covered in mosaics, but this has yet to happen. There is not even a lick of paint.

Meanwhile, the ground floor has progressed as Bentley intended and is now an almost alarming contrast. Installation of the marble veneering did not begin until the 1950s, taking half a century to complete; before

Left
West End Byzantine: cathedral from west

then the cathedral must have looked dire. It is now of great richness and variety.

Each arcade is subdivided into double-arches, shielding galleries above. The space is ablaze with colour, with aisles and chapels glittering under the darkness above. Over 125 different marble types have been identified, some from the same Thessaly quarries as were used for Constantinople's Hagia Sophia.

The colours are green, blue, grey, yellow and red. This is no longer any prison, but the shallowness of the decoration leaves rather the impression of a sumptuous film set awaiting the arrival of the actors.

The arcade piers carry Eric Gill's fourteen stations of the cross. They are complex narrative scenes portrayed in a highly stylised fashion, at times art nouveau, at times almost Byzantine. Gill was commissioned as a relative unknown in 1914. He responded to a protest that they 'did not look nice' by saying the subject was not nice either. The guidebook says they are today considered his finest works.

The cathedral's most rewarding feature is its complete circuit of side-chapels. Their completed walls of marble and roofs of mosaic give some idea how Bentley envisaged the entire church to appear. The chapels all date from the 20th century and constitute one of England's finest collections of religious art.

Starting from the left of the entrance, the Holy Souls Chapel (1908) is by Bentley himself, its vault a mosaic of Christ as the new Adam crushing the serpent. The dark marble altar hints at art deco. Further round, the Chapel of St George has an altarpiece by Gill, his last work, of Christ with the martyrs St Thomas More and St John Fisher. More was originally holding a monkey but this was later chipped off as somehow undignified. In the same

Left
Nave: cathedral as stage set

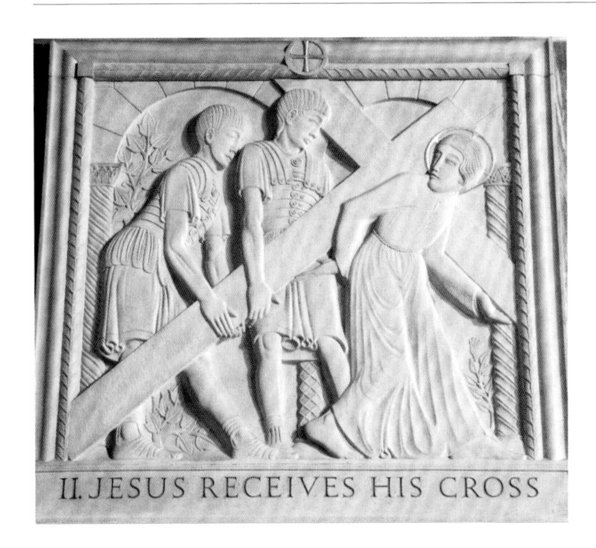

Opposite
Barnsley kneelers in St Andrew's Chapel

Left
Eric Gill: stations of the cross

chapel is the kneeler used by Elizabeth II in 1995, the first time an English monarch had attended a Catholic service since the Reformation.

The Chapel of St Joseph has a fierce modern mosaic by Christopher Hobbs of the Holy Family, looking as if they had just been visited by Westminster social services. The window has a column of *fior di pesco* (peach blossom) marble beneath a basket of doves, an exquisite work. The Vaughan chantry displays Hobbs' depiction of the death of Becket, mosaic used in the pointillist style of Georges Seurat.

We now cross the sanctuary in front of the baldacchino. It teeters on the edge of kitsch but is rescued by a lovely archbishop's throne, a facsimile of that in St John Lateran in Rome. The Lady Chapel is Bentley's masterpiece, guarded by two piers of black and grey marble. The chapel is proclaimed as Bentley's template for the entire cathedral. The ceiling drips with flowers and angels.

The most notable chapel on the north side is St Andrew's, devoted to all things Scottish. The murals depict the town of St Andrews, bizarrely flanked by Amalfi and Milan and gazing at Constantinople opposite. The chapel contains one of the finest works of the Arts and Crafts movement, Ernest Gimson's stalls of 1912. They are upright and slender, of ebony wood inlaid with bone. A decade later, Gimson's colleague, Sidney Barnsley, added kneelers in the same style, again of surpassing beauty. Ian Nairn was a great admirer of this chapel. It was 'a real work of being, style and expression pounding together'.

Westminster cathedral is a place of many such contrasts. We are left to imagine what it might be like if Bentley's vision were one day at last to be realised. It awaits enticingly.

WINCHESTER

The Holy Trinity, St Peter, St Paul and St Swithun

Longest nave, flooded crypt, Norman transepts, choir stalls carvings, Gardiner's chantry

Winchester has never been love at first sight. Externally, it is big rather than beautiful. It is big when seen from St Catherine's Hill where, as Pevsner says, it lies 'brooding in its valley bottom'. It looms big across its lawn to visitors emerging down alleys from the high street. It is big inside. Nor is bigness offset by any tower or spire. Winchester is also very long.

The city was capital of Saxon England and its cathedral therefore took precedence over London. Here kings were crowned, treasure was stored and power resided. The outline of Alfred the Great's church can still be seen plotted in the grass outside the north-west wall – though it looks desperately small compared with its Norman neighbour.

The cathedral's then patron was St Swithun, adviser to Alfred's father, Aethelwulf. He was canonised for performing such useful miracles as repairing a basket of eggs which a woman dropped on her way to market. When his body was moved from outside to inside the old church (on 15 July 971), his posthumous anger was such that it rained for forty days. If it now rains on St Swithun's Day, even weather forecasters feel obliged to mention it. The path between Canterbury and Winchester along the North Downs was one of the great pilgrim ways of England.

After the Conquest, Norman respect for Saxon pride ensured Winchester's swift replacement by something bigger. The first Norman bishop, Walkelin, began work as early as 1079 with a nave that, at 558ft, was to be (and remains) the longest medieval nave in the world. Unfortunately, he paid no thought to foundations. The ground on which they were built was so damp that the crypt is regularly under water during rainy months. The unstable tower fell into the transept as early as 1107 and no one has dared replace it.

Winchester's story then followed the familiar pattern, of a gothic rebuilding of the eastern arm to meet the needs of St Swithun pilgrims, followed, two centuries later, by a Perpendicular rebuilding of the nave. This rebuilding, under the patronage of the most powerful statesman of late 14th-century England, William Wykeham, was sensational.

Wykeham was in a line of self-made grandee bishops that held England together under the ever-warring Plantagenets. He was the son of a local peasant, rising through the church and royal administration

Left
Conqueror's romanesque: Norman north transept

12th CENTURY TOMB

to become clerk of works at Dover, Windsor and most of the royal castles. His talents as an administrator were prodigious. He was provost of Wells in 1365 when he met and became patron of a talented young architect, William Winford, with whom he was to be associated for the rest of his career. Winford was awarded the privilege of 'dining rights' at Wykeham's table for life.

By 1367, at the age of forty-three, Wykeham had become, among other offices, chancellor of England, bishop of Winchester and close confidant of the ageing Edward III. He was reputedly the richest man in the land, holding no fewer than twelve prebends (absentee but paid canonries). He survived the turbulent politics of Richard II's reign and devoted his later years to his home town where he founded what was to be a celebrated school, feeding pupils to his 'new' college at Oxford. He began rebuilding Winchester's nave in 1387 at his own expense, and died in 1404 before it was completed. To this day, alumni of Winchester College are Wykehamists.

Winchester's much-restored exterior needs little comment: indeed, the only picture of it in the guidebook is of the entrance front. It is the inside view that is breathtaking. On entering, we immediate confront Winford's nave. Its west wall is entirely composed of traceried glass, as of a vast conservatory. John Ruskin may have disliked its tedium, its 'carving knife' tiers of mullions that climb the façade until they bump into the top. The criticism is just, but the window remains a mammoth of 14th-century engineering. The tracery is filled with medieval fragments swept up after the Civil War. Beneath stand statues of James I and Charles I which were salvaged from the cathedral's former Inigo Jones screen.

Left
Scott's restored stalls, looking towards nave

Opposite
Gormley in flooded crypt

Winchester nave has inspired many similes, from cascading fountains and jousting tournaments to a canopy of palm tree fronds. I choose the palm trees. By day, the twelve bays soar from darkness into clerestory light, cross-lit by the sun. At night, the vault is transformed into the ceiling of a great antechamber, leading the eye to the presbytery beyond. On special occasions, the nave is hung with giant banners, by Thetis Blacker, depicting the Creation in vivid reds, blues and yellows.

In a west bay of the nave is a font of black Tournai marble, one of ten brought to England from Belgium in the mid-1100s. The carvings on the side include scenes of St Nicholas giving dowries for poor girls, and what is said to be the first depiction of a boat with a stern rudder. Nearby is the grave of Jane Austen, the slab making no reference to her being an author. There is some compensation in a later brass plaque, quoting from Proverbs, that 'She openeth her mouth with wisdom and in her tongue is the law of kindness.'

On the nave's south side is the jutting box of Wykeham's chantry. This intrusion into the symmetry of the nave was allowed since this was the spot, so the great man said, where as a boy he first heard mass. It is a towering creation of crockets and gables rising the full height of the bay, as if eager to break through the arch above. Inside, Wykeham's effigy lies richly clothed and in full colour, hugging his bishop's crozier and attended by angels and monks praying for his soul. It is said the Cromwellian officer assigned to smash it proved to be a Wykehamist and stayed his hand.

The crossing suddenly reverts three centuries to Walkelin's Norman cathedral. The nave's courtly music of the reign of Edward III is silenced by the war drums of William the Conqueror. Winchester and St Albans are regarded as the only cathedral interiors he would recognise today. They are all muscle and no prettiness. To Saxons still worshipping in the old cathedral next door, these massive walls must have seemed bastions of an alien power. Three tiers of arches rise to the roof, each tier a complex of single and double spans. There is no decoration. The triforium in the north transept contains a gallery with relics of the old cathedral, including a Madonna's head with paint still attached.

The north transept would have marked the final entry of pilgrims to St Swithun's shrine. It starts with the 12th-century Holy Sepulchre Chapel whose wall paintings of *c*1170 are in excellent preservation, having been discovered only during restoration in the 1960s. They

Left and opposite
Medieval tiles in retrochoir

depict the deposition from the cross and the burial in the tomb. Also in the north transept is the Epiphany Chapel, with a set of four windows by Edward Burne-Jones and an Eric Gill roundel of the Lamb of God, its limbs strangely contorted.

Steps from this transept lead down to the crypt. Here Winchester can be seen, in effect, 'floating' on its water-table. A statue in the retrochoir above honours William Walker, the diver who 'saved the cathedral' in the early 1900s by digging out peat in the crypt and replacing it with concrete sacks. The statue is less of him than of his diving suit. The crypt still regularly floods. This is celebrated in a water sculpture by and of Antony Gormley (1986), in which he stands naked, gazing at an image of himself in his cupped hands.

Back in the south transept is the Fisherman's Chapel, dedicated not to the high seas but to hobby fishing, with a portrait of Izaak Walton, 17th-century patron of anglers and once a resident of the cathedral close. The 1996 altar by Peter Eugene Ball is carved from a solid trunk of oak, adorned with swirls of water and fish. Next door, the Venerable Chapel's modernist altar has an electronic frontal by Rachel Schwalm that glows. In the centre of the transept is a Victorian monument to Samuel Wilberforce, son of the reformer; it is by George Gilbert Scott at his most lavishly neo-Decorated.

The choir screen is Scott in more scholarly vein. He at first declined to restore the battered original as too precious but, on later inspection, agreed on the basis that he would not touch any 'old work' and only replicate it. The result is an immaculate exercise in gothic revival. Depending on the light, the screen forms either a delicate backdrop to the nave altar or a dramatic silhouette against the presbytery beyond. The stalls of *c*1300 are, to Pevsner, 'the earliest and finest set of choir furniture in Europe of its date'.

We might wonder if their carver, William Lyngwode, had travelled to Southwell. Like the Southwell carvers, he depicts oak, hawthorn, ivy and vine, and avoids simpler shapes such as lime and ash. He includes human faces, smiling, grimacing, gurning in this holiest of places. In a spandrel, a well-dressed falconer tends his bird amid enveloping vines. The misericords below are no less enjoyable, including gossips, a cat with a mouse and a ridiculed bishop.

Over the sanctuary looms a stone reredos, partner to Wykeham's reredos in New College, Oxford. Its statues were smashed in the Reformation and were restored by J. R. Sedding in the 1870s. His work took a

bashing in turn – from the critics. Olive Cook wrote that the machine-chiselled features, stances and sentimental gestures 'highlight the dubiousness of the whole attempted return to the art of the Middle Ages'. I disagree. The statues may be more baroque than medieval, but this shows only how well Victorian sculpture can sit in a gothic setting.

On the screens to the north and south of the sanctuary are mortuary chests said to contain the bones of Saxon kings buried in the old cathedral, including Egbert and Canute, apparently to emphasise Winchester's historic primacy. The bones were scattered in the Civil War, but afterwards lovingly gathered up and put back, albeit at random.

Beyond the presbytery, we enter Winchester's retrochoir, one of England's most evocative gothic spaces. An Early Gothic chamber of clustered piers and rhythmic vaults, built for St Swithun's shrine, is crowded with chapels and chantries of those later celebrities of the church, bishops. Much of the floor is laid with the most extensive spread of medieval tiles in England. An enlightened policy allows visitors to walk on them, with any decayed and missing tiles replicated. The bosses in the vault overhead are like planets peering from a dark sky.

The former site of St Swithun's shrine is at the rear of the reredos, represented by nine niches with ogees and gables. Medieval statues lost in the Reformation were replaced in 1996 with icons by the Russian artist Sergei Fyodorov. At the foot of the screen's rear is a small door, known as the 'holy hole', through which pilgrims could crawl to 'sense the aura' of the saint. Swithun himself is commemorated by a spindly memorial chest of 1962.

The retrochoir is dominated by Winchester's four principal chantries. Each is a distinctive example of late-gothic design, lined up like Tudor galleons at anchor. First on the south side is the chantry of Bishop Fox, dated 1518. The tomb has his cadaver beneath, and is surrounded by a façade of intricate Tudor panels. The interior is a calm place, where the blind bishop spent hours in prayer, living on ten years after it was built. Beyond is the chantry of Cardinal Beaufort (1447), a lofty structure of niches and pinnacles but missing its statues.

On the north side of the retrochoir stands Bishop Waynflete's chantry, dated 1486. He rivalled Wykeham as an ecclesiastical grandee and educational patron, founding Magdalen College, Oxford. Here we see Perpendicular at full stretch, a crowded forest of pinnacles. The delicate interior could pass for 18th-century Strawberry Hill 'gothick', with fan vaults, liernes and roundels.

Opposite
'Galleon at anchor': Waynflete's chantry

Adjacent to the reredos is the final chantry, of Stephen Gardiner, opponent of Cranmer's Reformation, imprisoned under Edward VI and restored to his Winchester diocese and made Lord Chancellor during the return to the 'old religion' under Mary I. Gardiner was a dominant figure of the brief English counter-Reformation. He personally negotiated and conducted Mary's unpopular marriage to Philip of Spain in 1554 which was held at Winchester apparently to avoid the risk of anti-Catholic riots in London. Gardiner died a year later. His chantry of 1556 was probably the last to be built in England, and its survival into the reign of Elizabeth I shows her tolerance towards her sister's bishops.

The design is intriguing. On the outside, Perpendicular windows are set below a renaissance frieze. This merging is familiar in the Tudor period. What is less familiar is seen inside, where there is no compromise. It is as if the entire gothic era had collided with history. The chantry has a gothic ceiling but its reredos is of the high renaissance, with portico, capitals and classical entablature. We are left wondering if the interior was all by the same hand, or if the reredos was inserted later. Either way, we are witnessing the ghosts of the Middle Ages dissolve and those of the Elizabethan renaissance come into focus. In no cathedral does the old pass its baton to the new as vividly as in Gardiner's Winchester chantry.

The retrochoir culminates in the Perpendicular Lady Chapel. Its window is a minor version of the west window, its roof a star burst of liernes and bosses. On either side are the Guardian Angels Chapel and Bishop Langton's chantry. The first is named after its 13th-century ceiling, the second repainted in what is now the approved gothic colouring, not pastel but fairground bright.

Winchester ranks as the archetypal English cathedral. Its story embraces the highpoints of the medieval church, from Saxon significance to Norman Conquest and on to Plantagenet greatness and Reformation trauma. It begins with the north transept's defiant massif and ends in the exquisite equivocation of Gardiner's chantry. It is an eloquent journey through the history of these times.

Trophy
SCRIVEN

WORCESTER

Christ and the Blessed Virgin Mary

Riverside setting, Scott restoration, King John tomb, Norman crypt

★★★★

There are two Worcesters, one in heaven and the other hell. Heaven sits on a mound overlooking the River Severn, where its tower and west window gaze towards Wales over the loveliest of cricket fields. Hell arrived in the 1960s when the local council decided to drive a stretch of dual carriageway yards from the cathedral's north-east wall, adding insult to injury by positioning a modern shopping piazza directly opposite. Worcester wins my hotly contested prize for worst abuse of a cathedral setting.

At the time of the Conquest, the local bishop, Wulfstan, was one of the few Saxon prelates to collaborate with – or certainly impress – the Norman invaders. He was the only one to survive the Conquest unscathed, becoming a champion of the Normans' religious discipline and commitment. His priory had been a monastic cathedral since the 10th century but had dwindled to a dozen monks. On his death thirty years later, it had over fifty.

Wulfstan's Worcester became a centre of the fight to keep alive the language and culture of Anglo-Saxon scholarship against that of the invading Normans. In this respect, resistance was successful. But Wulfstan agonised over the Norman craze to rebuild. As his old cathedral was demolished, the seventy-four-year-old bishop is said to have wept, 'We have destroyed the work of saints. We neglect our souls, so we can build up stones.' It has been a wail of many in the Church of England ever since.

Whatever Wulfstan's views, he was close to Lanfranc of Canterbury and obediently pushed ahead with rebuilding. He was eventually canonised, his shrine joining that of his predecessor, Bishop Oswald, on the pilgrim trail. The future King John became so attached to his memory that he demanded in his will that he be buried next to his shrine, as indeed he was.

I find Worcester hard to assess. Compared with the wayward brilliance of neighbouring Gloucester, it seems a text-book cathedral, a gothic history lesson rather than a place of inspiration. This is despite offering a royal flush of styles – Norman crypt, transitional west nave, Early Gothic presbytery, Decorated nave and Perpendicular tower. One trouble is that it was massively restored in the 19th century, mostly by

Left
Cricket pays homage

George Gilbert Scott, to the extent that the east end is essentially Victorian. As with many buildings in the limestone belt, the eye can find it hard to appreciate a medieval building whose surface has been so patched over time.

The tower is inevitably compared with that at Gloucester. John Harvey is an admirer, finding the balance of vertical and horizontal features giving it 'strong claims to be regarded as the finest individual tower design of the whole gothic period'. I find it a little too squat, its decorative features too pronounced. But this is quibbling: it remains a superb structure – and one that no lover of cricket on the ground below can fail to appreciate.

The interior begins with the two westernmost bays of the nave, rebuilt in *c*1175 in transitional Norman/gothic style. The arcade arches are barely pointed and those in the triforium are Norman inside and pointed outside. To stand at the join between these bays and the remainder of the nave, rebuilt in the early 14th century, is to sense the presence of a seismic shift in European art, one that here is accomplished with effortless elegance. The nave's north side is Decorated, the south closer to Perpendicular, with thinner lines and meagre capitals. The west window is a superb geometrical composition. Slender lancets rise to support a multi-petalled rose. The stained glass depicting the Creation is a masterpiece of neo-medievalism by Hardman & Co.

As we reach the crossing, Scott's restoration becomes more insistent and perhaps controversial. It is so reworked that even a tutored eye finds it hard to assess the medieval from the Victorian. With Scott's work at Ely and Lichfield, this is no problem, but at Worcester the rebuilding jars. An exasperated Alec Clifton-Taylor railed against the

Left
Scott screen with chancel beyond

Opposite
Tomb of King John

'platitudinous screen, some very nasty seating, horrible floor-tiles and a lamentable (and all too prominent) reredos'. This seems harsh, as we cannot know the condition of the work Scott was restoring, but that applies to all restoration.

The original eastern arm of the cathedral straddled the evolution from Early Gothic to Decorated, with the choir and retrochoir a last elaborate variation on a lancet theme. Some of the Purbeck shafts soar a full 65ft up the wall. The triforium is a complex double-plane of arches, each with a (Victorian) musician in its spandrel. Above rise the clerestory lancets, which are repeated emphatically in the five giant lancets of the east window.

Despite Clifton-Taylor's strictures, the choir is a fine ensemble. Scott's screen is one of his collaborations with the Coventry metalworker Francis Skidmore, and is mercifully still in place (neighbouring Hereford's screen went to the V&A). It is carefully 'see-through' so as not to block the view from nave to choir. The eleven gables on Scott's high altar reredos echo the east end lancets. Among the furnishings, the only medieval survivals are the misericords beneath the stalls. They include a woman naked under a net riding a goat, another writing poetry, and a knight toppling another from his horse.

The choir, aisles and retrochoir are lined with sumptuous blind arcades, with medieval and Victorian carvings in their spandrels. Some tell of the horrors awaiting the damned in hell. Some relate biblical scenes. Others are domestic, with monks laying bricks, novices being chastised and knights fighting wild beasts. The iconoclasts thankfully did not touch this gallery of medieval art.

Worcester's sanctuary is elevated above the rest of the presbytery, to allow for Wulfstan's crypt underneath. Here pride of place in front of the high altar goes to King John whose body was brought here in 1216 after his death in Newark. Carved in the decade after his death, John's effigy is a jewel of 13th-century carving. At the king's shoulder are the local saints Oswald and Wulfstan. His sceptre has been broken off and his left hand holds a sword. His hair and beard are delicately carved, which some might say is more than he deserved.

On the south side of the sanctuary lies the chantry tomb of John's descendant, Prince Arthur, son of Henry VII and husband of the unfortunate Catherine of Aragon. After his sudden death at Ludlow in 1502 at the age of fifteen, he was laid to rest in Worcester 'on the foulest old wyndye and rainey daye'. It was said 'he had a hard heart who wept not'. The king and queen were so grieved they could not

Left
Charlotte Digby by Chantrey

Opposite
Crypt with Pietà

bring themselves to attend. England got Henry VIII instead.

The chantry has florid openwork panelling and a pendant in the lierne vaulted ceiling. It is a faint foretaste of the great chapel that Henry VII was to build, eventually for himself, at Westminster Abbey. There is no effigy, just a tomb coated in Tudor heraldry, reflecting Henry VII's obsession with his dubious right to the throne. When the iconoclasts arrived to smash Worcester's chantries, they baulked at defacing this Tudor one, destroying only the saints inside.

Wulfstan's crypt is one of the loveliest in England. Some of its pillars are thought to have survived from the Saxon church, with single-scallop capitals. The Norman arches are tall and mark out a curved ambulatory at the east end. As in Durham's Galilee Chapel, Worcester's crypt arches have a hint of Cordoba's mosque-cathedral, a ghost of the orient trespassing on Norman design. The crypt contains a lovely Pietà by Glynn Williams (1984), in which the figure of Christ is supported only by the disembodied hands of love.

The cathedral is crowded with monuments. Notable in the nave is that of John Beauchamp (*c*1400) and his wife, lying in full colour, their feet on greyhounds and their heads cushioned on gorgeous black swans, the epitome of medieval ostentation. In the north transept is Louis-François Roubiliac's 1746 monument to Bishop Hough, whose expulsion as President of Magdalen College, Oxford, by James II was the final catalyst of the 1688 revolution. On the north side of the retrochoir is a celebrated work of Regency emotionalism, Charlotte Digby by Francis Chantrey (1825). She looks passively up to heaven, while her hands lie poignant in her lap. At the west end of the north aisle, the Gerontius window commemorates a son of Worcester, Sir Edward Elgar, by A. K. Nicholson (1935).

Worcester's cloister, a Victorian rebuild, may lack Gloucester's spectacular fan vault but the sandstone arcades and lierne vaults form a square of blood-red tunnels, with lavishly panelled window openings dividing the monks' study bays. Off the cloister is Worcester's circular Norman chapter house, with a central pier rising to a stone vault. Dating from the early 12th century, it is the first example of this uniquely English form of episcopal governance. Some scholars have even attributed it to the Saxon cathedral and, more imaginatively, to the Saxon concept of local democracy, in which the elders sat in a circle to deny supremacy to any one. Round the sides are not the usual stalls but intersecting arcades.

YORK

St Peter

View from city walls, Heart of Yorkshire window, Five Sisters window, chapter house stalls

I am in awe of York. It is the seat of England's second archbishop and, as such, the second church in the kingdom. It revels in superlatives, the largest gothic church by volume, the biggest chapter house, the finest windows, the most medieval glass. To me, its outstanding feature is its setting, towering over a city which is still defined by its medieval walls. The view of the minster from any point along York's city walls shows it rising in almost surreal majesty. Shimmering white in daylight, ablaze with the sun at dusk or coated in winter mist, it offers one of the most glorious urban views in England. York Minster and its city are one.

Bede records Christians in Roman York in AD 180 but firmer history began in 625, when the pagan king, Edwin of Northumbria (616–33), returned from wars in the south with a new Christian bride, Ethelburga, sister of Ealdwald of Kent. A condition of the match was that Edwin become a Christian and his wife be accompanied by her chaplain, Paulinus. This chaplain duly founded a new church at York, but under the Roman rite, not that of Northumbria's local missionaries from Iona. Later, at the Synod of Whitby in 664, Rome triumphed over the Ionans and the seat of the Roman church in the north was henceforth Paulinus's York, a minster never a monastery. Though a cathedral, it is always referred to as 'the minster'.

York was always politically significant. Its archbishop, Ealdred, crowned both Edward the Confessor and Harold Godwinson and was summoned to crown William the Conqueror in 1066, a gesture of national unity and continuity. But it was not until the 1080s that the north was sufficiently settled for a new church to be built under Thomas of Bayeux. Money came from a diocese whose lands and sixty-five tributary monasteries covered northern England south of Durham. The murder by poisoning of a bishop, William Fitzherbert, in 1154 gave York a (modest) candidate for sainthood and a shrine, although he was not canonised until 1227.

The minster's walls and stained glass went on to celebrate, not just the saints and princes of the church, but the heraldic devices of the great families of the north. Particular favour was shown to those who supported the Plantagenet monarchs in their wars against the Scots, the Nevilles, Percys, Mowbrays, Cliffords and Hastings, whose shields adorn

Left
Minster from the city walls

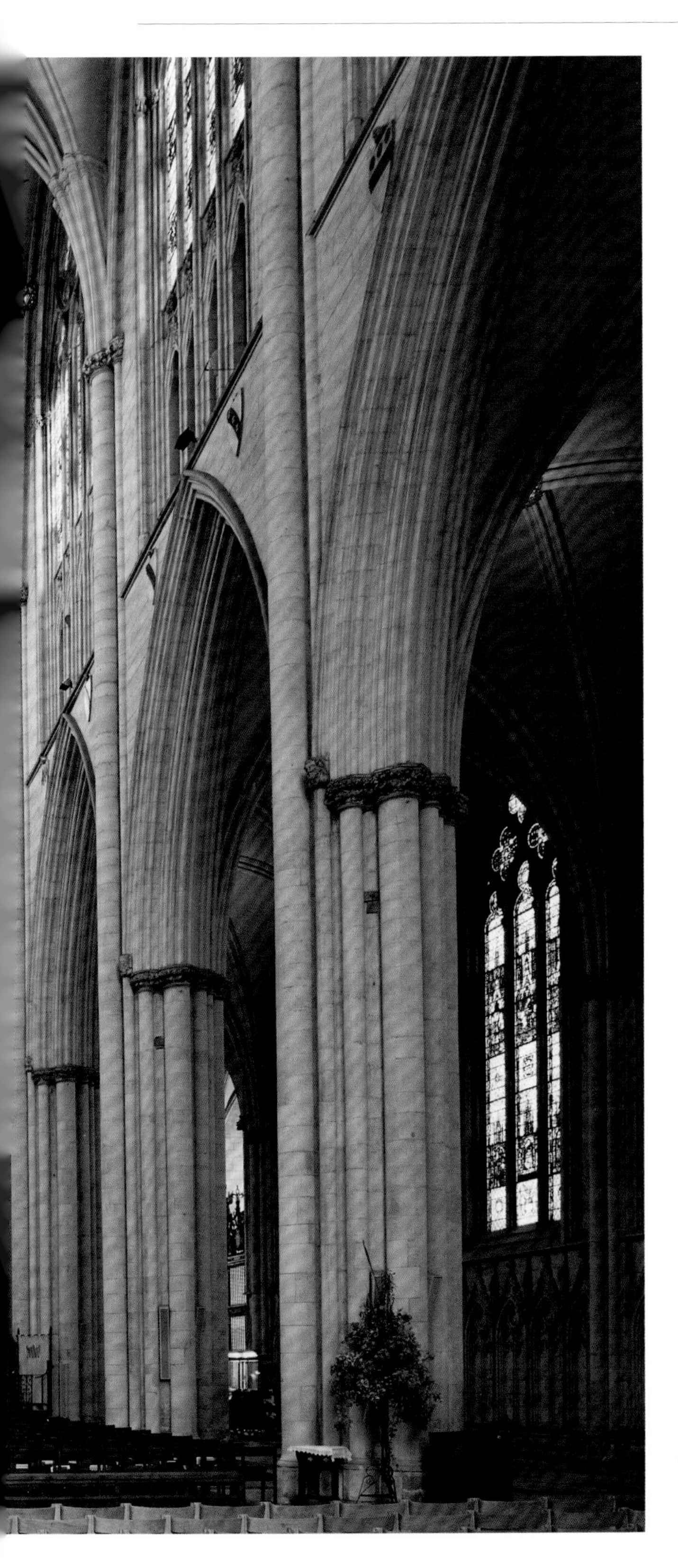

the nave. The crossing screen carries statues of the House of Lancaster (not of York). This was no isolated monastery but a church at one with the politics of the day, its territory and its rulers.

While the celebrated views of the exterior are from the city walls, equally rewarding are closer ones emerging from the press of surrounding streets. Towers, buttresses and windows are glimpsed from along Petergate or Stonegate, popping up from odd angles like a remembered friend. From the Middle Ages at least into the 16th century, we must imagine them rising in massive supremacy over a city of low cottages, roofed with thatch and oozing smoke. Even today, the planners have kept York's roofline blessedly low.

The minster rests on just 5ft of foundation, meaning that the exterior is visually compromised by the need for stability. There are buttresses everywhere, crowding the proportion of the walls and windows. While the west towers have pinnacles, the larger central tower was considered too delicate to support them, its plainness relieved by pairs of long bell-openings on each side. The exterior of the south transept exterior is extraordinary. Four ungainly tiers of lancets rise to the gable, with three triangular niches over the doorway. Clifton-Taylor calls the composition 'over-exuberant … deficient in horizontal articulation … lancets popping up all over the place'. To me it is a rare case of bad-taste gothic, as if the apprentices had run riot when their master was away.

York's exterior defers to its west front. Here the dominant feature is the celebrated west window known as the Heart of Yorkshire and a favourite backdrop to York wedding groups. While the glass is best studied inside, the

Left
Apotheosis of space: the nave

Opposite
'England's finest window': the Heart of Yorkshire

glorious Decorated tracery is visible outside. Completed in 1339, the window has eight slender lancets rising to a burst of ribs forming an oval pierced by another oval, hence the heart.

Beneath is now rightly the main entrance – previously in the south transept. The essence of the minster's iconography lies in a narrative progression from west to east, the story of human salvation, as told in windows, capitals and bosses. The initial view that greets the visitor is astonishing. Here is the largest interior volume in medieval England, dating from the reign of Edward II and a high point of the Decorated era. But unlike other naves of the period, York displays hints of a new 'perpendicularity'. Shafts rise uninterrupted from floor to roof. The triforium merges stylistically into the clerestory, creating a single, vertical panel. This is English gothic already in transition from the emotional expressionism of Decorated to a Perpendicular fascination with space.

Space is York's forte. The nave is too wide for its height, necessitating a wood rather than stone vault. The resulting volume forms a playground of light, with beams of sunlight roaming as if at will, dancing with piers and capitals, illuminating one object after another as if subject only to the seasons and the time of day.

From the west end of the nave we can now see the Heart of Yorkshire window in all its medieval glory, to my mind the finest window in all England. Its subject is the authority of the church, depicting bishops below, then saints, then the events of the Bible and finally a climax in the Coronation of the Virgin. It is a meticulous composition, by a craftsman in complete control of his medium. We know him only as Master Ivo, with glass by Master Robert.

Overhead, the vault is a Victorian replica following a fire in 1840. The copies of the original bosses are exact, except for one that was censored. Second from the west is Mary feeding Jesus anachronistically from a bottle, since the Victorians would not tolerate breast-feeding in church. Jutting out from the triforium above the north arcade is a strange wooden dragon, used to raise and lower a former font cover. In the north aisle, the sixth window from the west shows York's bell-founder Tunnoc (d.1330) making his donation of that window to the church.

We now ascend to the transepts. Both are Early Gothic and dominated by their windows. Most celebrated, in the north transept, is the Five Sisters window, dating from 1255. Five lancets, at 53ft the tallest in England, rise to

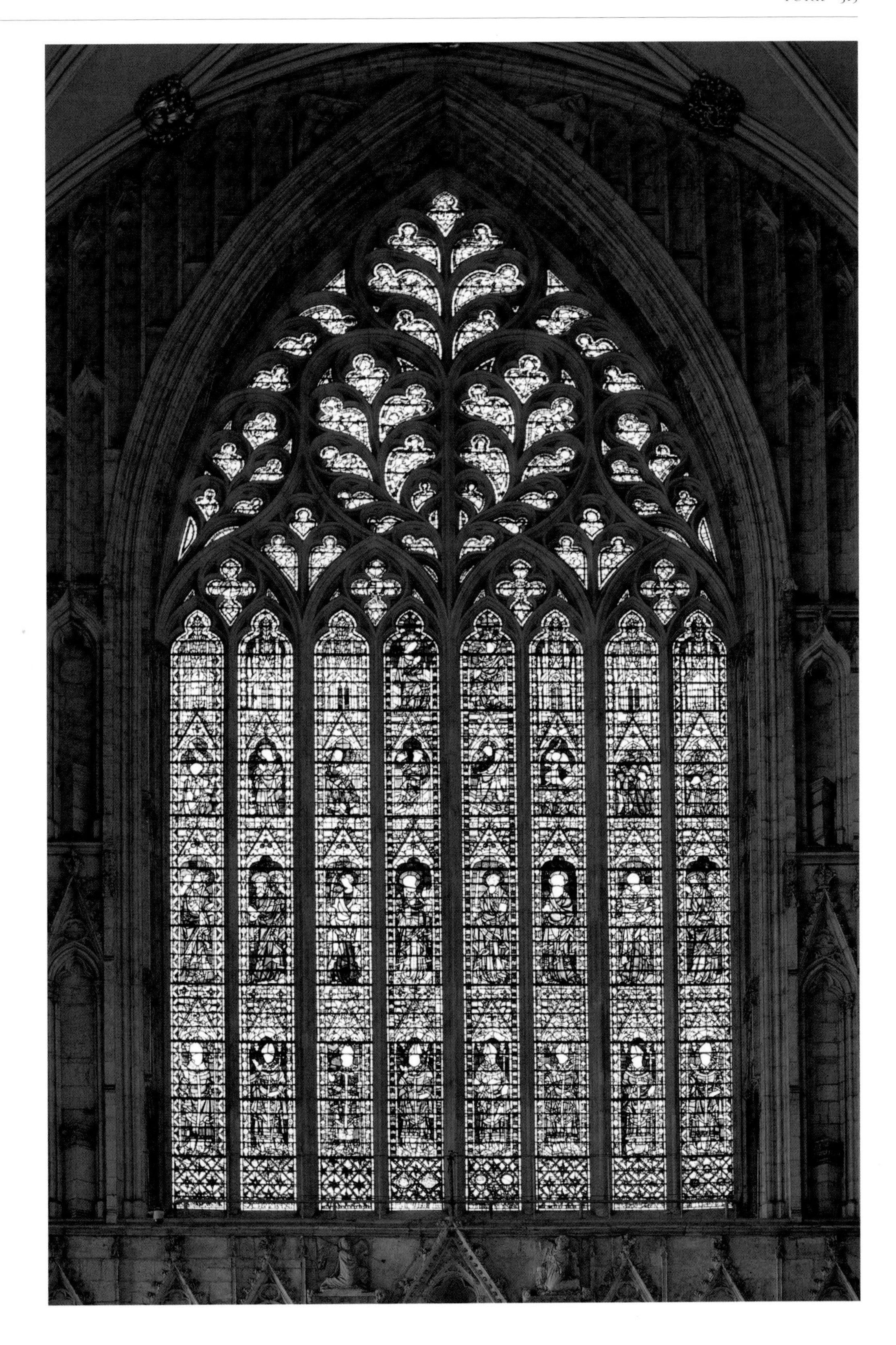

Left
Chapter house head

Opposite
Conquest of Space boss

support five stepped lancets in the gable. The glass is original, composed of over 100,000 tiny panes of grey dotted with points of colour, like carpets of semi-precious stones. It is tempting to try to find patterns in the glass, like a giant Rorschach test, but there is none. At the foot of the central light is a tiny panel of Daniel in the lion's den, transferred from an earlier Norman light.

Next to the window is an astronomical clock, a memorial to wartime aircrews. It depicts the position of the sun in relation to York, and the stars by which the aircrews were often required to navigate. In the south transept is a rose window. This was known as a marigold window from its tracery pattern, but this changed in the 1500s with the insertion of lights depicting red and white roses in honour of the union of Lancaster and York. The south transept roof was rebuilt after a fire in 1984. Sixty-eight new bosses were carved for it, including on such contemporary topics as 'saving the whale' and 'man on the moon'.

York's central crossing embraces a tower vault almost as exhilarating as Ely's, its roof of elegant fans seeming to float on a cloud of light from side windows. Below is the 14th-century pulpitum. Its off-centre doorway is due to the screen (like that of Canterbury) being a work of propaganda. It displays fifteen statues of monarchs from William I to Henry V, glorifying the house of Lancaster. The early death of Henry V necessitated a hurried redesign, with the asymmetric insertion of Henry VI. His subsequent murder led to a cult of veneration of this one statue, leading first to its removal and then to a Victorian replacement. There is more politics to a cathedral than we can imagine.

The Norman choir survived long into the gothic era, and was not finally rebuilt until the 1360s, in the Perpendicular style. However, the furnishings are Victorian replacements following a fire started by a madman in 1829. They look authentic enough, although a decision was made not to supply new misericords. The stalls in the sanctuary are by Robert 'Mousey' Thompson, with his mouse trademark carved on many of them.

York now rather runs out of steam, so much so that many critics find it lacks the sense of mystery needed to uplift a great English cathedral. There is a brief burst of Perpendicular excitement in the eastern transepts, short stubs that are in effect tall bay windows. But there is no real retrochoir and the east end barely exists. Clifton-Taylor describes York as becoming 'staid and earth-bound', and even Paul Johnson reports the view that it has 'splendour without beauty,

magnificence without charm'. A modest Lady Chapel is set into the east wall.

Instead, all eyes turn up to the east window, at 1680 sq ft reputedly the largest expanse of medieval glass in the world (but *see* Gloucester). The survival in the minster of so much glass – a quarter of England's medieval total – is York's pride and joy, albeit much of it plain grisaille in the clerestory. The glazier of the east window was John Thornton of Coventry, commissioned to complete the task in just three years from 1405. It was saved from destruction in the Civil War by an explicit treaty with Fairfax's besieging army.

The window lacks the curvilinear vitality of the Heart of Yorkshire, but still has panache. Rockets of colour shoot upwards to fracture into hearts and tulips. Four mouchettes hover like teardrops from the apex. The glass depicts angels, patriarchs and saints above scenes from the Bible and the Apocalypse. At the bottom are scenes from York's history. The window is an illuminated manuscript in glass, the medieval mind in faith, work and play, metaphysics interwoven with the workaday. When the burghers of York saw the finished work, they made Thornton a freeman of the city on the spot. The east window has been undergoing one of the most ambitious works known to medieval restoration.

York minster is strangely poor in monuments. No kings are buried here. The county's great families preferred to patronise their local churches. Most memorials are therefore to bishops, the north and south choir aisles being crowded with them. In the south transept is the tomb of Walter de Gray (d.1255), with swirling lines and dragons playing at his feet. The north choir aisle has the tomb of Edward III's baby son, Prince William (d.1337), depicted as older than his infant years, with flowing mantle and under a painted canopy. Illustrative of the post-Restoration mood is a pompous tomb of Archbishop Dolben (d.1686) in the south choir aisle, reclining arrogantly among cherubs.

York's chapter house is the largest and most impressive in England. It is reached through a vestibule with blind arcading and foliate carving. Above is a mason's loft, a rare survival (*see* Wells) of a medieval architects' workshop, or tracing floor, and with some of its drawings extant.

The chamber is entered through a modest double doorway under a trefoil arch, which has on its central pier a lovely statue of the Virgin. Begun towards the end of the 13th century, the roof has no central support and is thus of wood rather than stone. The span of 58ft is supported on a network of beams that continues to amaze engineers.

The chapter house windows are perhaps the first in England to act as walls in themselves, rather than openings in walls. Seven in number, they carry geometrical tracery of great subtlety. In each, five lights rise to a maze of bars, from which emerge three circles filling the gable. Their cusps spin before our eyes. The stained glass is a programme of figures set in grisaille backgrounds. There are 140 panels that depict Christ's Passion and a plethora of saints.

The chapter house's stone stalls and their canopies rival the medieval glass among the minster's treasures. Each is flanked by free-standing Purbeck shafts, rising to an octagonal crown with gables. They ripple round the edge of the chamber with an almost musical rhythm. From each canopy drop pendants heavy with stiff-leaf and birds. Kings, queens, bishops and green men seem to dart in and out of forests of vegetation. Here is a gallery of medieval faces, laughing, scowling, gurning, representing the joys and fears, deeds and misdeeds of their creators. Here, in the 'board room' of the great enterprise that was a medieval cathedral, we see all of humanity on display.

Left
Chapter house with 'gallery of faces' on stall capitals

GLOSSARY

ambulatory — *an aisle surrounding the chancel, usually with chapels on the outside.*

apse — *semi-circular or polygonal extension at the east end of the chancel.*

arcade — *row of arches usually between nave and aisle, divided by columns or other forms of pier. Arcading can also be blank or 'blind', a decorative form applied to a wall.*

baldacchino — *canopy of stone or wood over the altar, usually supported by four columns.*

ballflower — *stone ornament of crudely petalled flower inside a ball, usually arranged in a chain round the moulding of an arch. Feature of Decorated gothic at the turn of the 14th century.*

bay — *division of a wall defined by a single arch or window and continuing up into the vault.*

boss — *roof decoration covering the join or intersection of ribs, often elaborately carved.*

canon — *member of a cathedral chapter, normally in receipt of estate revenues or prebends, and thus a prebendary canon.*

capital — *architectural feature on top of column, focus of decorative invention since classical times and typically indicating date. Norman capitals were mostly cushion, trumpet or scallop; gothic were various forms of stiff-leaf.*

chancel — *term for the east end of a church, traditionally reserved for the clergy and separated from the nave by a screen; it can embrace choir, sanctuary and retrochoir. It is most often called a presbytery in a cathedral.*

chantry — *miniature chapel with altar at which masses could be said for the soul of a wealthy benefactor. Outlawed at the Reformation.*

chapter — *governing body of a cathedral, headed by the dean (not the bishop) and composed of canons.*

chevron — *Norman decoration in the form of zigzags.*

Left
Monks' carrels, Chester

clerestory — *top tier of cathedral interior containing a row of windows.*

corbel — *wall projection usually supporting a feature of the roof above, often elaborately carved, sometimes with grotesques.*

crocket — *decoration of stone curled leaves 'crawling' up a slope of a gable or pinnacle.*

cusp — *projection between the interior lobes of a gothic arch.*

Decorated — *second phase of gothic building in England, after Early (English) Gothic. Chiefly typified by window tracery and multi-shafted arcades. Roughly 1250–1340.*

dogtooth — *tooth-like – or, rather, fang-like – decoration set into the moulding of an arch, Early Gothic successor to Norman chevron.*

Early Gothic — *first phase of gothic architecture in England, arriving from France and characterised by the pointed lancet window. Formerly termed Early English, now more correctly Early Gothic. Roughly 1190–1250.*

fan vault — *later Perpendicular roof decoration, in which panels of ribs in each bay are formed into a fan.*

galilee — *confusing term applied to a porch or vestibule used in the Easter ritual as Christ's point of departure. In Durham, it is a Lady Chapel.*

garth — *area enclosed by a cloister, usually a garden.*

green man — *a face carved on a wall or capital with foliage emerging from mouth, ears and even eyes. Assumed to be related to pre-Christian forest rituals, sometimes as symbols of evil, sometimes of fertility and rebirth.*

grisaille — *grey-white opaque glass, admitting more light than coloured glass, often used in late-gothic clerestories.*

hammerbeam — *wooden arm projecting from wall to carry support for a roof, thus narrowing its span.*

Jesse window	*window depicting Christ's ancestry back to Jesse, usually depicted at the foot of the window, with the tree emerging from his navel.*
Lady Chapel	*special chapel devoted to the Virgin Mary, often erected in pride of place at the east end of a cathedral.*
lancet	*narrow pointed window without internal division, typical of Early Gothic period. Also a 'blind' version in wall decoration.*
lierne rib	*subsidiary rib in a vault not linked to pier or ridge and thus purely decorative; feature of Decorated and Perpendicular gothic.*
minster	*originally Anglo-Saxon missionary church (from monastery) but later an honorific title of certain churches and cathedrals.*
misericord	*underside of ledge in a choir stall on which monks and choristers could rest without seeming to sit. Often elaborately carved with domestic – rarely religious – scenes. From the Latin* misericordia *(compassion). Too often invisible to visitors.*
moulding	*concave and convex fashioning of piers and arches to convey contrasts of light and shade.*
nave	*western arm of church, customary for the use of the laity to hear mass conducted behind the screen in the eastern arm. From the Latin* navis, *reflecting the upturned hull of a ship.*
ogee	*complex arch composed of a double-curve, convex then concave, typical of late-Decorated style. Sometimes the upper element is thrust forward as into a third dimension, hence nodding ogee.*
Perpendicular	*third and final period of English gothic architecture, roughly 1340–1530, and merging into Tudor. It saw a move from decorative richness to space and height. Arches became flatter, vaults more complex and windows exceptionally large.*
pier	*general term for the internal support of a cathedral, columns, etc.*

prebendary	*member of cathedral staff with specific functions and usually in receipt of income (or a prebend) from the cathedral estate. Usually a canon and thus a member of the chapter.*
presbytery	*the name more usually given to the chancel area in a cathedral.*
pulpitum	*solid divide between nave and eastern arm of a cathedral, often incorporating a gallery or organ loft and sometimes containing a chapel. Often replaced with simpler screens after the Reformation.*
Purbeck marble	*not marble but stone from the Isle of Purbeck in Dorset (and later elsewhere), celebrated for taking a glossy black stain; much used for Early Gothic shafts.*
quatrefoil	*four-leafed or -lobed feature of window tracery. Hence* trefoil, cinquefoil, *etc.*
Reformation	*Protestant movement against the Roman church that spread across northern Europe at the turn of the 16th century. In England, it took the form of Henry VIII's revolt against the papacy in 1534 and the subsequent dissolution of the monasteries.*
reredos	*carved or painted panel forming the backing of an altar.*
retrochoir	*eastern part of cathedral lying beyond the sanctuary and high altar, often used to display a saint's shrine. Retrochoirs tended to replace earlier apses in 13th-century cathedrals.*
rib	*projecting feature of a vault, sometimes structural, sometimes decorative.*
rood	*crucifix, hence the rood group of the Calvary scene that traditionally stood on the pulpitum or screen facing the nave. Torn down at the Reformation but widely replaced later.*
sanctuary	*holiest part of the east arm of a cathedral where the high altar is located.*
sedilia	*three seats to the right of the high altar, for participants in the mass. Often the object of a cathedral's richest decoration.*

shaft	*slender column attached to pier or window opening.*
spandrel	*triangular space above a pier and between the splaying arms of an arch.*
springer:	*the point, usually a corbel, above a pier where the vaulting rib departs from the vertical and begins its climb to the ridge.*
steeple	*the entirety of the tower and spire (if there is one) of a cathedral.*
stiff-leaf	*floral decoration of the Early and Decorated gothic eras, usually stone-carved, on capitals, corbels and bosses. Subject of the most elaborate stylistic development, hence* undercut *and* wind-blown.
tierceron rib	*diagonal cross ribs from a vault springer to a central ridge, later joined by lierne ribs.*
tracery	*stone dividers to Decorated and later windows, often in stylised patterns. Hence* intersecting, reticulated *(like a net),* curvilinear *and* flamboyant *(waving).*
transept	*the north and south arms projecting from the crossing.*
triforium	*portion of the interior wall between the arcade below and the clerestory above. Often a wall passage or merely an arcaded feature. Tended to die out in the Perpendicular era.*
tympanum	*area above the door lintel and enclosed by an arch, often richly ornamented.*
vault	*arched interior of roof, initially made of wood in the Norman period, later of ever more complex stone ribs and ceiling. Sometimes also an underground burial chamber.*
vestibule	*small chamber between an inner and an outer entrance.*

VISITOR INFORMATION

ARUNDEL RC
BN18 9AY
arundelcathedral.org

BIRMINGHAM
B3 2QB
birminghamcathedral.com

BIRMINGHAM RC
B4 6EU
stchadscathedral.org.uk

BLACKBURN
BB1 5AA
blackburncathedral.co.uk

BRADFORD
BD1 4EH
bradfordcathedral.org

BRENTWOOD RC
CM15 8AT
cathedral-brentwood.org

BRISTOL
BS1 5TJ
bristol-cathedral-co.uk

BRISTOL RC
BS8 3BX
cliftoncathedral.org

BURY ST EDMUNDS
IP33 1LS
stedscathedral.co.uk

CANTERBURY
CT1 2EH
canterbury-cathedral.org

CARLISLE
CA3 8TZ
carlislecathedral.org.uk

CHELMSFORD
CM1 1TY
chelmsfordcathedral.org.uk

CHESTER
CH1 2HU
chestercathedral.com

CHICHESTER
PO19 1PX
chichestercathedral.org.uk

COVENTRY
CV1 5AB
coventrycathedral.org.uk

DERBY
DE1 3GP
derbycathedral.org

DURHAM
DH1 3EH
durhamcathedral.co.uk

ELY
CB7 4DL
elycathedral.org

EXETER
EX1 1HA
exeter-cathedral.org.uk

GLOUCESTER
GL1 2LX
gloucestercathedral.co.uk

GUILDFORD
GU2 7UP
guildford-cathedral.org

HEREFORD
HR1 2NG
herefordcathedral.org

LEEDS RC
LS2 8BE
dioceseofleeds.org.uk/
cathedral/

LEICESTER
LE1 5PZ
leicestercathedral.org

LICHFIELD
WS13 7LD
lichfield-cathedral.org

LINCOLN
LN2 1PX
lincolncathedral.com

LIVERPOOL
L1 7AZ
liverpoolcathedral.org.uk

LIVERPOOL RC
L3 5TQ

MANCHESTER
M3 1SX
manchestercathedral.org

NEWCASTLE
NE1 1PF
stnicholascathedral.co.uk

NEWCASTLE RC
NE1 5HH
stmaryscathedral.org.uk

NORWICH
NR1 4DH
cathedral.org.uk

NORWICH RC
NR2 2PA
sjbcathedral.org.uk

NOTTINGHAM RC
NG1 5AE
stbarnabascathedral.org.uk

OXFORD
OX1 1DP
chch.ox.ac.uk/cathedral

PETERBOROUGH
PE1 1XS
peterborough-cathedral.
org.uk

PORTSMOUTH
PO1 2HH
portsmouthcathedral.org.uk

RIPON
HG4 1QS
riponcathedral.info

ROCHESTER
ME1 1SX
rochestercathedral.org

ST ALBANS
AL1 1BY
stalbanscathedral.org

ST PAUL'S
EC4M 8AD
stpauls.co.uk

SALISBURY
SP1 2EF
salisburycathedral.org.uk

SHEFFIELD
S1 1HA
sheffieldcathedral.org

SOUTHWARK
SE1 9DA
cathedral.southwark.
anglican.org

SOUTHWELL
NG25 0HD
southwellminster.org

TRURO
TR1 2AF
trurocathedral.org.uk

WAKEFIELD
WF1 1PJ
wakefieldcathedral.org.uk

WELLS
BA5 2US
wellscathedral.org.uk

WESTMINSTER ABBEY
SW1P 3PA
westminster-abbey.org

WESTMINSTER RC
SW1P 1QW
westminstercathedral.org.uk

WINCHESTER
SO23 9LS
winchester-cathedral.org.uk

WORCESTER
WR1 2LA
worcestercathedral.co.uk

YORK
YO1 7JN
yorkminster.org

SOURCES

There are dozens of general books on English cathedrals, and hundreds embracing individual ones. Here are those most recently published which I found useful. The indispensable Pevsner guides have almost all be revised by a number of hands, though I tend to refer to them as 'Pevsner'. I have used the most up-to-date editions. Cannon's book has the most comprehensive cathedral bibliography.

Cannon, Jon,
Cathedral: The Great English Cathedrals and the World that Made Them,
Constable, 2007

Clifton-Taylor, Alec,
The Cathedrals of England,
Thames and Hudson, 1967

Cobb, Gerald,
English Cathedrals: The Forgotten Centuries: Restoration and Change from 1530 to the Present Day,
Thames and Hudson, 1980

Gough, Janet,
Cathedrals of the Church of England,
Scala Arts & Heritage, 2015

Harvey, John,
Cathedrals of England and Wales,
Batsford, 1963

Johnson, Paul,
Cathedrals of England, Scotland and Wales,
Weidenfeld & Nicolson, 1990

Marlow, Peter,
The English Cathedral, Merrell, 2012

Martin, Christopher,
A Glimpse of Heaven: Catholic Churches of England and Wales, English Heritage, 2006

Pevsner, Nikolaus and Priscilla Metcalf,
The Cathedrals of England,
Viking, 2 volumes, 1985

Pevsner, Nikolaus and other authors,
The Buildings of England,
Yale, 1966–2016

Ralls, Karen,
Gothic Cathedrals: A Guide to the History, Places, Art, and Symbolism,
Ibis, 2015

Smith, Edwin and Olive Cook,
English Cathedrals,
Herbert, 1989

Tatton-Brown, Tim,
Great Cathedrals of Britain,
BBC Books, 1989

INDEX

CREDITS

Andrew Sharpe/Alamy Stock Photo: vi
Dorling Kindersley/UIG/Bridgeman Images: x
VisitBritain/Martin Brent/Getty Images: xvi
© Colin Underhill/Alamy Stock Photo: xxii
© Simon Jenkins: xxv
© Martin Meehan/iStock: xxx
Adam Lister/Getty Images: 2–3
© Paul Barker: 4, 46, 49, 50, 78, 80–1, 83, 102–3, 134, 154, 156, 200, 202, 204, 205, 206–7, 208, 210, 240, 251, 254, 260, 307
© Neil McAllister/Alamy Stock Photo: 6–7, 309
Allan Baxter/Getty Images: 8
© Fr James Bradley: 10
© Lancashire Images/Alamy Stock Photo: 12
© Angelo Hornak/Alamy Stock Photo: 14–15, 32, 40, 41, 52, 54–5, 56, 57, 70, 96, 97, 104, 110, 113, 124 (right), 126, 140, 149, 167, 213, 226, 228, 230, 244, 247, 281, 284, 288–9, 290, 316, 320
© Ian Dagnall/Alamy Stock Photo: 16, 144
© Alex Ramsay: 18, 128, 186
© Jane Tregelles/Alamy Stock Photo: 20
© World History Archive/Alamy Stock Photo: 22–3, 25
© Nick Cable 2012: 24
© Jonny White/Alamy Stock Photo: 26
© Michael Brooks/Alamy Stock Photo: 28
© Steve Vidler/Alamy Stock Photo: 30–1
© Stephen Giardina/Alamy Stock Photo: 34
© Franz-Marc Frei/Getty Images: 36–7
© imageBROKER/Alamy Stock Photo: 38, 64, 98, 315
© Ross Jolliffe/Alamy Stock Photo: 42
© UK Churches/Alamy Stock Photo: 43, 182–3
Bridgeman Images: 44–5, 66, 141, 238, 239
© Linda Kennedy/Alamy Stock Photo: 58
Peter Noyce/age fotostock/SuperStock: 60
© dbphots/Alamy Stock Photo: 62–3
© Neale Clark/Robert Harding: 68–9
World History Archive/TopFoto: 72, 73
Stephen Spraggon/Getty Images: 74
Robin Weaver/Collections Picture Library: 76–7, 142–3
© QEDimages/Alamy Stock Photo: 84
Malcolm Crowthers/Collections Picture Library: 87
© Country Life: 88, 136–7, 138, 274, 276–7
© Stefano Baldini/Bridgeman Images: 90–1
© Holmes Garden Photos/Alamy Stock Photo: 92, 178–9
© David Keith Jones/Alamy Stock Photo: 94
© Wojtek Buss/Robert Harding: 100–1
© David Pearson/Alamy Stock Photo: 105
© Greg Balfour Evans/Alamy Stock Photo: 106
© Stephen Dorey/Alamy Stock Photo: 108, 116
Heritage Images/Getty Images: 114–15
© Peter Noyce GBR/Alamy Stock Photo: 118–19
© Colin Palmer Photography/Alamy Stock Photo: 120
© Jeff Morgan 04/Alamy Stock Photo: 122–3
© Robin Weaver/Alamy Stock Photo: 124 (*left*)
© Hereford Mappa Mundi Trust and the Dean and Chapter of Hereford Cathedral: 127
Photo by Carlo Draisci. Copyright Leicester Cathedral: 130
© David Warren/Alamy Stock Photo: 132–3
© Angelo Hornak/Getty Images: 146, 218, 225
Topham/Woodmansterne: 150, 285
© David Mark/Alamy Stock Photo: 151
© Kumar Sriskandan/Alamy Stock Photo: 152–3
© Mike Kirk/Loop Images/Getty Images: 158
© Loop Images Ltd/Alamy Stock Photo: 160, 312
© 2004 Woodmansterne/TopFoto: 163
© Paul Melling/Alamy Stock Photo: 164
© Jackie Ellis/Alamy Stock Photo: 166
© PHOTOBYTE/Alamy Stock Photo: 168, 298, 299 (left)
© Wilf Doyle/Alamy Stock Photo: 170
© Nikreates/Alamy Stock Photo: 171
© A.J.D. Foto Ltd/Alamy Stock Photo: 172
David Porter Peterborough UK/Getty Images: 174, 248
© Ian G. Dagnall/Alamy Stock Photo: 176
© Paul Hurst ARPS all rights reserved: 177
© Granger, NYC/Alamy Stock Photo: 180, 278
The Granger Collection/TopFoto: 181

© Sid Frisby/Alamy Stock Photo: 184
© eye35/Alamy Stock Photo: 188
© Peter Barritt/Alamy Stock Photo: 190 (*left*), 222–3
© 2004 TopFoto/Woodmansterne: 190 (*right*)
© David Gee/Alamy Stock Photo: 192–3
Brian Lawrence/Getty Images: 194
Ivan Vdovin/age fotostock/SuperStock: 196–7
© Stuart Forster/Alamy Stock Photo: 198
© Andrew Aitchison/In Pictures/Getty Images: 199
© Ian Dagnall Commercial Collection/Alamy Stock Photo: 211
TopFoto/Woodmansterne: 214, 308
© Neil Holmes/Bridgeman Images: 216
© Donato Cinicolo. Courtesy of St Albans Cathedral: 217
© Doug Pearson/JAI/Getty Images: 220
© James Davidson/Alamy Stock Photo: 224
Julian Elliott Photography/Getty Images: 232, 304–5
© Michael Hudson/Alamy Stock Photo: 234–5
© Sonia Halliday Photo Library/Alamy Stock Photo: 236
© 2005 TopFoto/Woodmansterne: 242–3
© Peter Vallance/Alamy Stock Photo: 246
© Bildarchiv Monheim GmbH/Alamy Stock Photo: 252–3
© Steve Taylor ARPS/Alamy Stock Photo: 255
© Heritage Image Partners Ltd/Alamy Stock Photo: 256
aaronnaps/iStock: 258–9
Latitudestock/Getty Images: 262
© church/Alamy Stock Photo: 264
© Markus Keller/Robert Harding: 266–7, 294
© Bygone Collection/Alamy Stock Photo: 268 (*left*)
© Manor Photography/Alamy Stock Photo: 268 (*right*), 269
MyLoupe/Getty Images: 271
Stephen Dorey/Getty Images: 273
Werner Forman Archive/Bridgeman Images: 279
© Hemis/Alamy Stock Photo: 282
Andy Williams/Getty Images: 286
© Alex Ramsay/Alamy Stock Photo: 291
Photo Joe Low www.joelow.com: 292
© Nik Wheeler/Corbis: 297
© Andrew Duke/Alamy Stock Photo: 299 (*right*)
© Robert Stainforth/Alamy Stock Photo: 301
Bob Thomas/Getty Images: 302
Neale Clark/Robert Harding/SuperStock: 310
Courtesy of the Chapter of York: 317
© UK City Images/Alamy Stock Photo: 318–19

The lines from 'Church Going' on p. xxiv are taken from *The Collected Poems* by Philip Larkin. © Estate of Philip Larkin.

The lines from 'Here on the cropped grass' on p. 48 are taken from *Look, Stranger!* by W. H. Auden. © Estate of W. H. Auden.